PEARSON
my World
Social Studies
Leveled Reader
Lesson Plans

PEARSON

Boston, Massachusetts
Chandler, Arizona
Glenview, Illinois
Upper Saddle River, New Jersey

ISBN 13: 978-0-328-67318-6
ISBN-10:   0-328-67318-8

12 13 14 15 16 V011 19 18 17 16 15

Contents

Grades 3–5

Leveled Readers Help Build Common Core State Standards Knowledge and Skills

myWorld Social Studies Leveled Readers from Pearson provide a progressive development program to promote proficiency and confidence in reading and comprehension.

Students read biographies of people from various backgrounds who have contributed to the development of the United States. Each reader gives students more experience with reading and analyzing informational texts.

Each chapter in the program includes three leveled readers—all biographies of the same person but written below, on, and above grade level. This enables you to assign "just the right" level reader for each student—easy enough to build confidence, but challenging enough to improve and enhance your students' reading skills. As students build their reading and comprehension skills, they move to the next level of text complexity.

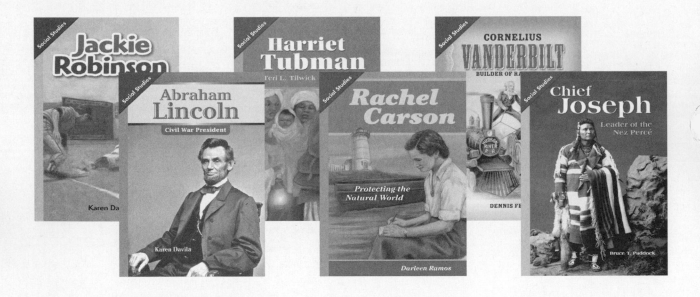

◉ Target Reading Skills

Target Reading Skills in each leveled reader help students develop reading skills and strategies so they will gain more understanding from what they read and be able to progress to more complex texts.

> **Target Reading Skills include:**
>
> - Main Idea and Details
> - Classify and Categorize
> - Fact and Opinion
> - Draw Conclusions
> - Sequence
> - Generalize
> - Cause and Effect
> - Compare and Contrast
> - Summarize

Built-In Reading Support

The inside front and back covers of each reader guide students to help them get the most from their reading.

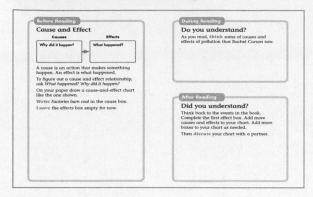

Lesson Plans

Lesson Plans for each leveled reader show you how to guide students as they improve their skills in reading informational texts. Graphic Organizer suggestions help students organize and analyze content to improve comprehension.

Before Reading

Students prepare to read with activities that build background knowledge and key vocabulary skills.

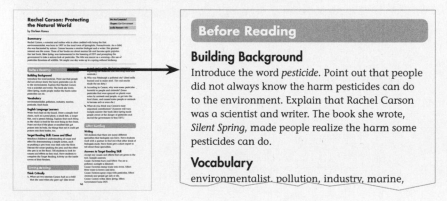

Before Reading

Building Background

Introduce the word *pesticide*. Point out that people did not always know the harm pesticides can do to the environment. Explain that Rachel Carson was a scientist and writer. The book she wrote, *Silent Spring*, made people realize the harm some pesticides can do.

Vocabulary

environmentalist, pollution, industry, marine,

During Reading

Students practice active reading and critical thinking.

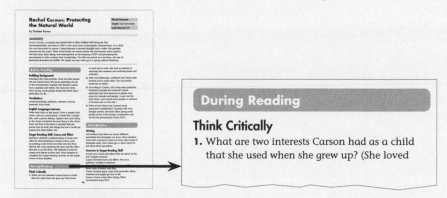

During Reading

Think Critically

1. What are two interests Carson had as a child that she used when she grew up? (She loved

After Reading

Students demonstrate their understanding of the text through written and verbal responses.

George Washington
by Karen Davila

Summary

George Washington had qualities that made him a good and important leader. He played many roles in our nation's history. He led the army, ran meetings where leaders made important decisions about the country, and was president of the United States.

Before Reading

Building Background

Point to the book title as you read it aloud. Invite children to share what they may already know about George Washington. Explain, if necessary, that he was the first president, or leader, of our country.

Vocabulary

leader, country, president

English Language Learners

Have children take turns acting out ways to lead in school or at home. (lead a parade, lead a band, lead exercises, lead a game of Simon Says, and so on.) Respond to each by saying, *You are a good leader.* Then read the text aloud, pausing at each page to clarify meaning, especially for the vocabulary words.

Target Reading Skill: Main Idea and Details

Draw a simple model of a Main Idea and Details graphic organizer on chart paper. Explain that the main idea tells what the story is about. Details tell more about the main idea. Tell them that this book is about George Washington. As you read the book together, they should think about what the book is telling them about George Washington.

During Reading

Read and Respond

On the first page of the book, read the question. Ask children to tell how they would answer the question. Have them predict what kind of answers might be in the book. Then continue to read the story aloud while children follow in their books. Pause after each page to discuss the text. Ask questions such as, *What does this page tell us about George Washington? What is George Washington doing?*

After Reading

Drawing or Writing

After reading, help children state the main idea of the story, *George Washington was a great leader.* Write the sentence on the Main Idea and Details graphic organizer and read it aloud with the children. Then have children recall the details the book told about Washington, such as, *He was a strong leader. He was our first president.*

Distribute copies of the Main Idea and Details graphic organizer or a graphic organizer you create. Restate the main idea, *George Washington was a great leader.* Have children draw a picture of George Washington in the center oval, that shows him as a great leader.

Speaking

Guide children to follow the directions on the inside back cover under Did you understand? Have children use their drawings to retell the story, telling the main idea and then telling one detail they learned about George Washington.

Answers to Target Reading Skill

Sample details: People chose him. He led an army. He rode a horse. He led meetings. He helped start our country. He was president.

George Washington Our First President

by Karen Davila

Summary

George Washington had qualities that made him a good and important leader. He played many roles in our nation's history. He led the army, ran meetings where leaders made important decisions about the country, and was president of the United States.

Before Reading

Building Background

Point to the book title and read it aloud. Invite children to share what they may already know about George Washington and their understanding of the word *president*. Tell children that in this book they will read about George Washington and some ways that he was a great leader of our country.

Vocabulary

leader, country, president

English Language Learners

Have children take turns acting out ways to lead in school or at home. (lead a parade, lead a band, lead exercises, lead a game of Simon Says, etc.) Respond to each by saying, *You are a good leader.* Then read the text aloud, pausing at each page to clarify meaning, especially the vocabulary words.

Target Reading Skill: Main Idea and Details

Draw a simple model of a Main Idea and Details graphic organizer on chart paper. Explain that the main idea tells what the story is about. Details tell more about the main idea. Tell them that this book is about George Washington. As you read the book together, they should think about what the book is telling them about George Washington.

During Reading

Read and Respond

On the first page of the book, read the question. Ask children to tell how they would answer the question. Have them predict what kind of answers might be in the book. Then continue to read the story aloud while children follow in their books. Pause after each page to discuss the text. Ask questions such as, *What does this page tell us about George Washington? What is George Washington doing?*

After Reading

Writing

After reading, help children state the main idea of the story, *George Washington was a great leader.* Write the sentence on the Main Idea and Details graphic organizer and read it aloud with the children. Then have children recall the details the book told about Washington, such as, *He was a strong leader. He was our first president.*

Distribute copies of a Main Idea and Details graphic organizer. Restate the main idea, *George Washington was a great leader.* Have children draw a picture of George Washington in the center oval that shows him as a great leader.

Speaking

Guide children to follow the directions on the inside back cover under Did you understand? Have children use their graphic organizers to retell the story to a partner or to the class, telling the main idea and then telling one detail they learned about George Washington.

Reading Skill Answers

Sample details: *People chose him. He led an army. He rode a horse. He led meetings. He helped start our country. He was president.*

Steve Jobs

by Karen Davila

Summary

Steve Jobs (born 1955, California) was fascinated by electronics. At thirteen, he won a science fair prize for designing a calculator. In high school, he met Steve Wozniak. In 1975, they produced a new kind of computer that was small and accessible enough for home use. The company, Apple Computers, was soon a success and Jobs continued to develop other valuable products.

Before Reading

Building Background

Tell children that in this book they will read about how Steve Jobs made and sold a new kind of computer. More than thirty years ago, computers were big and complex. People didn't use them in homes.

Ask children to point to any computers in the classroom and name other places in school, at home, in libraries, and in stores where they might see computers. Today computers are part of our daily lives, but when Steve Jobs was a boy they weren't.

Vocabulary

inventor, computer, company

Target Reading Skill: Cause and Effect

Read the directions in Before Reading on the inside front cover with children. Draw a cause-and-effect chart on the board. On the top of the left column write the heading Cause. On the top of the right column write the heading Effect. In the left column, write: Many people bought his computer. In the right column, write: His company grew and grew.

Have children read the headings aloud with you and follow along as you point to the words and read the two sentences aloud. Say that these sentences tell a cause and effect in the life of Steve Jobs. Help clarify how the cause and effect are related.

Say that children will help to add another cause and effect to the chart after they have read the book about Steve Jobs.

During Reading

Read and Respond

Read aloud while children follow in their books. After the first two pages, ask: *What is something that you learned so far?* Share additional information about his childhood from the Summary. Say that the rest of the book is about his work as a grown-up.

As you read the remaining pages, help children relate text to the pictures and understand how computers changed. Ask what they found out about Steve Jobs.

English Language Learners

After reading each page aloud, pause and ask children to look at the photo or illustration on that page. Ask them to use a simple sentence, such as I see_____. Help summarize their observations and clarify connections to the text on the page.

After Reading

Speaking

Turn to the inside back cover and read the After Reading section with children. Review with them the cause and effect on the chart you introduced earlier. Then ask: *What is another cause and effect you read about Steve Jobs?* Help to simplify answers as you record them under Cause and Effect.

Answers to Target Reading Skill

Possible cause-and-effect statements:

Cause: Many people bought his computer.
Effect: His company became very successful.

Cause: His computer was easy to use.
Effect: He changed computers.

Steve Jobs and the Computer Business

by Karen Davila

Summary

At thirteen, Steve Jobs (born 1955, California) won a science fair prize for his own design of a calculator. In high school, he spent nonschool time at a nearby computer company, where he met Steve Wozniak. In 1975, they teamed up to produce a computer that was small and easy to use at home. This was a new idea. Together, Jobs and Wozniak made people see that the new product was valuable, reliable, and unique. The company, Apple Computers, was soon a financial success and Jobs continued to develop useful products.

Before Reading

Building Background

Tell students that more than thirty years ago computers were big and complicated. Computers were kept in large buildings and run by experts. Today computers are part of our daily lives.

Ask children to point to any computers in the classroom and name other places where people might use computers.

Vocabulary

inventor, computer, company, business

English Language Learners

Write the vocabulary words on separate index cards with definitions on the back. Read aloud a sentence for each word, with the word left blank. Example: Steve Jobs was a young _____. He made a _____ that was easy to use. Invite children to select the word that fits and say the sentence aloud. Ask children to create additional sentences.

Target Reading Skill: Cause and Effect

Read the directions in Before Reading on the inside front cover with children. Create a cause-and-effect chart on the board. On the top of the left column, write the heading Cause. On the top of the right column, write the heading Effect. In the left column, write: Many people bought his computer. In the right column, write: His company grew bigger.

Have volunteers read the headings and the sentences aloud with you as you point to the words. Say that these sentences tell a cause and an effect in the life of Steve Jobs. Help clarify how the cause and effect are related. Say a cause happens before an effect. A cause makes the effect happen.

Say that children will help to add some other causes and effects to the chart after they have read the book about Steve Jobs.

During Reading

Read and Respond

Read aloud while children follow along. After reading each page, pause to discuss how the text and pictures relate. After the first two pages, ask: *What is something you learned about Steve Jobs?* Throughout, reinforce the idea that his computers were new and different at the time.

Turn to the inside front cover and read the directions for During Reading. Remind children to think about which sentences might tell a cause and which might tell an effect. Then have children work with partners, taking turns to read pages of the book aloud to each other. Support individuals as needed.

After Reading

Speaking

Turn to the inside back cover and read the After Reading section with children. Review the cause and effect on the chart you introduced earlier. Then ask: *What is another cause and effect you read or learned about Steve Jobs?* Clarify and simplify answers as you record them on the board.

Answers to Target Reading Skill

Possible cause-and-effect statements:

Cause : People wanted the new kind of computer.
Effect: The company grew.

Cause: Steve Jobs had many ideas.
Effect : He changed computers.

Mish Michaels

by Karen Davila

Summary

Mish Michaels loves weather and knows its power. At age five, she watched a tornado destroy parts of her hometown. This experience influenced her career choice—to become a weather scientist. She studies storms and reports weather news on television.

Before Reading

Building Background

Point to the lines of the book title as you read them aloud. Do a picture walk through the book and invite children to predict what kind of job they think Mish Michaels has. Invite children to tell what they know about the jobs of people who report weather on television.

Vocabulary

weather, tornado

English Language Learners

Reinforce the meaning of the word *weather* with students. Show pictures of various kinds of weather and invite children to "report" the weather, using the following sentence: The weather is _____. Prompt with examples (cold, sunny, windy, rainy, cloudy) as needed. Introduce the word *tornado*. Explain that a tornado is a storm with very high winds. Some Spanish-speaking ELLs may know the word *tornado*, which is a cognate.

Target Reading Skill: Classify and Categorize

Teach or review the idea of classifying and categorizing. Draw a simple T-Chart on the board. On one side, write *Mish Michaels* and draw a simple stick figure of her. On the other side, write *Weather* and draw a shining sun. Show labeled pictures of the following, in mixed order: (weather) reporter, scientist, storm, snow, rain, tornado. Have children identify each picture. Then work with children to decide where the pictures should go on the chart. Use tape to stick the pictures into the correct column as children respond.

During Reading

Read and Respond

Read the story aloud while children follow along in their books. After you read each page, pause to discuss any the text and the picture. Ask questions such as *What is Mish Michaels's job? What are some things you learned about weather?* When you have finished reading the text, ask *How do you think Mish Michaels feels about weather? What did you learn about weather?*

Turn to the inside back cover and read the directions for During Reading. Then have children work with partners, taking turns to retell the story to each other. When they are done, have them work together to complete the Target Reading activity.

After Reading

Review to the chart you made for the Target Reading Skill. Have children take turns telling things they learned from the book about Mish Michaels. Then have them take turns telling things they learned from the book about weather.

Read the After Reading activity with children. Have them work with a partner to retell the story and to complete the Target Reading activity.

Answers to Target Reading Skill

Possible chart entries in the *Mish Michaels* column: loves weather, saw tornado as a girl, is a weather scientist, loves to study storms, reports on weather.

Possible chart entries in the *Weather* column: tornado is one kind of storm, storms can be trouble, weather is important news.

Mish Michaels Weather Chaser

by Karen Davila

Summary

Mish Michaels loves weather and knows its power. At age five, she watched a tornado destroy parts of her hometown. This experience influenced her career choice—to become a weather scientist. She studies storms and reports weather news on television.

Before Reading

Building Background

Point to the lines of the book title as you read them aloud. Do a picture walk through the book and invite children to predict what kind of job they think Mish Michaels has. Invite children to tell what they know about the jobs of people who report weather on television.

Vocabulary

weather, tornado, scientist

English Language Learners

Reinforce the meaning of the word *weather* with students. Show pictures of various kinds of weather and invite children to "report" the weather, using the following sentence: The weather is _____. Prompt with examples (cold, sunny, windy, rainy, cloudy) as needed. Preview other vocabulary words. Spanish-speaking ELLs may know the word *tornado*, which is a cognate.

Target Reading Skill: Classify and Categorize

Teach or review the idea of classifying and categorizing. Draw a simple T-Chart on the board or on chart paper. On one side, write *Mish Michaels* and draw a simple stick figure of her. On the other side, write *Weather* and draw a shining sun. Show labeled pictures of the following, in mixed order: reporter (weather), scientist, storm, rain, and tornado. Have children identify each picture. Then work with children to decide where the pictures should go on the chart. Use tape to stick the pictures into the correct column as children respond. Save the chart for later.

During Reading

Read and Respond

Read the story aloud while children follow in their books. After you read each page, pause to discuss any the text and the picture. Ask questions such as *What is Mish Michaels's job? What are some things you found out about weather?* When you have finished reading the text, ask *How do you think Mish Michaels feels about weather? What can we learn from her about weather?*

Turn to the inside front cover and read the directions for During Reading.

After Reading

Refer to the chart you made for the Target Reading Skills. Have children take turns telling things they learned from the book about Mish Michaels. Then have them take turns telling things they learned from the book about weather.

Read the After Reading activity with children. Have them work with a partner to retell the story and to complete the Target Reading activity.

Answers to Target Reading Skill

Accept drawings that show any of the following in the *Mish Michaels* column: loves weather, saw tornado as a girl, is a weather scientist, is a weather reporter, loves to chase storms, reports on weather.

Accept drawings that show any of the following in the *Weather* column: tornado is one kind of storm, tornados can tear down walls and trees, storms can have rain and wind, weather has great power, weather is important news.

Jackie Robinson

by Karen Davila

Summary

Jackie Robinson (1919–1972) was a star athlete who excelled in many sports when he was young. After serving in the U.S. Army, he began a baseball career. As an African American, he found baseball to be a racially segregated sport. Major League teams were only open to whites. Based on his talent and willingness to deal patiently with prejudice, Robinson was hired by a major league team manager who wanted to integrate baseball. In 1947, Robinson joined the Brooklyn Dodgers and became the first African American major league player of the 20th century. His athletic skills and personal values enabled him to open up opportunities for other players.

Before Reading

Building Background

Point to the book title as you read it aloud. Invite children to look at the image on the cover and share anything they know about Jackie Robinson.

Vocabulary

champion

English Language Learners

In your own words, explain the meaning of key terms used in the book (sports, baseball, African American, etc.).

Target Reading Skill: Compare and Contrast

Read aloud the directions in Before Reading on the inside front cover. Point to a compare-and-contrast chart you have drawn on the board. Model the reading skill by comparing and contrasting some aspect of your life. (Example: I loved reading as a child. I love reading now. I didn't like to play sports then. I like to play sports now.) Tell students that the class will be doing the same for Robinson.

During Reading

Read and Respond

Read the book aloud while children follow in their books. After you read the text for each page, pause to discuss any vocabulary words and how the text relates to the picture. Point out which part of the book discusses Robinson's youth and which discusses his life as an adult.

After Reading

Speaking

Turn to the inside back cover and read the After Reading section with children. Ask students to tell one way that Robinson's was the same as a student and as adult. Then ask students to share one way in which his life was different. Summarize and write the responses in the chart on the board.

Answers to Target Reading Skill

Possible answers: Compare (what is alike): played sports as student and adult. Contrast (what is different): Played on many teams; played on one team. Was allowed to play on baseball team; adult baseball teams didn't allow African Americans.

Jackie Robinson Changes the Game

by Karen Davila

Summary

Jackie Robinson (1919–1972) was a star athlete who excelled in football, baseball, track, and basketball when he was young. After serving in the U.S. Army, he began a baseball career. As an African American, he found baseball to be a racially segregated sport. Major League teams were open only to whites. Based on his talent and his willingness to deal patiently with prejudiced attitudes, he was hired by a team manager who wanted to integrate baseball. In 1947, Robinson joined the Brooklyn Dodgers and became the first African American major league player of the 20th century. His athletic skills and personal values enabled him to open up opportunities for others.

Before Reading

Building Background

Point to the book title and read it aloud. Invite children to look at the image on the cover and share anything they may know about Jackie Robinson.

Discuss the idea that there was a time in this country when things were not fair for some people.

Vocabulary

major league, champion, equal rights

English Language Learners

In your own words, explain the meaning of key terms used in the book (sports, baseball, African American, etc.).

Target Reading Skill: Compare and Contrast

Read aloud the directions in Before Reading on the inside front cover. Point to a compare-and-contrast chart you have drawn on the board. Model the reading skill by comparing and contrasting some aspect of your life. (Example: I loved to read as a child. I love to read as an adult. I didn't like to play sports then. I love to play sports now.) Tell students that the class will be doing the same for Robinson.

During Reading

Read and Respond

Read the book aloud while children follow in their books. After you read the text for each page, pause to discuss any vocabulary words and how the text relates to the picture. Point out which part of the book discusses Robinson's youth and which discusses his life as an adult.

After Reading

Speaking

Turn to the inside back cover and read the After Reading section with children. Ask students to tell one way that Robinson's life was the same as a student and as adult. Then ask students to share one way in which his life was different. Summarize and write the responses in chart on the board.

Answers to Target Reading Skill

Possible answers: Compare (what is alike): played sport as student and adult. Contrast (what is different): Played on many teams; played on one team. Was allowed to play on baseball team; adult baseball teams didn't allow African Americans.

Rosa Parks

by Karen Davila

Summary

Rosa Parks (1913–2005) grew up in a small town in Alabama. As an African American, Parks was affected by segregation and racial prejudice. She and her husband were both active in groups working for racial equality for many years. On December 1, 1955, Rosa Parks refused to give up her bus seat to a white person. She acted from a deep belief in equal rights. Martin Luther King, Jr., organized support for her action to challenge city rules that maintained segregation. Forming the Montgomery Bus Boycott, African Americans and white supporters refused to ride the buses until the city buses granted them equal rights. More than a year later, the boycott ended. Rosa Parks and others rode the buses again and could sit wherever they pleased.

Before Reading

Building Background

Point to the title and read it aloud. Tell students that Rosa Parks grew up in Alabama. Show Alabama on a map of the United States. Tell them that in that part of the country and at that time, there were unfair rules. African Americans were forced to sit separately from whites on buses and in other public places. The illustration of the water fountain is another example of segregated facilities.

Vocabulary

rules, equal rights, hero

Target Reading Skill: Sequence

Turn to the inside front cover and read the meaning of *order*. Write two sentences on the board: *Rosa Parks got on the bus. She sat down on a seat on the bus.* Read the two sentences aloud with children and ask them to give their ideas about the order of the two sentences. Say that after reading the book, they will review these sentences and decide on their order.

During Reading

Read and Respond

Read the story aloud while children follow in their books. Pause before turning a page and ask, *What do you think might happen next?* Ask other questions that help clarify the sequence of events and ideas in the text.

English Language Learners

After reading the book to the students, ask children to tell something they learned about Rosa Parks. Guide them to form a sentence, using a simple frame, such as: Rosa Parks is _____.

After Reading

Speaking

Turn to the inside back cover and read the After Reading section with children. Have them review the two sentences you wrote earlier and confirm their order based on events in the text.

Answers to Target Reading Skill

Possible events and order: First, Rosa Parks broke a bus rule that was unfair. Then, people stopped riding the buses. Last, they made the rules change.

Rosa Parks Stands Up for Freedom

by Karen Davila

Summary

Rosa Parks (1913–2005) grew up in a small town in Alabama. As an African American, she was affected by segregation and racial prejudice. She and her husband were both active in groups working for racial equality for many years. On December 1, 1955, Rosa Parks refused to give up her bus seat to a white person. She acted from a deep belief in equal rights. Martin Luther King, Jr., organized support for her action to challenge city rules that maintained segregation. Forming the Montgomery Bus Boycott, African Americans and white supporters refused to ride the buses until the city bus rules granted them equal rights. More than a year later, the boycott ended. Rosa Parks and others rode the buses again.

Before Reading

Building Background

Examine the image and title on the cover. Make sure children understand the title by explaining that to *stand up* can mean "to defend or fight for something." Point out Alabama on a map of the United States and explain that during the time when Rosa Parks was growing up, there were unfair rules, and whites and African Americans did not share equal rights. African Americans were forced to stay apart from whites in buses and other kinds of places. The illustration of segregated water fountains in also an example.

Vocabulary

rules, equal rights, hero

Target Reading Skill: Sequence

Turn to the inside front cover and read the meaning of *sequence*. Write two sentences on the board: *Rosa Parks sat in the front seat. She went to jail.* Have volunteers read the two sentences aloud. Ask children to offer their ideas about the order of the two sentences. Say that after reading the book, they will review these sentences and decide on their order based on the book.

During Reading

Read and Respond

Read the story aloud while children follow in their books. Pause before turning a page and ask: *What do you think might happen next?* Ask other questions that help clarify the sequence of events and ideas in the text.

English Language Learners

After reading the book together with children, ask children to tell something that they learned about Rosa Parks. Guide them to form a sentence, using a sentence frame such as *Rosa Parks was _____*.

After Reading

Speaking

First have volunteers read aloud the two sentences you had introduced before they read they book. Ask them to conclude the order based on the sequence of events in the book.

Answers to Target Reading Skill

Possible events in order: First, Rosa Parks did not follow a bus rule that was unfair. Then, people stopped riding city buses. Last, the city buses finally had fair rules.

Eleanor Roosevelt

by Karen Davila

Summary

Eleanor Roosevelt (1884–1962) was a shy girl who grew up to be a highly respected first lady. As a young woman, Roosevelt worked to change conditions and practices that she saw as unfair. Roosevelt took an active role as first lady when her husband Franklin D. Roosevelt was president (1933 to 1945). Through her public speaking and her writing, she did much to convey her beliefs to people throughout the country.

Before Reading

Building Background

Read the title aloud. Identify the current president and first lady. Tell students that Franklin and Eleanor Roosevelt were the president and first lady many years ago. Note that Eleanor Roosevelt did many valuable things as first lady and throughout her long life.

Vocabulary

president, first lady, rights

English Language Learners

Have children make vocabulary cards for the words in the glossary. Go through the text and suggest other words for which they could also make cards. Provide meanings in your own words.

Target Reading Skill: Fact and Opinion

Show children a copy of the T-chart graphic organizer. Prepare copies of the T-chart to distribute after reading. Have headings already filled in.

Turn to the inside front cover and read the definitions and directions under Before Reading with children. Give some examples of facts, such as student ages or the day of the week. Give examples of opinions. (Our school is the best school.)

Ask students to compare these sentences: 1. George Washington was the first president of this country. (fact) 2. George Washington was the best president of this country. (opinion) Note and underline the words *first* and *best* as clues.

During Reading

Read and Respond

Periodically read a sentence aloud and ask students whether it is fact or opinion. Ask them whether or not they can prove the statement. Remind them that if they can, it is a fact. If they can't, it is an opinion.

After Reading

Writing

Distribute the T-charts. Have children find one sentence that is a fact and another that is an opinion. Ask them to copy the sentence or just the page number and the first two words of the sentence in their chart so they can identify it.

Answers to Target Reading Skill

Possible facts: She was very shy. She married Franklin Roosevelt.

Possible opinions: She was a remarkable first lady.

Eleanor Roosevelt First Lady

by Karen Davila

Summary

Eleanor Roosevelt (1884–1962) was a shy girl who grew into a brave and remarkable woman. As a young woman, Roosevelt worked to change conditions and practices that she saw as unfair. Roosevelt was a particularly active first lady while her husband Franklin D. Roosevelt was president (1933 to 1945). Through her public speaking and her writing, she did many things and conveyed her beliefs and goals to people around the country.

Before Reading

Building Background

Read the title aloud. Identify the current president and first lady. Tell students that Franklin and Eleanor Roosevelt were the president and first lady many years ago. Note that Eleanor Roosevelt did many valuable things as first lady and throughout her long life.

Vocabulary

president, first lady, government, rights

English Language Learners

Have children make vocabulary cards for the words in the glossary. Go through the text and suggest other words for which they can also make cards. Provide meanings in your own words.

Target Reading Skill: Fact and Opinion

Show children a copy of the T-chart graphic organizer. Provide copies of the T-chart with the headings *Fact* and *Opinion* already filled in. Distribute for After Reading.

Turn to the inside front cover and read the definitions and directions. Give some examples of facts, such as student ages or the day of the week. Give examples of opinions. (Our school is the best.)

Ask students to compare these sentences: 1. George Washington was the first president of this country. (fact) 2. George Washington was the best president of this country. (opinion) Note and underline the words *first* and *best* as clues.

Say that during reading, children will have a chance to look for two sentences, one that tells a fact and another that tells an opinion. Then they will fill out their charts for the After Reading activity.

During Reading

Read and Respond

Periodically read a sentence aloud and ask students whether it is fact or opinion. Ask them whether or not they can prove the statement. Remind them that if they can, it is a fact. If they can't, it is an opinion.

After Reading

Writing

Distribute the T-charts and have students write or read aloud the headings *Fact* and *Opinion*. Have children find one sentence that is a fact and one that is an opinion. They should copy each sentence into the organizer.

Answers to Target Reading Skill

Possible facts: She was very shy. She married Franklin Roosevelt.

Possible opinions: She felt that she must do more. She was a remarkable first lady.

Eleanor Roosevelt Speaks Out

by Karen Davila

Summary

Eleanor Roosevelt (1884–1962) was a shy girl who became a brave woman and a remarkable first lady. As a young woman, Roosevelt worked to change conditions or practices that she saw as unfair. Roosevelt took an active role in being first lady when her husband Franklin D. Roosevelt was president (1933 to 1945). Through her public speaking and her writing, she conveyed her beliefs and goals to people around the country. After Franklin's death, she continued to work to improve the country and the world.

Before Reading

Building Background

Read the title aloud. Ask for or supply examples of what the phrase *speak out* means. Identify the current president and first lady. Tell students that Franklin and Eleanor Roosevelt were the president and first lady many years ago. Note that Eleanor Roosevelt often spoke out and wrote about the things she believed in.

Vocabulary

communities, government, first lady, rights

English Language Learners

Have children make vocabulary cards for the words in the glossary. Go through the text and suggest other words that they could also make cards for. Help them look up the words in a dictionary.

Target Reading Skill: Fact and Opinion

Show children a copy or model of the T-chart graphic organizer. Write the word *Fact* at the top of the left column and *Opinion* at the top of the right column. You may want to provide copies of the T-chart with the headings already filled in. Distribute them for After Reading.

Turn to the inside front cover and read the definitions and directions under Before Reading with children. Give some examples of facts, such as student ages or the current date. Give examples of opinions. (Our pool is the best place to swim.)

Ask students to compare these sentences: 1. George Washington was the first President of this country. (fact) 2. George Washington was the best President of this country. (opinion) Note and underline the words *first* and *best* as clues.

Say that during reading, children will have a chance to look for two sentences, one that tells a fact and another that tells an opinion. Then they will fill out their charts for the After Reading activity.

During Reading

Read and Respond

Periodically read a sentence aloud and ask students whether it is fact or opinion. Encourage students to explain their answers. Ask them whether or not they can prove the statement. Remind them that if they can, it is a fact. If they can't, it is an opinion.

After Reading

Writing

Distribute the T-charts and have students write or read aloud the headings *Fact* and *Opinion*. Have children find at least one sentence that is a fact and one that is an opinion. They should copy the sentence into the organizer.

Answers to Target Reading Skill

Possible facts: She was very shy. She married Franklin Roosevelt.

Possible opinions: She felt that she must do more. She was a remarkable first lady.

13

Marian Wright Edelman

by Karen Davila

Summary

Marian Wright Edelman (born in 1939) speaks for the needs of children, especially those who are poor, members of racial minorities, or have disabilities. Her childhood experience in an African American family committed to community service greatly influenced her. Her approach has been to help children as a way to help the communities in which they live. In 1973, she founded the Children's Defense Fund. It continues to provide valuable health care, education, and leadership programs to communities around the country.

Before Reading

Building Background

Share information about Marian Wright Edelman based on the Summary to convey that her work has helped children in many ways. Note that Edelman started a fund that provides help to children and their communities.

Vocabulary

fund, education

English Language Learners

Help children make their own vocabulary cards for the words in the Glossary. Have them write the word on one side and then copy its definition from the Glossary page. Have them take turns with a partner holding up the word side as well as providing the definition in their own words.

Target Reading Skill: Cause and Effect

Turn to Before Reading on the inside front cover and read the definitions of *cause* and *effect* with children. Offer a concrete example of cause and effect, such as: I like to ride my bike, so I rode it yesterday.

Fold a sheet of paper in half lengthwise and write Cause at the top of the left side. Write Effect at the top of the right side and fill in both with your example. Explain that children will use the sample to write more about cause and effect after they read about Marian Wright Edelman.

During Reading

Read and Respond

Read the sentences, pointing to each word, as children follow in their books. Pause after each page or spread to discuss the images in context.

Raise questions that help children think in terms of cause and effect, such as, What caused Marian Wright Edelman to start a fund?

After Reading

Drawing and Writing

Read directions for After Reading on the inside back cover. Distribute copy paper that has been folded in half lengthwise and then opened again. Following the sample, have children write Cause at the top of the left side and Effect at the top of the right side. Help children write down or draw a cause and an effect from the book.

Speaking

Invite children to read or show what they have put on their papers to tell a cause and effect in the book. Encourage them to describe any drawing in terms of cause and effect. Ask volunteers to read aloud their sentences describing a cause and effect. You may list or summarize the cause and effect sentences that children have shared. You may post their writing and drawings on a bulletin board about Marian Wright Edelman's work.

Answers to Target Reading Skill

Possible example of statements of cause and effect: Marian Wright Edelman wanted to help children (cause), so she started a fund (effect).

Marian Wright Edelman
Helping Children and Families

by Karen Davila

Summary

Marian Wright Edelman (born in 1939) speaks for the needs of children, especially those who are poor or have disabilities. Her own childhood experience in an African American family committed to community service, as well as her later work with people such as Dr. Martin Luther King, Jr., greatly influenced her. Her approach has been to help children as a way to help the communities in which they live. In 1973, she founded the Children's Defense Fund that continues to provide valuable health care, education and leadership programs around the country.

Before Reading

Building Background

Share facts about Marian Wright Edelman from the Summary that relate to her helping children and families through the Children's Defense Fund. Write *Children's Defense Fund* on the board. Underline the word *Fund* and have children locate *fund* and its definition in the Glossary. Read other Glossary terms and have volunteers locate them within the pages.

Vocabulary

communities, fund, education

English Language Learners

Read or have volunteers read aloud each page of the book. After each page or spread, ask, *What did you learn about Marian Wright Edelman?* Guide them to answer in simple sentences, rephrasing the text in their own words.

Target Reading Skill: Cause and Effect

Turn to Before Reading on the inside front cover and read the definitions of *cause* and *effect* with children. Offer a concrete example of cause and effect, such as: I wanted to learn about Marian Wright Edelman (cause) so I read this book (effect). Invite children to give examples, and help them specify which element is a cause and which is an effect. For example, I love to bike (cause), so I rode it to the park (effect).

Display a copy of a cause-and-effect graphic organizer. Read the labels and clarify connections between the cause and effect boxes. Explain that children will help to complete the chart after they have read the book.

During Reading

Read and Respond

Read the steps in During Reading on the inside front cover. Point to examples of words that are clues to information about cause and effect, such as *why* and *because*.

Support children as needed as they read the text independently. Then have them take turns reading pages of the text aloud with a partner. Model how to pause after reading a page to identify any statements of cause or effect.

After Reading

Writing

Read directions for After Reading on the inside back cover. Children may work with partners or independently to write one or two sentences that tell a cause and effect they read about in the book.

Speaking

Invite volunteers to read aloud their sentences describing a cause and effect. You may use their statements to fill in boxes of a large version of the cause-and-effect graphic organizer. You may prefer to create a list of their sentences, reviewing each one to identify which part describes a cause and which describes an effect.

Answers to Target Reading Skill

Possible statements of cause and effect: Marian Wright Edelman started a fund (cause) to help children (effect). Children are taught skills (cause) so that they can get good jobs as adults (effect). Children get health care (cause) so they can stay heathy (effect).

Marian Wright Edelman
A Voice for Children

by Karen Davila

Summary

Marian Wright Edelman (born in 1939) speaks for the needs of children, especially those who are poor or have disabilities. Her own childhood experience in an African American family committed to community service, as well as her later work with people such as Dr. Martin Luther King, Jr., greatly influenced her. Her approach has been to help children as a way to help the communities in which they live. In 1973 she founded the Children's Defense Fund that continues to provide valuable health care, education and leadership programs around the country.

Before Reading

Building Background

Share facts about Marian Wright Edelman from the Summary that relate to her helping children and families through the Children's Defense Fund. Write *Children's Defense Fund* on the board. Underline the word *Fund* and have children locate *fund* and its definition in the Glossary. Read other Glossary terms and have volunteers locate them within the pages.

Vocabulary

communities, fund, education, health care

English Language Learners

Read or have volunteers read aloud each page of the book. After each page or spread, ask, What did you learn about Marian Wright Edelman? Guide them to answer in simple sentences, rephrasing the text in their own words.

Target Reading Skill: Cause and Effect

Turn to Before Reading on the inside front cover and read the definitions of *cause* and *effect* with children. Offer a concrete example of cause and effect, such as: I wanted to learn about Marian Wright Edelman (cause) so I read this book (effect). Invite children to give examples, and help them specify which element is a cause and which is an effect. For example, I love to bike (cause), so I rode it to the park (effect).

Display a copy of a cause-and-effect graphic organizer. Read the labels and clarify connections between the cause and effect boxes. Explain that children will help to complete the chart after they have read the book.

During Reading

Read and Respond

Read the steps in During Reading on the inside front cover. Point to examples of words that are clues to information about cause and effect, such as *why* and *because*.

Support children as needed as they read the text independently. Then have them take turns reading pages of the text aloud with a partner. Model how to pause after reading a page to identify any statements of cause or effect.

After Reading

Writing

Read directions for After Reading on the inside back cover. Children may work with partners or independently to write one or two sentences that tell a cause and effect they read about in the book.

Speaking

Invite volunteers to read aloud their sentences describing a cause and effect. You may use their statements to fill in boxes of a large version of the cause-and-effect graphic organizer. You may prefer to create a list of their sentences, reviewing each one to identify which part describes a cause and which describes an effect.

Answers to Target Reading Skill

Possible statements of cause and effect: Marian Wright Edelman started a fund to (cause) help children (effect). Children are taught skills (cause) so that they can get good jobs as adults (effect). Children get health care (cause) so they can stay heathy (effect).

Ernest Shackleton

by Karen Davila

Summary

As a boy in Ireland and then England, Ernest Shackleton (1874–1922) showed his love of adventure. Though his father wanted him to study medicine, Shackleton joined the merchant navy at age 16. Then, in 1901, he joined an Antarctic expedition led by Robert Scott. Illness forced Shackleton to leave the expedition early, but he was determined to explore Antarctica. On the first expedition that he planned and led, he came within 97 miles of the South Pole. On the next, beginning in 1914, his ship, the *Endurance,* became stuck in ice. It finally sank, stranding his crew. Shackleton's successful efforts to get the entire crew to safety, and ultimately home, became the best-known adventure of his life.

Before Reading

Building Background

Ask children to read the title with you. Use a globe or map to locate Antarctica and the South Pole. Preview the pictures to give children a sense of the climate and conditions of Antarctica.

Vocabulary

explorer, South Pole, crew

English Language Learners

Encourage children to use pictures to help them learn details about Ernest Shackleton's life. Model how to make observations aloud. For example, say: *In this picture, I see a man standing on a ship.* Invite children to make their own observations about the pictures.

Target Reading Skill: Main Idea and Details

Turn to the inside front cover and read the Before Reading section with children. Show them the main idea graphic organizer and have them read the labels with you. Say that the main idea of this kind of book is often on the first page. Read and discuss the sentence. Then write it under Main Idea in the graphic organizer and post it for reference. Say that children will help you complete the chart after reading the book.

During Reading

Read and Respond

Read the text aloud while children read along quietly. Guide children in determining the meanings of challenging words by using context clues and the Glossary.

As you read, model how to stop to identify supporting details in the text. Then read the text with children. Help them to identify the main idea and details as you read with them.

After Reading

Speaking and Drawing

Turn to the inside back cover and read the After Reading section with children. Review the Main Idea graphic organizer with children. Invite children to share details that tell more about the main idea. Simplify and record their details in the graphic organizer. Add other boxes as needed. Have children draw a picture to go with the main idea. Post their pictures around a statement of the main idea.

Answers to Target Reading Skill

Main Idea: Ernest Shackleton was a brave leader. Supporting Details: He sailed and explored. He explored Antarctica. He came near the South Pole. His ship was trapped in ice. He saved his crew.

Explorer Ernest Shackleton

by Karen Davila

Summary

As a boy in Ireland and then England, Ernest Shackleton (1874–1922) showed his love of adventure. Though his father wanted him to study medicine, Shackleton joined the merchant navy at age 16. Then in 1901, he joined an Antarctic expedition led by Robert Scott. Illness forced Shackleton to leave the expedition early, but he was determined to further explore Antarctica. On the first expedition that he planned and led, Shackleton came within 97 miles of the South Pole. On the next trip, in 1914, his ship, the *Endurance,* got crushed in packed ice. It finally sank, stranding his crew. His successful effort to get his whole crew to safety, and ultimately home, became the best-known adventure of his life.

Before Reading

Building Background

Ask children to read the title with you. Confirm their understanding of the term *explorer* by asking them to name other explorers they may know of (Christopher Columbus, among others). Use a globe or map to locate Antarctica and the South Pole. Preview the pictures to give children a sense of the climate and conditions of Antarctica.

Vocabulary

explore, South Pole, continent, crew

English Language Learners

Create a simple word web on chart paper. Write the name *Ernest Shackleton* in the center circle. Ask children to find words in the text that describe him or his actions (explorer, sailor, leader, brave). Write or assign children to write the descriptions in circles that connect to the center. Guide each child to make up a sentence about Ernest Shackleton using one of the words.

Target Reading Skill: Main Idea and Details

Turn to the inside front cover and have children read the Before Reading section. Show them the main idea graphic organizer and have them read the labels with you. Based on the title and the first paragraph of the book, suggest that the main idea of the book is: *Ernest Shackleton was a brave explorer.* Write the sentence under Main Idea in the graphic organizer and post it for reference. Say that children will help fill in Supporting Details after reading the book.

During Reading

Read and Respond

Turn to the inside front cover and read the During Reading section. Provide sticky notes for children to flag pages that contain supporting details. Model how they can take turns with a partner reading pages aloud and pointing to details that tell more about the main idea.

After Reading

Speaking and Writing

Turn to the inside back cover and read the After Reading section with children. Review the model chart for Main Idea and Details with children. Ask one child to read aloud the main idea and another to tell what makes it the main idea. Invite children to share supporting details they have flagged in their books. Record their details in the boxes.

Answers to Target Reading Skill

Main Idea: Ernest Shackleton was a brave explorer.

Supporting Details: He wanted to explore. He sailed to new places. He explored Antarctica. He led trips there. He came close to the South Pole. His ship got stuck and sank. He led his crew to a safe place.

Ernest Shackleton Exploring the South Pole

by Karen Davila

Summary

As a boy in Ireland and then England, Ernest Shackleton (1874–1922) showed his love of adventure. Though his father wanted him to study medicine, Shackleton joined the merchant navy at age 16. Then in 1901, he joined an Antarctic expedition. Illness forced Shackleton to leave the expedition early, but he remained determined to further explore Antarctica. On the first expedition that he planned and led, Shackleton came within 97 miles of the South Pole. On the next, in 1914, his ship, the *Endurance,* got stuck in ice. It finally sank, stranding his crew. Shackleton's successful efforts to get his whole crew to safety, and ultimately home, became the best-known adventure of his life.

Before Reading

Building Background

Show students that forms of two words in the title are defined in the Glossary. Use a globe or map to locate Antarctica and the South Pole. Have students describe what they think that Antarctica might be like.

Vocabulary

explore, continent, expedition, South Pole, crew

English Language Learners

Point out the name of Shackleton's ship, the *Endurance.* Explain that the word *endurance* means being able to keep going through hard times. Ask them to explain why this name might be a good one for the ship and an expedition.

Target Reading Skill: Main Idea and Details

Turn to the inside front cover and have children read the Before Reading section. Show them the main idea graphic organizer and have them read the labels with you. Point out that sometimes the main idea of a book is found at the beginning or the end of the book. In this case it can be found at the end: *Ernest Shackleton was a brave leader and explorer.* Write the sentence under Main Idea in the graphic organizer and post it for reference.

During Reading

Read and Respond

Turn to the inside front cover and read the During Reading section. Provide sticky notes for children to flag pages that contain supporting details. Model how they can take turns with a partner reading pages aloud and pointing to details that tell more about the main idea.

After Reading

Speaking and Writing

Turn to the inside back cover and read the After Reading section with children. Distribute copies of the main idea graphic organizer. Have children fill them in using the supporting details they have flagged in their books. Gather as a group or have children work with partners to share details.

Answers to Target Reading Skill

Main Idea: Ernest Shackleton was a brave leader and explorer.

Details: He loved adventure. He became a sailor. He explored Antarctica. He planned and led expeditions. He came close to the South Pole. His ship got stuck and sank. He got everyone back safely.

Abraham Lincoln

by Karen Davila

Summary

Abraham Lincoln (1809–1865) is remembered and honored as a great president who maintained the Union during a difficult war and ended slavery. Born in the log cabin of his pioneer family, he learned to build and farm at an early age. Though he had little formal schooling, he loved to read and taught himself surveying and law. His reading of news and history led him into politics. Lincoln's own words, as well as stories about his life, are part of the history and culture of the United States.

Before Reading

Building Background

Have children look together at the cover and read the title. Ask children to name some places where they may have seen pictures of Abraham Lincoln (*penny, five dollar bill, Presidents' Day posters*). If possible, show children the bill and coin. Explain that Lincoln was president during a terrible time in our country.

Vocabulary

honor, pioneers, president, slavery, unite

English Language Learners

Write the word *president* on the board and have children pronounce it. Show children a picture of the current president of the United States. Explain that the president is elected by the people of our country. Display pictures of George Washington and Abraham Lincoln. Explain that Lincoln was our president about 150 years ago. Have children make up a sentence about one of the presidents, such as _____ *is our president now.*

Target Reading Skill: Compare and Contrast

Show children two items that are similar, but not exactly alike, such as two different books. Model comparing and contrasting the two books. Explain that when we compare things, we tell how they are alike. When we contrast things, we tell how they are different. After children have read the book, work with them to compare and contrast two pictures of Lincoln, such as the ones on page 2 and page 6.

During Reading

Read and Respond

Read the text aloud while children read along quietly. Pause after each page and invite children to retell what they learned about Lincoln. Then continue to read the story aloud while children follow in their books. Pause after each page to discuss the text. Ask questions, such as, *What was Lincoln like as a boy? What did Lincoln do when he was older?*

After Reading

Drawing

After reading the book, discuss the illustrations. Then have children draw two pictures of Lincoln. One should show something Lincoln did when he was younger. The other should show something Lincoln did when he was grown up. Invite volunteers to compare and contrast their drawings.

Speaking

Have children sit with a partner and take turns retelling the story to each other. Then call on volunteers to stand and say a sentence that tells something they learned about Lincoln. If children need prompting, give them a sentence starter, such as "Abraham Lincoln worked _____."

Answers to Target Reading Skill

Alike: Both pictures show Lincoln.

Different: The first shows a statue of Lincoln. The second is a drawing. He is standing.

President Abraham Lincoln

by Karen Davila

Summary

Abraham Lincoln (1809–1865) is remembered and honored as a great president who maintained the Union during a difficult war and ended slavery. Born in the log cabin of his pioneer family, he learned to build and farm at an early age. Though he had little formal schooling, he loved to read and taught himself surveying and law. His reading of news and history led him into politics. Lincoln's own words, as well as stories about his life, are part of the history and culture of the United States.

Before Reading

Building Background

Have children look together at the cover and read the title. Ask children to name some places where they may have seen pictures of Abraham Lincoln (*penny, five dollar bill, Presidents' Day posters*). If possible, show children the bill and coin, or pictures of the Lincoln Memorial and Mt. Rushmore. Tell children that these are examples of how Lincoln is still honored today.

Vocabulary

president, honor, pioneers, government, elected, slavery

English Language Learners

After you read the book aloud to children, write sentence frames, such as, *When Lincoln was a boy, he _____* on the board. Have children take turns filling in the frame orally with something they learned from the book. Repeat the procedure with *When Lincoln was a man, he _____.*

Target Reading Skill: Compare and Contrast

Display two items that are similar, but not exactly alike, such as two different books. Model comparing and contrasting them. Explain that when we compare things, we tell how they are alike. When we contrast things, we tell how they are different. After children have read the book, work with them to compare and contrast two pictures of Lincoln, such as the ones on page 4 and page 7.

During Reading

Read and Respond

Read the text aloud while children read along quietly. Pause after each page and invite children to talk about the illustrations and to retell what they learned about Lincoln. Ask questions, such as, *What was Lincoln like as a boy? What kind of work did Lincoln do when he was a ___? How did Lincoln help our country?*

After Reading

Speaking
Drawing and Writing

Distribute drawing paper and have children a picture of something they learned about Lin Their pictures should show Lincoln as a boy or a man. Have them write a sentence that tells about their picture. You may wish to supply sentence starters on the board, such as, *When Lincoln was a boy, he ____* and *When Lincoln was a man he ____.* When the drawings are finished, call on volunteers to read their sentences aloud.

Answers to Target Reading Skill

Children's drawings and sentences should show Lincoln as a boy or as a man.

Abraham Lincoln
Civil War President
by Karen Davila

Summary

Abraham Lincoln (1809–1865) is remembered and honored as a great president who maintained the Union during a difficult war and ended slavery. Born in the log cabin of his pioneer family, he learned to build and farm at an early age. Though he had little formal schooling, he loved to read and taught himself surveying and law. His reading of news and history led him into politics. Lincoln's own words, as well as stories about his life, are part of the history and culture of the United States.

Before Reading

Building Background

Display a picture of Lincoln. Ask children to identify him and to tell where they have seen pictures of Lincoln (*penny, five dollar bill, Presidents' Day posters*). Show children the bill and coin, or pictures of the Lincoln Memorial and Mt. Rushmore. Tell children that these things are examples of how Lincoln is still honored today. Explain that Lincoln was president during a time when one part of our country was at war with another part. He worked to keep the country together.

Vocabulary

Civil War, pioneers, lawyer, government, elected, slavery

English Language Learners

Write *elect* on the board and discuss its meaning. Then write *Lincoln was elected president*. Show a picture of George Washington and of the current president. Invite children to use the words *elected* and *president* to tell about the pictures. Encourage children to use complete sentences, or if this is too challenging, provide sentence frames for them, such as ____ *is our president now*.

Target Reading Skill: Compare and Contrast

Display two items that are similar, but not exactly alike, such as two different books. Model comparing and contrasting them. Explain that when we compare things, we tell how they are alike. When we contrast things, we tell how they are different. Then choose two pictures in the book and invite children to compare and contrast them.

During Reading

Read and Respond

Read the text aloud. Pause after each page to discuss the content of each page. Ask questions, such as, *What was Lincoln's life like when he was a boy? What happened when Lincoln was nine?*

After Reading

After children have read the book, show or draw a large copy of a Venn diagram. Write *Abraham Lincoln* as a heading. Then write *Boy* above the left circle and *Man* above the right circle. Write *Both* above the intersecting area. Have children read these labels and note their placement above the circles. Work with children to fill in information in each of the three sections of the diagram. Allow time for children to complete the rest of the After Reading activity on the inside cover of their Readers.

Speaking

Ask children to work with a partner to practice telling things they learned about Lincoln from the book. Then call on volunteers to tell two things about Linclon as a boy and two things about him as a man.

Answers to Target Reading Skill

Possible notes for Venn diagram:

Boy: lived in log cabin, mother died, helped run farm, learned to read

Both: loved to read, worked hard, helped others, learned and studied

Man: lawyer, ran a store, won votes, elected president, helped end slavery

Sacagawea

by Karen Davila

Summary

Sacagawea (sa kuh juh WEE uh) was a Shoshone Native American born around 1788. In 1805, she and her husband joined the expedition of Meriwether Lewis and William Clark. The couple used their knowledge of Native American languages to help the expedition members communicate with people. Sacagawea's knowledge of land, plants, and animals was also valuable. Her role in this significant piece of American history has been honored in stories, statues, and commemorative coins.

Before Reading

Building Background

Provide context by explaining that the United States was not always as large as it is today. Other countries owned a great deal of land in the West. After much of that land was purchased by the U.S., Lewis and Clark were sent to explore the West. Sacagawea and her husband acted as guides on that expedition. Invite students to preview the book by looking at the pictures. Preview vocabulary words as well.

Vocabulary

explore, languages, history, honor

Target Reading Skill: Sequence

Create a sequence chart by folding a sheet of standard copy paper into three horizontal sections. Unfold the paper and label the sections *First, Next,* and *Last.* Write the heading *Sequence* at the top. Make copies to distribute later for the After Reading activity.

With children, read directions under Before Reading on the inside front cover. Show one copy or a large-scale model of the sequence chart. Help them read the heading and then the words *First, Next,* and *Last.*

English Language Learners

Have students note the word *explore.* Discuss how adding suffixes can change the meaning.

During Reading

Read and Respond

Read the text aloud while children follow in their books. As you read, ask children questions that will help establish sequence of events in the book. For example: What skills did Sacagawea learn as a child? (She learned to fish and hunt. She learned languages.) How did she use her skills when she joined the expedition? (She helped people talk to each other. She found food.) How do people honor her today? (They create stories, statues, and coins.)

After Reading

Writing

Distribute copies of the sequence chart and read directions under After Reading on the inside back cover. Help children use their understanding of the text and pictures in the book to write in the three sections.

Speaking

Invite children to share what they have written in their sequence charts. Model how they can use statements starting with *First, Next,* and *Last* to tell the order.

Have children work with partners or a group. Help them check back in the book to see if their answers reflect the sequence of events.

Answers to Target Reading Skill

Possible sequence:
First Sacagawea was born.
Next She learned to hunt and fish.
Last She was a guide.

Sacagawea Guide to the West

by Karen Davila

Summary

Sacagawea (sa kuh juh WEE uh) was a Shoshone Native American born around 1788. Almost twenty years later, she and her husband joined the expedition of Meriwether Lewis and William Clark. She used her knowledge of Native American languages as well as knowledge of land, plants, and animals and proved a valuable guide. Her role in this significant piece of American history has been honored in stories, statues, as well as commemorative coins.

Before Reading

Building Background

Provide context by explaining that the United States was not always as large as it is today. Other countries had owned or controlled land in the West. When the U.S. bought much of the land, Lewis and Clark were sent to explore the West and see what was there. Sacagawea and her husband acted as guides on that expedition. Use a map of the U.S. to point out the western U.S. and the Lewis and Clark expedition route. You may want to gather additional resources. Invite students to preview the book by looking at pictures. Preview vocabulary words.

Vocabulary

explore, expedition, guide, history, honor

Target Reading Skill: Sequence

Create a sequence chart by folding a sheet of paper into three horizontal sections. Label the sections *First*, *Next*, and *Last*. Write the heading *Sequence* at the top. Make copies to distribute later for the After Reading activity.

With children, read directions under Before Reading on the inside front cover. Show one copy or a large model of the sequence chart. Help them read the heading and *First*, *Next,* and *Last*.

English Language Learners

Point to the model sequence chart and read the words *First*, *Next*, and *Last* with children. Then ask them to volunteer their understanding of those words.

During Reading

Read and Respond

Read the text aloud while children follow in their books. As you read, ask children questions that will help establish the sequence of events in the book. For example: What skills did Sacagawea learn as a child? (She learned to fish and hunt. She learned languages.) How did she use her skills when she joined the expedition? (She helped people talk to each other. She found food.) How do people honor her today? (They create stories, statues, and coins.)

After Reading

Drawing

Distribute copies of the sequence chart and read directions under After Reading on the inside back cover. Help children understand the headings and how to use their understanding of the text and pictures to draw in the three sections.

Speaking

Invite children to share what they have written or drawn in their sequence charts. Model how they can use statements starting with *First*, *Next*, and *Last* to explain the order. Have children work with partners or a group to see if their answers reflect the page order of the book.

Answers to Target Reading Skill

Possible sequence:
First Sacagawea was born.
Next she learned to hunt and fish.
Last she was a guide.

Sacagawea
Trail Guide and Explorer

by Karen Davila

Summary

Sacagawea (sa kuh juh WEE uh) was a Shoshone Native American born around 1788. She and her husband joined the expedition of Meriwether Lewis and William Clark. The couple used their knowledge of Native American languages to help people communicate along the way. Sacagawea's knowledge of land, plants, and animals was also valuable. Her role in this significant piece of American history has been honored in stories, statues, and commemorative coins.

Before Reading

Building Background

Provide context by explaining that the United States was not always as large as it is today. Other countries owned a great deal of land in the West. After the U.S. purchased much of it, Lewis and Clark were sent to explore the West. Sacagawea and her husband acted as guides on that expedition.

Use a map of the U.S. to point out the Lewis and Clark expedition route. For additional context, you may want to gather additional resources.

Invite students to preview the book by looking at the pictures. Preview vocabulary words as well.

Vocabulary

expedition, history, interpreters, diary, honor

Target Reading Skill: Sequence

Create a sequence chart by folding a sheet of paper into three horizontal sections. Unfold the paper and label the sections *First*, *Next*, and *Last*. Write the heading *Sequence* at the top. Make copies to distribute later for the After Reading activity. With children, read directions under Before Reading on the inside front cover. Show one copy or a large-scale model of the sequence chart. Help them read the heading and then the words *First*, *Next*, and *Last*.

English Language Learners

Have students note the word *explore*. Discuss how adding suffixes can change the meaning.

During Reading

Read and Respond

Read the text aloud while children follow in their books. As you read, ask children questions that will help establish the book's sequence of events. For example: What skills did Sacagawea learn as a girl? (She learned to fish and hunt. She learned languages.) How did she use her skills when she joined the expedition? (She helped people talk to each other. She found food.) How do people honor her today? (They create stories, statues, and coins.)

After Reading

Writing

Distribute copies of the sequence chart and read the directions under After Reading on the inside back cover. Help children utilize their understanding of the text and pictures in the book to write in the three sections.

Speaking

Invite children to share what they have written in their sequence charts. Model how they can use statements starting with *First*, *Next*, and *Last* to tell the order. Have children work with partners or a group to check the book to see if their answers reflect the page order of the book.

Answers to Target Reading Skill

First Sacagawea was born.
Next she learned to hunt and fish.
Last she guided an expedition.

John Adams

by Teri L. Tilwick

We Do Our Part

Chapter: My Community, My Country

Lexile Measure: 240

Summary

John Adams, our second president, grew up on a Massachusetts farm in Massachusetts. In 1764, he married Abigail Smith. America was ruled by Great Britain at that time, and Adams (among others) wanted America to be an independent country. After helping America win its war of independence from Great Britain, Adams served as the second president of the United States. He was the first president to live in the White House.

Before Reading

Building Background

Build background for the book by directing children's attention to the illustrations. Invite them to identify how the costumes and setting in the images provide evidence that the events occurred long ago. Also invite students to discuss what they know about the American Revolutionary War period.

Vocabulary

colonies, freedom

English Language Learners

To help communicate content, have students work in pairs or as a group to paraphrase words and vocabulary words in the text. Model how to do this by reading a selected passage aloud and restating it in your own words.

Target Reading Skill: Draw Conclusions

Explain to children that when we read, we can put facts together to make a decision about a person, a place, or an event. This helps us to better understand what we read. To make this kind of decision is called *drawing a conclusion*.

Tell children that they are about to read a book about John Adams, our second president, and they will learn new things about his life.

Have each child write *Things I Learn About John Adams* at the top of a sheet of paper, and list new facts about him as they read. Point out that children can also learn facts by looking at the pictures.

When children finish the book, have them read their facts to a partner. Children may work together to draw a conclusion about Adams based on these facts. Have students write it at the bottom of their papers.

During Reading

Think Critically

1. When Adams was young, what did he want to be? (a farmer)
2. Why did American leaders want a Declaration of Independence? (They wanted to be free from Great Britain.)
3. What was Adams first to do? (He was the first president to live in the White House.)

After Reading

Writing

Tell children to think about Adams and write a word or sentence or two about him.

Answers to Target Reading Skill

Possible facts: Adams grew up on a farm. He became a lawyer. He worked for freedom. He was the second president of the United States.

Possible conclusions: John Adams was a busy man. He helped America become free.

President John Adams

by Teri L. Tilwick

Summary

John Adams, the country's second president, was born in Braintree, Massachusetts, in 1735. His father, a farmer, shoemaker, and town leader, urged Adams to stay in school. Adams attended college, taught school, and then became a lawyer. In 1764, he married Abigail Smith. Because Adams frequently traveled, they often wrote letters and shared their thoughts and ideas. At this time, the colonies were ruled by Great Britain. Adams and other American leaders met in Philadelphia and requested a declaration of independence be written. The colonies had to fight for their independence. In 1797, Adams became the second president of the United States and the first to live in the White House.

Before Reading

Building Background

Build background for the book by inviting children to discuss what they know about the founding fathers, the thirteen colonies, and the Revolutionary War. What events might John Adams have participated in?

Vocabulary

founder, colonies, declaration, independence, elected

English Language Learners

To help communicate content, have students work in pairs or as a group to paraphrase key ideas and vocabulary words and phrases from the text. Model how to do this by reading a selected passage aloud and restating it in your own words.

Target Reading Skill: Draw Conclusions

Explain to children that when we read, we can put facts together to make a decision or form an opinion about a person, a place, or an event. This helps us to better understand what we read. To make this kind of decision is called *drawing a conclusion*.

Have each child write *Things I Learn About John Adams* at the top of a sheet of paper, and list new facts about him as they read and as they look at the pictures. Point out that not all the facts in this book have to do with John Adams.

When children finish the book, have them reread their list of facts to a partner. Have children think about the facts and draw a conclusion about Adams, and then write it at the bottom of their papers.

During Reading

Think Critically

1. Why do you think John Adams wanted to be a farmer? (His father was a farmer.)

2. What was the purpose of the Declaration of Independence? (To state that the colonies will be free of British rule.)

3. Why did the colonies wanted to be free? (It was unfair for someone else to make the rules for the colonies.)

After Reading

Writing

Work with a partner and write a short letter to the King of England saying why the colonies should be free.

Answers to Target Reading Skill

Possible facts include: (1.) John Adams was our second president. (2.) He was born in Braintree, Massachusetts in 1735. (3.) He wanted to be a farmer, but his father wanted him to stay in school. (4.) He became a lawyer. (5.) He met with other leaders in Philadelphia. (6.) The leaders asked for a declaration of independence. (7.) Adams made sure America had a navy during its war with Great Britain. (8.) He was elected president in 1796. (9.) He was the first to live in the White House.

Possible conclusion: John Adams did a lot to help the United States.

John Adams
Our Second President

by Teri L. Tilwick

We Do Our Part

Chapter: My Community, My Country

Lexile Msasure: 540

Summary

John Adams, our second president, was born in Massachusetts, in 1735. His father was a farmer, shoemaker and town leader. While Adams wanted to become a farmer, his father urged him to stay in school. Adams attended college and became a lawyer. In 1764, John Adams and Abigail Smith married. Because John Adams was often traveling, they wrote letters in which they shared thoughts and ideas. Adams was a member of the Continental Congress that approved the Declaration of Independence stating the colonies should be free. When the colonies won their independence, Adams became the second president of the new country.

Before Reading

Building Background

Build background for the book by inviting students to discuss what they may know about the founding fathers, the thirteen colonies, and the American Revolution. What events might John Adams have participated in?

Vocabulary

founder, colonies, congress, declaration, independence, elected

English Language Learners

To help communicate content, have students work in pairs to paraphrase key ideas and vocabulary words and phrases from the text. Model how to do this by reading a selected passage aloud and restating it in your own words.

Target Reading Skill: Draw Conclusions

Explain to children that when we read, we can put facts together to make a decision about a person, a place, or an event. This helps us better understand what we read. This is called drawing a conclusion.

Tell children that they are about to read a book about the life of John Adams. Have each child write *Things I Learn About John Adams* at the top of a sheet of paper. Then tell them to list facts about Adams as they read each section. Ask children to make a line after each section with enough room to write on it. When children have finished reading each section, have them draw a conclusion based on the facts and write it on the line.

During Reading

Think Critically

1. Why do you think Adams wanted to be a farmer? (His father was a farmer.)

2. What changed before and after the war with Great Britain? (Before, the colonies were ruled by Britain. After, America was free.)

3. Why did President Adams say, "May none but honest and wise men ever rule under this roof"? (He hoped all presidents would be great leaders.)

After Reading

Writing

Adams wrote his thoughts about freedom in the *Boston Gazette*. Work with a partner to list several points Adams might have raised in his article.

Answers to Target Reading Skill

Possible facts in *From Farm Boy to Lawyer:* (1.) John Adams went to college. (2.) Adams taught school. (3.) Adams became a lawyer. Possible conclusion: Being a teacher and a lawyer helped Adams become a leader.

A Leader for American Freedom: (1.) Adams wrote about freedom for the colonies. (2.) Adams was a member of the Continental Congress. (3.) He helped Thomas Jefferson write the Declaration of Independence. Possible conclusion: John Adams helped create the government of the United States.

The War for Independence: (1.) Adams was the first vice president. (2.) Adams was elected president in 1797. (3.) Adams and his family were the first to live in the White House. Possible conclusion: Adams was an important leader.

Elizabeth Blackwell

by Teri Tilwick

Summary

In 1849, Elizabeth Blackwell became the first woman to graduate from medical school. Only men went to medical school in the mid-1800s. When Blackwell applied, only Geneva Medical College in Geneva, New York, accepted her. Blackwell was a top student. After graduation she got a job in a maternity hospital in Paris, France. During the Civil War, Blackwell trained nurses in the United States. She later opened a medical college for women.

Before Reading

Building Background

Build background for the book by having children read aloud the title with you. Then take a picture walk through the book. Point out the old-fashioned clothing, and explain that Elizabeth Blackwell lived a long time ago. Ask children to tell what they think Elizabeth Blackwell did that made her famous. Tell them that as they read they will find out what was special about Blackwell's life.

Vocabulary

medical, maternity

English Language Learners

Have children review the words *woman* and *man* by pointing out individuals in the illustrations. Then have them review the plural forms, *women* and *men*, by pointing out groups on pages 3, 5, and 7. Call on volunteers to use the words *woman*, *women*, *man* and *men* in their own sentences about the pictures in this book. Point out that most words add *s* to make the plural, so these words are irregular plurals. Underline the *a* and *e* to point out the spelling difference.

Target Reading Skill: Main Idea and Details

Help children understand the concepts of main idea and details. Display the following sentence and read it aloud. *Firefighters help people.* Have children give examples of the things firefighters do to help people, such as *put out fires, teach people about fire safety* and *help people escape from a fire.* Explain that *Firefighters help people* is a main idea. The ways they help people are details that tell more about the main idea. You may wish to write the main idea and details in a graphic organizer as you teach the skill.

During Reading

Think Critically

1. What was Elizabeth Blackwell's dream? (She wanted to be a doctor.)
2. Why was it hard for her to make her dream come true? (There were no women doctors then.)
3. Name three ways that Blackwell helped women. (She became America's first woman doctor; she worked at a maternity hospital; she opened a women's medical school.)

After Reading

Using the Graphic Organizer

Now distribute the Main Idea graphic organizer or create one of your own for children. Discuss with children that the book tells about what important thing Blackwell did. (She was America's first woman doctor.) Have children find facts that tell about her medical career, and tell them that these are details that support the main idea. Guide children to write these details in the boxes labeled Supporting Detail. Allow children time to complete the Target Reading Skill activity on the inside cover of their Readers.

Answers to Target Reading Skill

Main Idea: Blackwell was the first woman doctor. Supporting Details: Accept drawings that show any of the following possible details: worked hard in school, worked in a maternity hospital, trained nurses, started a medical school for women.

Doctor Elizabeth Blackwell

by Teri Tilwick

Summary

In the middle 1800s, when no other women went to medical school or became doctors, Elizabeth Blackwell managed to accomplish both. Shunned at first, she graduated first in her class to become the first female doctor. American hospitals would not hire her, so her first job was in France at a maternity hospital. Returning to America she adopted 7-year-old Kitty Barry, opened a medical center for poor women and children, trained nurses for the Civil War, and opened a medical college for women. She spent her last years with Kitty in England, and wrote many books.

Before Reading

Building Background

Build background for the book by talking about doctors. (Make sure some are women.) Then take a picture walk through the book with children. Ask them what they see. Guide children to conclude that these events took place long ago, and that they have to do with doctors.

Vocabulary

applied, medical, maternity, orphan, wounded

English Language Learners

Write the words *medicine* and *medical* on the board and help children read them. Underline the *medi* in each word. Help children use each word in a sentence. Spanish-speaking ELLs may know the words *medicina* (medicine), *médica* (medical) and *médico* (doctor).

Target Reading Skill: Main Idea and Details

Draw a main idea and details graphic organizer on the board. Then display the following and read it aloud: *Firefighters help people.* Explain that *Firefighters help people* is a main idea.

Then have children give examples of the things firefighters do to help people, such as *put out fires, teach people about fire safety* and *help people escape from a fire.* As children give examples, write them in the Supporting Details boxes. Explain that the ways firefighters help people are details that tell more about the main idea.

During Reading

Think Critically

1. What is one reason Elizabeth Blackwell wanted to be a doctor? (Possible answers: She disagreed that this was not a job for women; a friend gave her the idea of becoming a doctor; she wanted to help others.)

2. Why did students at Geneva College vote that Blackwell should go to their school? (They thought it was a joke.)

3. How did Blackwell help women during her lifetime? (She became a doctor; she helped mothers with newborns; she set up a clinic for poor women and children; she adopted an orphan, Kitty Barry; she trained nurses; she opened a medical college.)

4. Which of the things Blackwell did do you think was most important? Why? (Accept any of the following, with a reason children can support: became first woman doctor; treated mothers, newborns, poor women, and poor children; trained nurses; trained women to become doctors; adopted an orphan; wrote books.)

After Reading

Target Reading Skill: Main Idea and Details

Distribute the Main Idea graphic organizer or create one of your own. Tell children to turn to page 5 and help them reread that page. Guide them to write, *Blackwell needed a job* in the box labeled Main Idea. Then guide them to write *Hospitals in America would not hire her* in a box labeled Supporting Detail. Allow children time to complete the Target Reading Skill activity on the inside cover of their Readers.

Answers to Target Reading Skill

Main idea: Now Blackwell needed a job.
Supporting details: Blackwell went to France; Blackwell worked at a maternity hospital; Blackwell liked working with the babies.

Elizabeth Blackwell America's First Woman Doctor

by Teri Tilwick

Summary

In the mid 1800s, when no other women went to medical school or became doctors, Elizabeth Blackwell managed to do both. Shunned at first, she graduated first in her class at Geneva Medical College, the first woman to graduate from a medical college. American hospitals would not hire her, so her first job was in France at a maternity hospital. Returning to America, she adopted a child, opened a medical center for poor women and children, trained nurses for the Civil War, and opened a medical college for women. She spent her last years in England.

Before Reading

Building Background

Read the title aloud. Explain that Blackwell lived a long time *ago*, when no women became doctors. Ask them to tell what they think Blackwell did that made her famous.

Vocabulary

medical, maternity, orphan, wounded, pioneer

Target Reading Skill: Main Idea and Details

Write the following on the board. *Firefighters help people.* Have children name things firefighters do to help people such as, *put out fires, teach people about fire safety, help people escape from a fire.* As children give their ideas. Write them in sentences under the main idea sentence. Tell children the first sentence is a main idea, and the other sentences tell details. Tell children to look for main ideas and details about Blackwell as you read the book.

During Reading

Think Critically

1. What is one reason Elizabeth Blackwell wanted to be a doctor? (Possible answer: A friend gave her the idea of becoming a doctor; she wanted to help others.)

2. How did Blackwell finally get into medical school? (Geneva Medical College students voted on whether she could attend. Since they thought it was a joke, they voted to let her in.)

3. What kinds of things became possible for women because of Blackwell? (She opened the way for other women to become doctors. She trained nurses. She opened a medical college for women in New York.)

English Language Learners

Write the words *man/men* and *woman/women* on the board. Review the irregular plurals *men* and *women.* Have children use the words in sentences.

Write the words *medicine* and *medical* on the board and help children read them. Underline *medi* in each word. Help children use each word in a sentence. Spanish-speaking ELLs may know the words *medicina* (medicine), *médica* (medical) and *médico* (doctor).

After Reading

Complete Graphic Organizer

Distribute the Main Idea graphic organizer or create one of your own for children. Have children reread pages 6 and 7 or reread it with them. Help children find the main idea of these two pages. Then allow children time to complete the Target Reading Skill activity.

Answers to Target Reading Skill

Main Idea: Elizabeth Blackwell did many things that made a difference.

Supporting Details: (Accept any of the following) She adopted Kitty, she opened a medical center for poor women and children; she trained nurses; she opened a medical college for women.

John Muir

by Teri L. Tilwick

We Do Our Part

Chapter: The World
Around Us

Lexile Measure: 230

Summary

John Muir, known as the "Father of Our National Parks," was one of America's early conservationists. Born in Scotland in 1838, Muir came to America with his family as a child. He lived on a farm and made clever inventions that people noticed. Muir attended college, where he studied nature, among other subjects. After leaving college, he devoted himself to the appreciation and protection of nature. This began with his 1,000-mile walk from Indiana to Florida and continued with his efforts to protect Yosemite and other natural lands. The Sierra Club was established; Muir was their first president. President Theodore Roosevelt helped create the national parks.

Before Reading

Building Background

Build background for the book by having children share experiences seeing or being in natural settings. Tell them that John Muir worked to protect nature.

Vocabulary

national, inventor, hiked

Target Reading Skill: Cause and Effect

Explain to children that an effect is something that happens, and a cause is the reason why it happens. Give children this example: Joe was so hungry that he gobbled down his sandwich. Ask: *What did Joe do?* (He gobbled down his sandwich.) *What was the reason?* (He was so hungry.) Explain that identifying causes and effects can help us better understand what we read. Note that sometimes there are clue words such as *so, because,* or *since* which can help identify cause and effect.

Distribute a cause-and-effect organizer and tell children to take notes on cause-and-effect relationships they find as they read. Provide guidance as needed.

English Language Learners

Find cause-and-effect situations in the classroom, and guide children to construct sentences about them. (Example: The bell rings, so I sit down.) Children may point to pictures if they need vocabulary support.

During Reading

Think Critically

Why is John Muir known as "Father of Our National Parks"? (He helped create our national parks.) What talent did Muir show as a boy and a young man? (He was an inventor.) What did Muir mean by "University of the Wilderness"? (He meant that he could learn a great deal by studying nature outdoors.)

After Reading

Writing

Discuss the graphic organizer and remind children that the answer to the question "What happened?" is the effect, and the answer to "Why did it happen?" is the cause. Have them reread their notes with a partner and write one or more cause-and-effect relationships on the chart.

Writing

Ask students to write about or draw something they have seen or imagined in nature (a river, a mountain, a bird's nest.)

Answers to Target Reading Skill

Possible effects are listed first because the first column is headed "What happened?" Possible causes are second because the column is headed "Why did it happen?"

(1.) John Muir is called the "Father of Our National Parks." Muir cared about protecting nature. (2.) Muir was excited. His family went to America. (3.) A desk helped him study. Muir invented a desk.

John Muir
Protector of Nature

by Teri L. Tilwick

We Do Our Part

Chapter: The World Around Us

Lexile Measure: 450

Summary

John Muir, known as the "Father of Our National Parks," was one of America's early conservationists. Born in Scotland in 1838, Muir came to America with his family as a child. Living on a farm left him time to invent, and his inventions gained him recognition at the state fair. Muir attended the University of Wisconsin. After leaving college he sustained a serious eye injury. When it healed, he devoted himself to the appreciation and protection of nature. This began with his 1,000-mile walk from Indiana to Florida and continued with his efforts to protect Yosemite and other natural lands. The Sierra Club was established; Muir was its first president. President Theodore Roosevelt was persuaded by Muir to help create the national parks and preserve millions of acres of wilderness.

Before Reading

Building Background

Build background by having children share experiences seeing or being in nature. Tell them that John Muir worked to protect nature.

Vocabulary

national, inventing, University, compass, acre

Target Reading Skill: Cause and Effect

Explain to children that an effect is something that happens, and a cause is the reason why it happens. Give children this example: Joe was so hungry that he gobbled down his sandwich. Ask: *What did Joe do?* (He gobbled down his sandwich.) *What was the reason?* (He was so hungry.) Use the words *cause and effect*. Explain that identifying causes and effects can help us better understand what we read. Note that sometimes there are clue words such as *so, because* or *since* which can help identify cause and effect.

Distribute a cause-and-effect organizer and tell children to take notes on cause-and-effect relationships they find as they read.

English Language Learners

Find cause-and-effect situations in the classroom, and guide children to construct sentences about them. (Example: The bell rings, so I sit down.) Children may point to pictures if needed.

During Reading

Think Critically

Why is John Muir known as "Father of Our National Parks"? (He helped create our national parks.) What talent did Muir show as a young man? (He was an inventor.) What did Muir mean by "University of the Wilderness"? (He meant that he could learn by studying nature.)

After Reading

Writing

Discuss the graphic organizer and remind children that the answer to the question "What happened?" is the effect. The answer to "Why did it happen?" is the cause. Have them reread their notes with a partner and write two or more cause-and-effect relationships on the chart.

Writing

Ask students to write about something they have seen or imagined in nature (a river, a mountain) and why they think it should be protected.

Answers to Target Reading Skill

Possible effects are listed first under "What happened?" Possible causes are listed second under the heading "Why did it happen?"

(1.) John Muir is called the "Father of Our National Parks." Muir cared about protecting nature.
(2.) Muir was excited. His family would sail to America. (3.) Muir moved to Madison, Wisconsin. He wanted to attend the University of Wisconsin.

John Muir and Our National Parks

by Teri L. Tilwick

We Do Our Part

Chapter: The World Around Us

Lexile Measure: 590

Summary

John Muir, known as the "Father of Our National Parks," was one of America's early conservationists. Born in Scotland in 1838, Muir came to America with his family as a child. Living on a farm left him time to tinker, and his clever inventions gained him recognition at the Wisconsin State Fair. Muir attended the University of Wisconsin. After leaving college, he sustained a serious eye injury. When it healed, he devoted himself to the appreciation and protection of nature. This began with his 1,000-mile walk from Indiana to Florida and continued with his efforts to protect Yosemite and other natural lands. The Sierra Club was established; Muir was their first president. President Theodore Roosevelt helped create the national parks and preserved millions of acres of land.

Before Reading

Building Background

Build background for the book by having children share experiences seeing or being in natural settings. Tell them that John Muir worked to protect nature.

Vocabulary

inventor, exhibit, University, acres

Target Reading Skill: Cause and Effect

Explain to children that an effect is something that happens, and a cause is the reason why it happens. Give children this example: Joe was so hungry that he gobbled down his sandwich. Ask: *What did Joe do?* (He gobbled down his sandwich.) *What was the reason?* (He was so hungry.) Use the words *cause and effect*. Explain that identifying causes and effects can help us better understand what we read. Note that sometimes there are clue words such as *so*, *because*, or *since* which can help identify cause and effect.

Distribute the cause and effect organizer and tell children to take notes on cause-and-effect relationships they find as they read.

English Language Learners

Find cause-and-effect situations in the classroom, and guide children to construct sentences about them. (Example: The bell rings, so I sit down.) Children may point to pictures for support.

During Reading

Think Critically

Why is John Muir known as "Father of Our National Parks"? (He helped create our national parks.) What talent did Muir show as a young man? (inventing) What did Muir mean by "University of the Wilderness"? (He meant that he could learn a great deal by studying nature.)

After Reading

Writing

Discuss the graphic organizer and remind children that the answer to the question "What happened?" is the effect, and the answer to "Why did it happen?" is the cause. Have them reread their notes with a partner and write two or more cause-and-effect relationships on the chart.

Writing

Ask students to write about something they have seen or imagined in nature (a river, a mountain) and why they think it should be protected.

Answers to Target Reading Skill

Possible effects are listed first because the first column is headed "What happened?" Possible causes are second because the column is headed "Why did it happen?"

(1.) John Muir is called the "Father of Our National Parks." Muir cared about protecting nature.
(2.) Muir was excited. His family would sail to America. (3.) Muir moved to Madison, Wisconsin. He wanted to attend the University of Wisconsin.

Paul Revere

by Teri L. Tilwick

Summary

Paul Revere (1734–1818) spent his life in Boston and was a well-known silversmith and engraver. Revere was also a Patriot, and his actions for this cause took many forms. Among them, he participated in the Boston Tea Party and served as a messenger and a spy. His most famous "message delivery" was the dramatic midnight ride to warn Patriots of the British advance.

Before Reading

Building Background

Build background for the book by explaining to students that the United States was once ruled by Great Britain and that Paul Revere lived during this time.

Vocabulary

Patriots, taxes, spy, independence

English Language Learners

Display the following time words and phrases from the text: *long ago* (page 2), and *then* (page 13) on the board. Help reinforce the meanings of these words and phrases by helping children use them in simple sentences. Discuss other words that help readers know when something happened.

Target Reading Skill: Compare and Contrast

Tell children that to compare is to find how things are alike and to contrast is to find how things are different. Write *Compare* on the board. Hold up an orange and an apple. Say, "Look at these two fruits. How are they alike?" Write children's answers on the board under *Compare*. (They are both fruits, round, sweet, healthy.) Next, write *Contrast*. Hold up the fruits again. Say, "Tell me how they are different." Write their answers under the word *Contrast*. (They are different colors, sizes, and so on.)

Have children reread pages 9 through 11. Ask: What is the same about the lamp signals? What is different?

Have children work with a partner to list the similarities and differences on a separate sheet of paper.

Display a large Venn diagram and show children how you would use it to organize the information on the lists. Label the left outer circle *One Lamp*, and the right outer circle *Two Lamps*. Explain that they are to write in the middle how the signals were the same, and in the outer circles how the signals were different. Work through the Target Reading Skill activity as a class.

During Reading

Think Critically

1. What are some words that describe Paul Revere? (Patriot, hero, American, colonist)

2. Where did Revere live? (He lived in Boston.)

3. What did the lanterns mean? (The British were about to attack—one lantern meant they were coming by land and two by sea.)

4. What did Paul Revere do during his famous ride? (He woke Patriots up and told them that the British were coming.)

After Reading

Target Reading Skill

Give out the diagrams. Have children work with a partner to complete one, using their lists. Review the information together as a class.

Answers to Target Reading Skill

One lamp: The British were coming by land. This signal was not used.

Two lamps: The British were coming by sea. This is the signal that was used.

Same: Both would send a message. Both would shine in the tower.

Paul Revere
Ride for Liberty

by Teri L. Tilwick

We Do Our Part

Chapter: We Share Our Traditions

Lexile Measure: 530

Summary

Paul Revere (1735–1818) spent his life in Boston and was a well-known silversmith and engraver. Revere was a Patriot, and his actions for this cause took many forms. Among them, he participated in the Boston Tea Party and served as a messenger and a spy. His most famous "message delivery" was the dramatic midnight ride to warn Patriots of the British advance. In 1860, Henry Wadsworth Longfellow wrote a poem about Revere that helped enshrine Revere's ride in American culture.

Before Reading

Building Background

Build background for the book by explaining that the United States was once ruled by a country called Great Britain. Have children scan the images and captions to learn more about Revere's life. Next have children read the title. Tell children that *liberty* means "freedom." Ask children why the author used the word "ride" in the title. (Revere rides a horse.) Then, if possible, read the opening stanza to "Paul Revere's Ride."

Vocabulary

colonies, independence, engraved, taxes, Patriots, spies

English Language Learners

Display the time words and phrases *long ago* (page 2), *back then* (page 3), as well as such dates as 1735 (page 2) and 1775 (pages 10 and 11). Review these dates and time phrases before children read the book. Help children practice using the words and phrases in sentences of their own.

Target Reading Skill: Compare and Contrast

Write *Compare* and *Contrast* on the board. Hold up two books that vary in size. Say, "Look at these two books. Tell me how they are alike." (They are books, you are holding them, we read them.) Write children's answers under *Compare*. Then ask: "How are they are different?" Write answers under *Contrast*. (Possible answers may include differences in color, size, title, details on cover.) Tell students that, as they read, they should note the ways in which Revere communicated with others. After reading, students will be asked to compare and contrast the ways that colonists communicated then with the ways that people communicate today. They will put this information in a Venn diagram that you provide for them.

During Reading

Think Critically

1. Why did people ring church bells? (The bells let people know when something important happened.)
2. What kind of work did Revere do? (He made things from silver.)
3. How did lanterns warn the Patriots? (They told that the British were coming. Two lanterns meant they were coming by water. One meant they were coming by land.)
4. What did Revere do during his ride? (He rode to villagers' houses in Lexington to tell them that the British were coming.)

After Reading

Writing

Have children look at the illustration on page 15 and write what they think that Revere might be say to his grandchildren. Encourage children to include examples of comparing and contrasting.

Answers to Target Reading Skill

Old ways: ring bells, knock on doors, light lanterns.

New way: phone, text, email

Same: All are about getting information to others.

Different: New ways are faster and easier.

Paul Revere
American Patriot

by Teri L. Tilwick

Summary

Paul Revere (1734–1818) spent his life in Boston and was a well-known silversmith and engraver. Revere was a Patriot, and his actions for this cause took many forms. Among them, he participated in the Boston Tea Party and served as a messenger and a spy. His most famous "message delivery" was the dramatic midnight ride to warn Patriots of the British advance. In 1860, Henry Wadsworth Longfellow wrote a poem about Revere that helped enshrine the ride in American culture.

Before Reading

Building Background

Build background for the book by explaining to students that much of what is now the United States was once ruled by a country called Great Britain. Have children scan the images, captions, and headings throughout the book. Tell them to look at the words *Patriots* and *independence* in the glossary. Next have them read the title and explain what it might mean.

Vocabulary

colonies, independence, Patriots, silversmith, engrave, taxes, harbor, spies

English Language Learners

Display the following time words and phrases from the text: *long ago* (page 2), *at that time* (page 2), *a few years later* (page 4), *the next day* (page 8), and *soon* (page 9) on the board. Help reinforce the meanings of these words and phrases by helping children use them in simple sentences.

Target Reading Skill: Compare and Contrast

Write *Compare* and *Contrast* on the board. Hold up a book and a magazine. Say, "Tell me how these are alike." (Both contain writing; you can read both.) Write answers under *Compare*. Then say, "Tell me how they are different." Write answers under *Contrast*. (Possible answers: different size; the book is about one subject while the magazine is about many.)

Then draw a compare and contrast Venn diagram on the board and demonstrate how to insert the information they have provided. Tell students that, as they read, they should take note of the ways that Revere communicated with others. After reading, students will create their own diagram. They will compare and contrast the ways that colonists communicated then with the ways that people communicate today.

During Reading

Think Critically

1. What was Revere's job? (He was a silversmith.)

2. Why did Revere and his friends ring church bells? (The bells told people when something important happened.)

3. What did the lanterns tell the Patriots? (If two were lit, the British were coming by water. If only one, they were coming by land.)

4. What words would you use to describe Paul Revere? (hero, brave, silversmith, artist, spy, Patriot, American)

After Reading

Writing

Have children write a poem about part of Revere's life, such as his job as a bell ringer, his business, his activities with the Sons of Liberty, or the famous ride of April 18, 1775.

Answers to Target Reading Skill

Old ways: ring bells, knock on doors, light lanterns.

New ways: phone, text, email

Same: All are about getting information to others.

Different: New ways are easier and faster.

Harriet Tubman

by Teri L. Tilwick

Summary

Harriet Tubman was born in Maryland around 1820 to a family of enslaved African Americans. She married a free African American named John Tubman, but she remained enslaved until her escape via the Underground Railroad. Tubman returned to the South many times to free hundreds of other enslaved African Americans. She assisted the North during the Civil War and finally settled in Auburn, New York. There, she opened the Harriet Tubman Home to help homeless and ill people.

Before Reading

Building Background

Tell children this story is about a brave African American woman who escaped from slavery and then helped others to do the same.

English Language Learners

To build background, help children break down the metaphor *Underground Railroad*. Explain that *underground* used in Underground Railroad does not mean something "below ground." Explain that *underground* can also mean "secret," because things that are underground are hidden from view. Then explain that the word *railroad* used in the term *Underground Railroad* does not mean steel tracks and real trains. Explain that it means a way for people to travel. Therefore, *Underground Railroad* means "a secret way for people to travel."

Vocabulary

slavery, plantation, overseer

Target Reading Skill: Fact and Opinion

Write on the board the words *fact* and *opinion*. Explain that a fact can be proven but an opinion is someone's feelings and cannot be proven. Present this example:

> Today is Monday.
> Matt thinks that Mondays are great.

Explain that the first sentence tells a fact. Because it can be proven to be true or not, it is a fact. Explain that the second sentence is an opinion. It is how Matt feels. Distribute the T-chart graphic organizer. Have children write *Fact* at the top of the left column and *Opinion* at the top of the right column. Tell students that, after reading, they will write one fact and one opinion from the book. After reading, record everyone's facts and opinions on the board and have students discuss what makes each one a fact or an opinion.

During Reading

Think Critically

1. Where did Tubman's grandparents come from? (West Africa)
2. What was the Underground Railroad? (a secret path to freedom for slaves)
3. Why was Tubman happy when she reached Pennsylvania? (She was free.)
4. How did Tubman help her family? (She helped her sister and her parents to escape.)

After Reading

Writing

Work with children to write a poem about Harriet Tubman's escape to Pennsylvania. When the poem is finished, have children read it chorally. They may wish to share their poem with other classes.

Answers to Target Reading Skill

Possible Facts: Harriet Tubman escaped slavery; she helped her parents and many others escape; the Underground Railroad was a secret way for slaves to escape. Possible opinions: She was brave; we think of her as an American hero.

Harriet Tubman: The Road to Freedom

by Teri L. Tilwick

Summary

Harriet Tubman was born in Maryland around 1820 to a family of enslaved African Americans. She married a free African American named John Tubman, but she remained enslaved until her escape via the Underground Railroad. Tubman returned to the South many times to free hundreds of other enslaved African Americans. She assisted the North during the Civil War. She lived out her days in Auburn, New York and is remembered as an American hero.

Before Reading

Building Background

Explain that this story takes place in a time when many Americans were enslaved and some tried to escape.

English Language Learners

To build background, help children break down the metaphor *Underground Railroad*. Explain that *underground* used in Underground Railroad does not mean something "below ground." Explain that *underground* can also mean "secret," because things that are underground are hidden from view. Then explain that the word *railroad* used in the term *Underground Railroad* is not referring to trains. Explain that it means a way for people to travel. The *Underground Railroad* was a secret way for people to travel.

Vocabulary

slavery, plantation, overseer

Target Reading Skill: Fact and Opinion

Write on the board the words *fact* and *opinion*. Explain that a fact can be proven but an opinion is someone's belief and cannot be proven. Present this example:

> It is raining outside.
> Keisha thinks rainy days are beautiful.

Explain that the first sentence tells a fact; you can prove whether it is raining or not. Explain that the second sentence is Keisha's opinion. Distribute the two-column T-chart graphic organizer to children. Have them write *Fact* at the top of the first column and *Opinion* at the top of the second column. Explain to them that, as they read, they will record two facts and opinions they find in the book. Collect and record answers on the board, and have students discuss why some statements are facts and others are opinions.

During Reading

Think Critically

1. Where and when was Harriet Tubman born? (She was born about 1820 in Maryland.)

2. What did Tubman know about her grandparents? (She knew they had lived in West Africa.)

3. Why did Tubman say she felt like she was in heaven when she crossed into Pennsylvania? (She was so happy to be free.)

4. Why did Harriet go back to the South? (She wanted to help other slaves escape.)

After Reading

Writing

Review the meaning of *opinion*. Ask students to write down their opinions. What did they think about the book? How did they feel about Harriet Tubman's story.

Activity

Have children act out Tubman's escape on the Underground Railroad. Assign roles to children based on the reader.

Answers to Target Reading Skill

Possible facts: Tubman escaped on the Underground Railroad; Tubman helped others escape; Tubman settled in Auburn, New York. Possible opinions: Harriet was a remarkable woman; her parents were brave; she was a fearless conductor; this is about a brave woman.

Harriet Tubman Conductor of the Underground Railroad

by Teri L. Tilwick

We Do Our Part

Chapter: Our Nation Past and Present

Lexile Measure: 610

Summary

Harriet Tubman was born in Maryland around 1820 to a family of enslaved African Americans. She married a free African American named John Tubman, but she remained enslaved until her escape via the Underground Railroad. Tubman returned to the South many times to free hundreds of other enslaved African Americans, including her parents, whom she had to take out by wagon. She assisted the North during the Civil War. She lived the rest of her life in Auburn, New York, where she opened a home for homeless and sick people.

Before Reading

Building Background

Explain that this story takes place in a time when many Americans lived in slavery and some tried to escape. Preview the glossary.

English Language Learners

Explain that *underground* used in Underground Railroad does not mean something "below ground." Explain that *underground* can also mean "secret," because things that are underground are hidden from view. Then explain that the word *railroad* used in the term *Underground Railroad* does not refer to trains. It means a way for people to travel. The *Underground Railroad* was a secret way for people to travel.

Vocabulary

slavery, enslaved, plantation, overseer

Target Reading Skill: Fact and Opinion

Write on the board the words *fact* and *opinion*. Explain that a fact can be proven but an opinion is someone's belief and cannot be proven. Present this example:

> It is raining outside.
> Jane thinks rainy days are beautiful.

Explain that the first sentence tells a fact; you can prove whether it is raining or not. Explain that the second sentence is someone's opinion. It can not be proved. Distribute the T-chart graphic organizer to children. Have them write *Fact* at the top of the first column and *Opinion* at the top of the second. Tell them that, as they read, they will write down in the organizer two facts and two opinions that they find in the book. Have students discuss why some statements are facts and others are opinions.

During Reading

Think Critically

1. Why didn't Tubman have any rights on the plantation? (She was an enslaved African American and had no rights.)

2. Why was Tubman glad she about the North Star? (She followed it when she escaped to the North.)

3. How did many enslaved African Americans escape? (by the Underground Railroad)

4. Who might not have agreed that Tubman was a hero? Why? (Slave owners did not think she was a hero because she helped others escape.)

After Reading

Drama

Have children act out Tubman's escape on the Underground Railroad. Ask children to re-enact the parts of the volunteers in the safe houses and of Tubman. Continue in similar fashion for other scenes in the book.

Answers to Target Reading Skill

Possible facts: Tubman escaped on the Underground Railroad; Tubman helped others escape; Tubman settled in Auburn, New York. Possible opinions: She was a brave women; Tubman was a great American hero; Tubman will always be remembered.

Bradford Washburn

by Jeri Cipriano

Summary

Bradford Washburn had a remarkable life as a mountain climber, photographer, and mapmaker. Throughout his life, Washburn was a leader among his community of fellow mountain climbers and explorers. His achievements include exploring mountains, mapping them, and taking remarkable photographs of the places he explored.

Before Reading

Building Background

Build background by allowing students to look at images on the cover and inside the book. Then preview and preteach vocabulary words.

Vocabulary

peak, photographs, explore

English Language Learners

Read the text aloud, pausing frequently to clarify meaning, especially of vocabulary. Note how knowing the definition of one form of a word can help students figure out the meaning of another form of the word. Discuss how adding suffixes can change the meaning of a word.

Target Reading Skill: Generalize

When reading a biography it can be helpful to make generalizations about a person's life. A generalization is a broad statement, conclusion, or big idea based on specific facts and details.

Draw a Generalize graphic organizer on the board with the following example:

Fact: Lee likes to hike.

Fact: Lee likes camping.

Fact: Lee likes bird-watching.

Generalization: Lee likes the outdoors.

Have students copy the Generalize graphic organizer before they have read the book or provide them with a Generalize organizer to use. Help students complete the Reading Skill activity on the inside cover of their Readers.

During Reading

Think Critically

1. What kinds of things did Bradford Washburn like to do when he was young? (He liked to climb. He liked to make maps.)

2. Why can it be dangerous to climb mountains in Alaska? (Climbers can die from the cold.)

3. What made Washburn a good climber? (He was careful.)

4. Why do you think Washburn was a hero to other climbers? (He climbed many mountains. He showed people safer ways to explore.)

After Reading

Writing

Ask students to look at the list of facts they made about Bradford Washburn. Tell them to pick three facts. What do the facts have in common? Are they all about Washburn's childhood? Or are they about his mountain climbing or writing? Students should write down a generalization about Bradford Washburn based on those three facts. Provide help to those students who have a generalization but find it hard to write down.

Answers to Target Reading Skill

Sample generalization: Washburn was a great mountain climber. Facts that support this generalization: Washburn first climbed a mountain at age 11; Washburn climbed three huge mountains in Europe at age 16; Washburn did not give up when he did not reach the peak of Mount Fairweather.

Bradford Washburn Mountain Climber

by Jeri Cipriano

We Are Connected

Chapter: Our Communities

Lexile Measure: 540

Summary

Bradford Washburn (1910–2007) was a remarkable mountaineer, photographer, and mapmaker. Washburn was a leader among his community of mountain climbers and explorers. Born in 1910, Washburn became an avid mountaineer at an early age. His achievements include the exploration of mountains in Alaska and northern Canada, making detailed maps of the Grand Canyon, taking remarkable photographs of mountains, and organizing an expedition to determine the exact height of Mount Everest.

Before Reading

Building Background

Build background for the book by allowing students to preview the images, captions, and headings throughout. Then preview and preteach the vocabulary words with them.

Vocabulary

explore, geography, sea level, expedition, achievement

English Language Learners

Read the text aloud, pausing frequently to clarify meaning. Note how knowing the definition of one form of a word can help students figure out the meaning of another form. Discuss how adding suffixes changes meaning.

Target Reading Skill: Generalize

Sometimes authors give facts and details about a person and expect readers to make generalizations. A generalization is a statement or big idea that is based on specific facts or examples.

Create a generalization graphic organizer on the board with the following example:

Fact: Lee likes to go hiking.

Fact: Lee likes to go camping.

Fact: _____.

Generalization: Lee likes the outdoors.

Ask the class for another fact that supports the generalization. (Example: Lee likes to go biking.) Have students copy the organizer after they have read the book or provide them with one. Allow students time to complete the Reading Skill activity on the inside cover of their Readers.

During Reading

Think Critically

1. What did Bradford Washburn accomplish when he was young? (He climbed his first mountain at age 11.)
2. What traits made Washburn a good climber? (He was careful but not foolhardy.)
3. Why do you think Washburn climbed mountains even though it could be dangerous? (He loved exploring new places.)
4. In what way did Washburn encourage other climbers? (He gave advice about how to be safe.)

After Reading

Writing

Ask students to write a letter that Bradford Washburn might write to his grandchildren encouraging them to do what they love best. They should use his life as an example.

Answers to Target Reading Skill

Sample generalization: Washburn was always an explorer. Facts: Washburn climbed a huge mountain at age 11; Washburn climbed three huge mountains in Europe at 16; Later, Washburn climbed mountains in Alaska and northern Canada.

Bradford Washburn Exploring Alaska's Mountains

by Jeri Cipriano

Summary

Bradford Washburn (1910–2007) was a remarkable mountaineer, aerial photographer, cartographer, and science educator, as well as a leader among his community of mountain climbers and explorers. Born in 1910 in Cambridge, Massachusetts, Washburn became an avid mountaineer at an early age. His achievements include leading expeditions in the mountains of Alaska and northern Canada, making detailed maps, and taking remarkable aerial photographs.

Before Reading

Building Background

Build background for the book by allowing students to preview the book. Make sure students are familiar with key concepts and key vocabulary words. Discuss genre.

Vocabulary

explore, geography, sea level, mountain range, expedition, glacier

English Language Learners

Read selected text aloud, pausing frequently to clarify meaning, especially of vocabulary. Note how knowing the definition of one form of a word can help students figure out the meaning of another form of the same word. Discuss how adding suffixes changes the meaning.

Target Reading Skill: Generalize

A generalization is a conclusion or big idea you make based on specific facts and details.

Draw a generalization graphic organizer on the board with the following example:

Fact: Lee likes to go camping.

Fact: Lee like to go bird-watching in the woods.

Fact: _____.

Generalization: Lee likes the outdoors.

Ask the class to think of two other supporting facts that would support the idea that Lee likes the outdoors.

Have students copy the graphic organizer after they have read the book. Allow students time to complete the Reading Skill activity on the inside cover of their Readers.

Encourage students to think of other generalizations they can make after reading the book (for example, Washburn was an excellent mountain climber and photographer) and to find supporting facts.

During Reading

Think Critically

1. What was Bradford Washburn like when he was young? (He loved learning about the outdoors. He gave advice to readers.)

2. What traits made Washburn a good leader on expeditions? (He was brave and careful.)

3. How did Washburn help people better understand the world? (He climbed unexplored mountains. He made detailed maps and he took amazing photographs.)

After Reading

Writing

Ask students to imagine they went mountain climbing in Alaska. Have them write about what the experienced.

Answers to Target Reading Skill

Sample generalization: Washburn was a great explorer. Facts: Washburn led many expeditions; Washburn wrote books about his experiences; Washburn took photos of unexplored mountains.

Rachel Carson

by Darleen Ramos

Summary

Rachel Carson, a scientist and author who is often credited with being the first environmentalist, was born in 1907 in the rural town of Springdale, Pennsylvania. As a child, she was fascinated by nature. After college, Carson became a scientist, noted for her gift of writing. As a scientist and writer, her greatest interest was the ocean. Her first three books were about ocean life. Her last book, *Silent Spring*, was instrumental in the banning of DDT and prompting the government to take a serious look at pesticides.

Before Reading

Building Background

Discuss with students what they know about things that cause pollution in our environment. Introduce the word *pesticide* and define it. Point out that people did not always know that pesticides can do harm. Explain that they will read about Rachel Carson, a scientist and writer. The book she wrote, *Silent Spring*, made people realize the harm some pesticides can do.

Vocabulary

environment, polluted, pesticides, banned

English Language Learners

Use pictures cards to orally teach or review words shown in the text, such as *bird, woods, stream, plants, ocean, insect, shell,* and *crab*. Read the book aloud as children follow along in their own books. After each pause, invite children to talk about the illustration and about what they learned from the text.

Target Reading Skill: Cause and Effect

Draw a cause-and-effect graphic organizer on the board. Reinforce children's understanding of cause and effect by discussing why the air in Pittsburgh was smoky and dirty. Fill in the cause on the graphic organizer: Factories burned coal. Have a volunteer state the effect: The air became dirty. Repeat this procedure for other causes and effects. Sample responses are given below.

During Reading

Think Critically

1. What did Carson like to do as a young child? (She liked to explore the woods, watch birds, and read and write stories.)

2. Why did Carson want to become a writer? (She liked to write. A magazine printed her story.)

3. What was Pittsburgh like when Carson went to college there? (It was polluted. Factories burned coal, and the air was smoky and dirty.)

4. What happened after Carson wrote *Silent Spring*? (People read it and became worried about pesticides. Laws were passed to protect nature, and some pesticides were banned.)

After Reading

Drawing

Discuss ways rivers, lakes, and oceans might get polluted. Have students draw a picture that shows some of the ways people pollute our water. Then have them write a sentence that tells how we can protect our water.

Answers to Target Reading Skill

Cause: Factories burn coal. Effect: Air turns smoky and dirty.

Cause: People and animals eat plants sprayed with pesticides. Effect: People and animals could get sick.

Cause: Pesticides get into water. Effect: People and animals could get sick.

Rachel Carson
Friend of Land and Sea

by Darleen Ramos

We Are Connected

Chapter: Our Environment

Lexile Measure: 540

Summary

Rachel Carson, a scientist and author who is often credited with being the first environmentalist, was born in 1907 in rural Springdale, Pennsylvania. As a child, she was fascinated by nature. After college, Carson became a scientist. As a scientist and writer, her greatest interest was the ocean. Her first three books were about marine life. Her last book, *Silent Spring*, was instrumental in the banning of DDT and prompting the government to take a serious look at pesticides. The title of the book was a warning—unless we stop polluting the environment, we may one day no longer have songbirds.

Before Reading

Building Background

Introduce the word *pesticide* and define it. Point out that people did not always know the harm pesticides can do to the environment. Explain that the book is a biography of Rachel Carson, a scientist and writer. The book she wrote, *Silent Spring*, made people realize the harm some pesticides can do.

Vocabulary

pollute, marine, pesticide, ban, environmentalist

English Language Learners

Write the words *pollute* and *pollution*. Explain their meanings. Draw a word web on the board. Write the word *pollution* in the center circle. Tell students that something that contaminates the air or water causes pollution. Using the illustrations in the book to prompt them, have students name places that could become polluted (air, rivers, streams, ocean). Add these words to the word map.

Target Reading Skill: Cause and Effect

Draw a cause-and-effect graphic organizer on the board. Reinforce children's understanding of cause and effect by demonstrating a simple action, such as pushing a pen from your desk onto the floor. Discuss the cause (pushing the pen) and the effect (the pen is on the floor). Tell students to look for causes and effects as they read. Allow time for students to complete the Target Reading Skill activity on the inside covers of their Readers.

During Reading

Think Critically

1. What are some things Carson liked to do when she was a child? (She liked to explore the woods, watch birds, and read and write stories.)

2. Why did Carson switch her focus in college from writing to science? (She took a biology class and decided she wanted to study more about nature, and to be a scientist.)

3. What event caused Carson to become interested in pesticides? (A friend told her that after pesticides were sprayed near her home, she found many dead birds. Carson wondered if the events were connected.)

4. Why were some pesticides banned? (People became aware of the harm they could do.)

After Reading

Writing

Tell students that it is not just farmers who use pesticides. People often use pesticides around their homes and in their gardens. Have students write a short paragraph telling why people should be careful how they use pesticides.

Answers to Target Reading Skill

Accept any causes and effects that are given in the text. Sample answers:
Cause: Factories burn coal. Effect: Air becomes smoky and dirty.
Cause: People and animals eat plants sprayed with pesticides. Effect: People and animals get sick.
Cause: Pesticides get into water. Effect: People and animals get sick.
Cause: Many people read Carson's book. Effect: People became concerned about pesticides.

Rachel Carson
Protecting the Natural World

by Darleen Ramos

Summary

Rachel Carson, a scientist and author who is often credited with being the first environmentalist, was born in 1907 in the rural town of Springdale, Pennsylvania. As a child, she was fascinated by nature. Carson became a marine biologist and a writer. Her greatest interest was the ocean. Three of her books were about marine life and became quite popular. Her last book, *Silent Spring*, was instrumental in the banning of DDT and prompting the government to take a serious look at pesticides. The title was meant as a warning—the use of pesticides threatens all wildlife. We might one day wake up to a spring without birdsong.

Before Reading

Building Background

Introduce the word *pesticide*. Point out that people did not always know the harm pesticides can do to the environment. Explain that Rachel Carson was a scientist and writer. The book she wrote, *Silent Spring*, made people realize the harm some pesticides can do.

Vocabulary

environmentalist, pollution, industry, marine, pesticide, food chain

English Language Learners

Write *food chain* on the board. Draw a simple food chain, such as a pond plant, a small fish, a larger fish, and a person fishing. Explain that each thing in the chain is food for the next thing in the chain. Point out that if the plant or smallest fish got poison into its body, the things that eat it could get poison into their bodies, too.

Target Reading Skill: Cause and Effect

Reinforce children's understanding of cause and effect by demonstrating a simple action, such as pushing a pen from your desk onto the floor. Discuss the cause (pushing the pen) and the effect (the pen is on the floor). Tell students to look for causes and effects as they read. Have students to complete the Target Reading Skill activity on the inside covers of their Readers.

During Reading

Think Critically

1. What are two interests Carson had as a child that she used when she grew up? (She loved to read and to write. She had an interest in exploring the outdoors and watching birds and animals.)

2. Why was Pittsburgh a polluted city? (Steel mills burned coal to make steel. The coal smoke made the air dirty.)

3. According to Carson, why were some pesticides harmful to people and animals? (Some pesticides that were sprayed on plants were eaten by animals and people, or got into the food chain, and caused some people or animals to become sick or even die.)

4. What do you think was Carson's most important contribution? (Answers will vary. Sample answer: Her book *Silent Spring* made people aware of the danger of pesticides and moved the government to ban DDT.)

After Reading

Writing

Tell students that there are many different specialties that biologists can have. Have students work with a partner to find out what other kinds of things biologists study. Have them give a short report to tell about these specialties.

Answers to Target Reading Skill

Accept any causes and effects that are given in the text. Sample answers:
Cause: Factories burn coal.
Effect: The air is polluted, sunlight is dimmed.
Cause: Factories dump waste into rivers. Effect: River water is brown and dirty.
Cause: Farmers spray crops with pesticides. Effect: Animals and people get sick or die.
Cause: Carson writes *Silent Spring*. Effect: Government bans DDT.

Sequoyah

by Jeri Cipriano

Summary

Sequoyah was a Cherokee, born about 1770, who began working on a writing system for the Cherokee language. Although he could not read or write himself, he created a writing system for the Cherokee based on syllables, enabling the Cherokee to write their history, constitution, and laws. Sequoyah was honored by his people by the presentation of a silver medal and is remembered today for his remarkable achievement. The system he invented remains in use today.

Before Reading

Building Background

Begin a discussion about how we use an alphabet to write down our words, by saying a three-letter word such as *mat*. Ask a volunteer to write the word. Then ask a student to explain how he or she knew which letters to write. Help understand that we choose the letters to write based on the sounds we hear. Explain that Sequoyah didn't know our alphabet, but he figured out a way to write the Cherokee language.

Vocabulary

silversmith, symbols, constitution

English Language Learners

Write or display the Roman alphabet. Have students practice saying the names of the letters in English. Write the word *symbol* and have students pronounce it. Display some common symbols, such as the peace sign, a heart, and an American flag. Point out that the letters of the alphabet are symbols. They stand for sounds.

Target Reading Skill: Sequence

Explain that the sequence is the order of events in a selection. In a biography, the events of a person's life are usually told in time order, in the order they happened. Explain that sometimes writers give clues to sequence by using signal words such as *first, next, then, after that,* or *before*. Allow time for students to complete the Target Reading Skill activity on the inside cover of their Readers.

During Reading

Think Critically

1. What made Sequoyah want to create a writing system? (Sample answer: He wished he could sign his name in the Cherokee language.)

2. What words would you use to describe Sequoyah? Why? (Sample answer: He was very determined. He didn't give up until he found a way.)

3. How did having a writing system help the Cherokee preserve their traditions? (Sample answer: Traditions could now be written down.)

4. What are some things we would not have today if we had no written system? (Sample answer: newspapers, magazines, books, letters, e-mail, written records)

After Reading

Drawing

Have students draw a picture showing something they can do because they can read. Have them write a sentence telling what their picture shows.

Answers to Target Reading Skill

Possible answers include:

Beginning: Sequoyah was born in Tennessee. Sequoyah became a silversmith.

Middle: Sequoyah started to work on a Cherokee alphabet.
His first idea (tiny picures for every word) didn't work.
He made symbols for each sound in Cherokee.

End: Sequoyah showed Cherokee leaders how his system works.
Leaders honored him with a silver medal.

Sequoyah and the Cherokee Language

by Jeri Cipriano

We Are Connected

Chapter: Communities Build a Nation

Lexile Measure: 610

Summary

Sequoyah was a Cherokee, born about 1770, who began working on a writing system for the Cherokee language. Although he could not read or write himself, he created a writing system for the Cherokee based on syllables, enabling the Cherokee to write their history, constitution, and laws. Sequoyah was honored by his people by the presentation of a silver medal and is remembered today for his remarkable achievement. The system he invented remains in use today.

Before Reading

Building Background

Begin a discussion about how we use an alphabet to write down words. Demonstrate writing the symbols that stand for the sounds in *mat*. Help understand that we choose the letters to write based on the sounds we hear. If you have students who can write in other alphabets, such as Hebrew, Greek, or Arabic, ask them to demonstrate. Explain that Sequoyah didn't know our alphabet, but he invented a way to write the Cherokee language.

Vocabulary

custom, generation, symbol, constitution

English Language Learners

Write or display the Roman alphabet. As needed, have students practice saying the names of the letters in English. Write the word *symbol*, explain its meaning, and have students pronounce it. Display some common symbols, such as the peace sign, a heart, and an American flag. Point out that the letters of the alphabet are symbols, too. They stand for sounds.

Target Reading Skill: Sequence

Explain that the sequence is the order in which events happen in a story or in history. Most stories have a beginning, middle, and end. In biographies, the events are usually told in time order. Read the Target Reading Skill activity on the inside cover of the Reader with students. After students have finished reading the book, allow time for them to complete the activity.

During Reading

Think Critically

1. Why did Sequoyah want to create a writing system? (Sample answer: He wanted the Cherokee to be able to write in their own language.)

2. What did Sequoyah's system allow his people to do? (Sample answer: They could read and write.)

3. Why didn't Sequoyah's first idea, of having a picture for every word, work? (It was taking too long for him to draw pictures for all the words.)

4. What are some things we would not have today if we had no written system? (Sample answer: newspapers, magazines, books, letters, e-mail, written records)

After Reading

Classroom Theater

Divide the group into three sections, one for the beginning, the middle, and the later part of Sequoyah's life. Have each section prepare a short skit of something that happened during that part of his life. Allow time for each group to perform.

Answers to Target Reading Skill

Possible answers include:

Beginning: Sequoyah was born in Tennessee. Sequoyah became a silversmith.

Middle: Sequoyah worked a long time to create an alphabet; his daughter helped him; friends did not understand what he was trying to do.

End: Sequoyah showed leaders that his system worked; leaders gave Sequoyah a medal; other Cherokee learned to read.

Sequoyah Inventor of the Cherokee Alphabet

by Jeri Cipriano

We Are Connected

Chapter: Communities Build a Nation

Lexile Measure: 680

Summary

Sequoyah was a Cherokee, born about 1770, who began working on a writing system for the Cherokee language. Although he could not read or write himself, he created a writing system for the Cherokee based on syllables, enabling the Cherokee to write their history, constitution, and laws. Sequoyah was honored by his people by the presentation of a silver medal and is remembered today for his remarkable achievement. The system he invented remains in use today.

Before Reading

Building Background

Ask children to imagine how they would write if they did not have the alphabet. What other ways could they think of to write a message? What if they had to invent a way to write from the beginning? Tell students that this is the challenge Sequoyah faced when he invented the Cherokee alphabet.

Vocabulary

custom, symbol, literacy, constitution

English Language Learners

Write and say the word *symbol* and have students pronounce it. Display some common symbols, such as the peace sign, a heart, and an American flag. Point out that the letters of the alphabet are symbols, too. They stand for sounds.

Target Reading Skill: Sequence

Explain that sequence is the order in which events happen. Most stories have a beginning, middle, and end. In biographies, events are usually told in time order. Explain that we can think of a person's life story as having a beginning, a middle, and an end. Allow time for students to complete the Target Reading Skill activity on the inside cover of their Readers.

During Reading

Think Critically

1. What was the first way Sequoyah tried to create a Cherokee writing system? Why did he decide it wouldn't work? (Sample answer: He first tried writing a picture for each word. He decided that method required too many pictures and took too long to learn.)

2. Why do you think his friends did not take Sequoyah seriously when he told them he was creating "talking leaves" for Cherokee words? (Sample answer: They probably didn't understand how reading works.)

3. Why do people honor Sequoyah today? (Sample answer: He made an important gift to his people.)

After Reading

Writing

Explain that a rebus is a message written with symbols and letters. In a rebus, the word *I* might be represented by a picture of an eye. Show an example. Have students work to create a simple rebus message. Then have them trade with a partner and decode each other's rebuses.

Answers to Target Reading Skill

Possible answers include:

Beginning: Sequoyah was born in 1770. He learned to be a hunter and fur trader; he learned to be a silversmith. He decided to invent a way to write Cherokee.

Middle: He fought in the War of 1812. He moved to Arkansas. Sequoyah changed his system from pictures to sounds. He taught the system to his daughter.

End: Sequoyah was given a medal for his invention; Sequoyah helped write a new constitution for the Cherokee. He died in 1842.

Thomas Jefferson

by Darleen Ramos

We Are Connected

Chapter: United States Government

Lexile Measure: 370

Summary

Thomas Jefferson was a talented man—a farmer, inventor, architect, and writer. He wrote about rights and freedoms in the Declaration of Independence and was the third president of the United States. As president, his most significant contribution was the purchase of the Louisiana Territory. During his retirement, he founded the University of Virginia. Thomas Jefferson's words and ideas helped shape our government and our country.

Before Reading

Building Background

Build background for the book by allowing students to observe the book's art and predict what some of the topics covered will be. Make sure students are familiar with key vocabulary and concepts. Encourage students to discuss and share what they may already know about Thomas Jefferson.

Vocabulary

colonies, government, congress, declaration, independence, elected

English Language Learners

Have students reread page 4. Ask them to say what the important idea is. They might say that Great Britain ruled the colonies. Choose one or two additional pages. Read each aloud and make a list of important ideas suggested by students. Discuss how and why they may or may not be important.

Target Reading Skill: Summarize

Explain to students that a summary is a short statement that retells the main idea. A summary includes the most important ideas of the book. Pause periodically to identify important ideas as you read the book.

During Reading

Comprehension and Critical Thinking

1. What did Jefferson think about Great Britain? (He thought the colonies should be free from Great Britain.)

2. What did Jefferson write to declare our freedom? (the Declaration of Independence)

3. Summarize what Jefferson did to serve his country. (He did many things. He wrote the Declaration of Independence and was President.)

4. In what ways do you think Jefferson helped form our government? (Sample answer: He wrote that the colonies should be free.)

After Reading

Writing

Thomas Jefferson was a great writer. He wrote many letters. Have students write a letter to a friend telling him or her what he or she learned about Jefferson.

Answers to Target Reading Skill

Possible important ideas:

Jefferson wrote the Declaration of Independence.

Jefferson was the third president of the United States.

Jefferson purchased land from France.

Possible summary:

Thomas Jefferson was a writer, leader, and president. His words and ideas helped shape our government.

Thomas Jefferson Our Third President

by Darleen Ramos

We Are Connected

Chapter: United States Government

Lexile Measure: 610

Summary

Thomas Jefferson was a talented man noted for his many accomplishments. He was a gifted writer whose moving ideas and words about rights and freedoms shaped the Declaration of Independence. Jefferson served his country in several capacities, including governor of Virginia and secretary of state. As the third president of the United States, one of his most significant contributions was the purchase of the Louisiana Territory. During his retirement, he founded the University of Virginia.

Before Reading

Building Background

Build background for the book by allowing students to observe the book's art and predict what some of the topics covered will be. Make sure students are familiar with key vocabulary and concepts. Encourage students to discuss and share what they already know about Thomas Jefferson.

Vocabulary

declaration, independence, government, colonies, representative, elect, Constitution

English Language Learners

Have students reread page 4. Ask them to say what the most important idea is. They might say that Jefferson agreed with others that the colonies should govern themselves. Next, choose a different page. Have students read it and then offer what they believe are the important ideas. Assess importance as you make a list of those ideas.

Target Reading Skill: Summarize

Explain to students that a summary is a short statement that retells the main idea. A summary includes the most important ideas of the book. Pause periodically to identify important ideas as you read the book.

During Reading

Comprehension and Critical Thinking

1. How did Jefferson help the colonies in their fight for freedom? (He wrote about the colonists and said they had rights.)

2. What were some of Jefferson's talents? (He spoke several languages and was a great writer, inventor, and architect.)

3. Summarize how Jefferson served his country. (Jefferson served the country as secretary of state, vice president, and president.)

4. What do you think was Jefferson's most important contribution? (Sample answers: He wrote the Declaration of Independence. He doubled the size of the United States without fighting a war.)

After Reading

Writing

Thomas Jefferson was a great writer who wrote many letters. Write a letter to a friend telling him or her what you have learned about Jefferson and why they might be interested in reading about Jefferson.

Answers to Target Reading Skill

Possible important ideas:

Thomas Jefferson was a writer, inventor, and designer.

Jefferson wrote about rights and freedoms in the Declaration of Independence.

Jefferson was the third president of the United States.

Jefferson purchased the Louisiana Territory from France.

Jefferson built the University of Virginia.

Possible summary:

Thomas Jefferson was a writer, leader, and president whose words, ideas, and actions helped shape our government and our country.

Thomas Jefferson
Writer, Leader, President

by Darleen Ramos

We Are Connected

Chapter: United States Government

Lexile Measure: 740

Summary

Thomas Jefferson was a talented man and a gifted writer whose moving ideas and words about rights and freedoms shaped the Declaration of Independence. Jefferson served his country in several capacities, including governor of Virginia and secretary of state. As president, his most significant contribution was the purchase of the Louisiana Territory. During his retirement, he founded the University of Virginia.

Before Reading

Building Background

Allow students to observe the book's art and make predictions about some of the topics covered. Make sure students are familiar with key vocabulary and concepts. Encourage students to discuss and share what they already know about Thomas Jefferson.

Vocabulary

declaration, independence, government, legislature, colonies, representative, Constitution

English Language Learners

Have students reread page 4. Ask them to say what the most important idea is. They might say that Jefferson agreed with others that the colonies should govern themselves. Next, have students turn to another page. Ask them to help make a list of the most important ideas on the page. As you make a list, discuss the relative importance of each idea.

Target Reading Skill: Summarize

Explain to students that a summary is a short statement that retells the main idea. A summary of a book includes the most important ideas of the book. Pause periodically to identify important ideas as you read.

During Reading

Comprehension and Critical Thinking

1. How did Jefferson help the colonies in their fight for freedom? (He wrote passionately about the rights and freedoms he believed the colonists deserved.)

2. What were some of Jefferson's talents? (He spoke several languages and was a gifted writer, inventor, and architect.)

3. Summarize how Jefferson served his country after its independence. (Jefferson served as secretary of state, vice president, and president.)

4. What do you think was Jefferson's most important contribution? (He wrote the Declaration of Independence. He doubled the size of the United States without fighting a war.)

After Reading

Writing

Thomas Jefferson was a great writer who wrote many letters. Write a letter to a friend about what you have learned about Jefferson and why they might be interested in him.

Answers to Target Reading Skill

Possible important ideas:

Thomas Jefferson was a writer, inventor, and designer.

Jefferson wrote the Declaration of Independence.

Jefferson was the third president of the United States.

Jefferson purchased the Louisiana Territory from France.

Jefferson built the University of Virginia.

Possible summary:

Thomas Jefferson was a writer, leader, and president whose words, ideas, and actions helped shape our government and our country.

Thurgood Marshall

by Jeri Cipriano

Summary

Thurgood Marshall (1908–1993) experienced racial discrimination and prejudice growing up. These experiences motivated him to become a lawyer to help African Americans achieve equality under the law. His 1954 landmark win in the *Brown v. Board of Education* case made segregation in public schools illegal. In 1967, he became the first African American to serve as a Supreme Court justice. By participating in court cases as a lawyer and a judge, Marshall helped all Americans achieve equal rights.

Before Reading

Building Background

Use the illustration of the segregated water fountain (p. 3) to begin a discussion of segregation and laws that treated African Americans unfairly. Explain that at one time, many places in our country had laws or customs that kept black people and white people separate. Have students share what they already may know about Rosa Parks, Martin Luther King, Jr., or other figures of the civil rights era.

Vocabulary

equality, Civil War, Constitution, segregated, Supreme Court

English Language Learners

Write the words *equal, equally,* and *equality* on the board. Use pictures of two unequal things, such as two different size slices of pie, to illustrate the meaning. Tell students that Marshall and others worked so all people would be treated equally and have equality.

Target Reading Skill: Fact and Opinion

Clarify students' understanding of fact and opinion by reading with them the Before Reading section on the inside cover of the Reader. After students have read the book, allow students time to complete the fact and opinion graphic organizer.

During Reading

Think Critically

1. What did Marshall learn from his father by going to courtrooms with him? (Sample answer: Marshall learned how lawyers worked.)

2. Why did Marshall go to a law school far from home? (Sample answer: The law school he wanted to go to that was close to home would not accept African Americans.)

3. What facts did Marshall give to show that segregated schools were not equal? (White schools had more money, were less crowded, and had newer books.)

4. Who was Ruby Bridges? (Sample answer: She was the first black student to go to a white school in New Orleans.)

5. What was special about Marshall becoming a Supreme Court justice? (Sample answer: Marshall was the first African American to become a Supreme Court justice.)

After Reading

Writing

Have students write two or three sentences to tell why they think Thurgood Marshall is someone whom all Americans should know about and remember. Have them draw a picture to go with their writing.

Answers to Target Reading Skill

Accept any facts supported by the text. If students give opinions as facts, model checking the facts in a reliable source.

Sample opinions: Having a separate section at the movies for blacks was unfair. Ending segregation was wrong. His decisions brought more equality to people's lives.

Justice Marshall Fighter for Equality

by Jeri Cipriano

Summary

Thurgood Marshall (1908–1993) experienced racial discrimination and prejudice growing up. These experiences motivated him to become a lawyer to help African Americans achieve equality under the law. His 1954 landmark win in the *Brown v. Board of Education* case made segregation in public schools illegal. In 1967, he became the first African American to serve as a Supreme Court justice. By participating in court cases as a lawyer and a judge, Marshall helped all Americans achieve equal rights.

Before Reading

Building Background

Use the illustration of the segregated water fountain (p. 3) to begin a discussion of segregation. Explain that at one time, many places in our country had laws or customs that kept black people and white people separate. Have students share what they already may know about Rosa Parks, Martin Luther King, Jr., or other figures of the civil rights era.

Vocabulary

segregation, Constitution, Civil War, Supreme Court, expert, justice

English Language Learners

Introduce the word *justice*. Explain that this word has more than one meaning. We often use it to mean "fair treatment" as when we say, "with liberty and justice for all." Then explain that *justice* can also mean a judge. The judges on the Supreme Court are called justices.

Target Reading Skill: Fact and Opinion

Review the definitions of *fact* and *opinion:* A fact can be checked with other sources and proven. An opinion is the way an individual feels about something. Give students oral examples of facts and opinions and have them identify which is which and explain how they know.

During Reading

Think Critically

1. What are some examples of unfair treatment Marshall experienced when he was growing up? (Sample answer: He was unfairly arrested for starting a fight; he was told to sit in a segregated area of a movie theater; he was denied admittance to law school because he was black.)

2. Why do you think Marshall became a lawyer? (Sample answer: He wanted to help African Americans get equal treatment.)

3. What kinds of cases did Marshall take as a lawyer? (Sample answer: He took cases that involved unfair laws.)

4. What happened because of the Supreme Court's decision in the case about school segregation? (Segregation of public schools became illegal. Over time, segregation ended in other areas, too.)

After Reading

Activity

Have students write a short paragraph about their school. Have them include both facts and opinions. Then have volunteers read their paragraphs aloud. Call on other students to identify statements of fact and opinion.

Answers to Target Reading Skill

Accept any facts stated in the text. Have students use an encyclopedia or other reliable source to check any statements they are not sure are facts. Sample opinions: Some whites thought that they were better than blacks. Marshall thought his original name, Thoroughgood, was too long. Marshall was lucky when his boss came to get him out of jail. Marshall became one of the country's best lawyers. Some whites thought ending school segregation was wrong. Marshall made the world a better place.

Thurgood Marshall
The Struggle for Legal Equality
by Jeri Cipriano

Summary

Thurgood Marshall (1908–1993) experienced racial discrimination and prejudice growing up. These experiences motivated him to become a lawyer to help African Americans achieve equality under the law. His 1954 landmark win in the *Brown v. Board of Education* case made segregation in public schools illegal. In 1967, he became the first African American to serve as a Supreme Court justice.

Before Reading

Building Background

Use the illustration of the water fountain (p. 3) to begin a discussion of segregation. Explain that at one time, many places in our country had laws or customs that kept black people and white people separate. Have students share what they may already know about Rosa Parks, or Martin Luther King, Jr. Relate these figures' lives to that of Marshall.

Vocabulary

Supreme Court, debate, segregation, Constitution, Civil War, expert, integrated

English Language Learners

Preview the book with students, discussing the illustrations. Point out the photograph of the segregated water fountain on page 3 and use it to give additional background. Discuss and define *Supreme Court*. Explain that saying the Supreme Court is the highest court in the country means that the Supreme Court decides whether state and local laws are fair or not.

Target Reading Skill: Fact and Opinion

Review *fact* and *opinion* with students. Give students some oral examples of facts and opinions, and have them tell which is which. After students read, allow time for them to complete the activity on the inside covers of their Readers.

During Reading

Think Critically

1. How did Marshall's father influence him? (His father taught him how to debate; he took him to courtrooms to see trials.)

2. Which school experiences do you think helped prepare Marshall for his work as a lawyer? (Sample answer: He got to know the Constitution well, so he knew what the law said. Experiencing segregation firsthand, as well as being denied admission to the University of Maryland, probably made him want to help others.)

3. What was Marshall's strategy to win the school segregation case? (He needed to show that segregated schools were not equal, and that separate schools were harmful to black students.)

4. How did Marshall's work change people's lives? (Sample answer: He helped bring an end to segregation.)

After Reading

Writing

Tell students that Ruby Bridges (now Ruby Bridges Hall) is now grown up. There are several children's books written about her. Have them find out more about her. Have them work with a partner to report their findings to the class.

Answers to Target Reading Skill

Accept any facts that can be supported by the text. If students disagree on which statements are facts, have them check the statements in a reliable source. There are several opinions expressed or described in the text. They include: Thurgood Marshall changed the lives of many people for the better. Whites are better than blacks. Marshall and the other Lincoln students were lucky not to be arrested at the movie theater. Marshall became one of the best lawyers in the country. Black students were less capable than white students.

Jane Addams

by Darleen Ramos

We Are Connected

Chapter: A Growing Nation

Lexile Measure: 370

Summary

This biography of Jane Addams (1860–1935) is the story of how she came to help the poor by establishing Hull House, one of the first settlement houses in the United States. Founded in Chicago's Nineteenth Ward, it provided support and a sense of community to the many immigrants and poor in the neighborhood.

Before Reading

Building Background

Make sure students are familiar with key vocabulary and concepts. Encourage students to discuss and share what they may already know about Jane Addams or other individuals who help those in need.

Vocabulary

extraordinary, settlement house, immigrants, community, inspector

Target Reading Skill: Draw Conclusions

Explain to students that when we draw conclusions, we make decisions or form an opinion about what we read. We base our conclusions on facts and details. Give students an example. Tell them that you have just read that a very popular book series is going to be turned into a TV show. Ask students what conclusion they might draw. (Conclusion: The TV series will be popular.)

Distribute copies of the web graphic organizer. Then, as students read the book, have them use it to write down the facts they select. After students finish the book, have them draw a conclusion based on the facts they have chosen. Invite students to share their conclusions with the class.

English Language Learners

Review Glossary words with students. Help students see the connection between the word *extraordinary* and the two words it is built from, *extra* and *ordinary*.

During Reading

Comprehension and Critical Thinking

1. What caused Jane Addams to think about the poor and needy? (She saw poor, hungry people and thought she could help them.)

2. Why did Jane Addams open Hull House where she did? (It was a poor neighborhood. There were many immigrants.)

3. Why did Addams care about the garbage on the streets in Chicago? (Children played near garbage. The garbage spread diseases and made them sick.)

4. Ask students if they agree with the conclusion: Jane Addams was a hero. Why? Ask them to support their answer with facts from the book. (Answers will vary. Sample answers: Addams cared about others. Jane Addams helped others. Jane Addams opened Hull House.)

After Reading

Activity

Jane Addams felt strongly about helping others by offering many activities in Hull House. If you ran a place like Hull House, what kinds of activities would you like to offer? Draw a poster to illustrate your ideas.

Answers to Target Reading Skill

Facts and conclusions will vary.

Possible Facts: Addams lost her mother when she was two. She had back pain. She started a successful settlement house.

Conclusion: Addams was a very strong person because she overcame challenges to achieve great things.

Possible Facts: Addams became upset when she saw people buy rotten food. She wanted to help the poor.

Conclusion: Addams cared about others.

Jane Addams Helping Neighbors in Need

by Darleen Ramos

We Are Connected

Chapter: A Growing Nation

Lexile Measure: 600

Summary

This biography of Jane Addams (1860–1935) recounts her achievement of establishing one of the first settlement houses in the United States. She established Hull House in Chicago's Nineteenth Ward, a community of poor immigrants. In addition to providing a place of culture and respite, Addams was an advocate for children, civil rights, and peace. She was the first woman to win a Nobel Peace Prize.

Before Reading

Building Background

Make sure students are familiar with key vocabulary and concepts. Encourage students to discuss and share what they may already know about community centers or people like Jane Addams who help those in need.

Vocabulary

settlement house, immigrant, tenement, community, culture, inspector, tradition, volunteer

Target Reading Skill: Draw Conclusions

Explain to students that when we draw conclusions, we make decisions or form an opinion about what we read. We base our conclusions on facts and details. Provide an example by writing a statement on the board. Then ask students to draw a conclusion. Write their responses on the board. Example: Many apartments in the 1880s did not have running water. (Conclusions: People could not take baths. People lived in unhealthy places.)

Pause periodically to discuss facts and details as you read the book. Have students draw conclusions after you complete the book. Invite students to share their conclusions with the class.

English Language Learners

Review the section headings with students before they read. Help them to understand any words they may not know. Help them rephrase headings in their own words.

During Reading

Comprehension and Critical Thinking

1. What made Addams realize she should help others? (She saw how hungry people struggled to find food. She felt her life had no purpose and helping others would make a difference.)

2. Why was Addams so concerned about the garbage on the streets in Chicago? (The garbage spread diseases, and children played near the garbage.)

3. Draw a conclusion about Jane Addams, and support your answer with information from the text. (Sample answers: Addams was a great woman. Addams cared about others and did something about it.)

4. How did Hull House help children learn about customs of different cultures? (Adults taught children skills and crafts. Addams brought together people of the same nationality and background so that they could share customs.)

After Reading

Activity

Jane Addams felt strongly about helping others by offering them help to make their lives better. What kind of help do you think would be useful to people today? Draw a picture of people helping people.

Answers to Target Reading Skill

Possible Conclusions:
Immigrants lived hard lives.
Addams was a strong, independent woman.
Addams cared about others and made a difference.

Jane Addams
Social Reformer

by Darleen Ramos

Summary

This biography of Jane Addams (1860–1935) recounts her achievement of establishing one of the first settlement houses in the United States. She established Hull House in Chicago's Nineteenth Ward, a community of poor immigrants. In addition to providing a place of culture and support, she was an advocate for children, civil rights, and peace, and was the first woman to win a Nobel Peace Prize.

Before Reading

Building Background

Make sure students are familiar with key vocabulary and concepts. Build background by asking students to discuss people like Jane Addams that help others in need.

Vocabulary

inherit, settlement house, immigrant, tenement, inspector, culture, tradition, volunteer, pacifist

Target Reading Skill: Draw Conclusions

Explain to students that when we draw conclusions, we make decisions or form an opinion about what we read. We base our conclusions on facts and details. Provide an example by writing a statement on the board. Then ask students to draw a conclusion. Write their responses on the board.

Example: Many apartments in the 1880s did not have running water. (Possible conclusions: People could not take baths. People lived in unhealthy places.)

English Language Learners

Have students preview headings and Glossary terms. Make sure they understand the meanings of a phrase such as *speaking out*, and how *speaking out* is different from *talking*.

During Reading

Comprehension and Critical Thinking

1. What made Addams realize she should help others? (She saw how hungry people struggled to find food. She felt her life had no purpose and helping others would make a difference.)

2. Why was Addams so concerned about the garbage on the streets in Chicago? (The garbage spread diseases, and children played near the garbage.)

3. Draw a conclusion about Jane Addams, and support your answer with information from the text. (Answers will vary. Sample answer: Addams was a great woman. Addams cared about others and did something about it.)

4. How did Hull House help children learn about native customs? (Adults taught children skills and crafts. Addams brought together people of the same nationality and background so that they could share customs.)

After Reading

Activity

Jane Addams felt strongly about helping others. Ask students what kind of things would help needy people today? Have them draw a poster of a place where people might get help and support in the neighborhood where they live.

Answers to Target Reading Skill

Possible conclusions:
Addams was a strong, independent woman.
Addams was a caring person.
Immigrants lived hard lives.

Wally Amos

by Jeri Cipriano

Summary

Wally Amos (born 1936) became a hugely successful entrepreneur in the 1970s, when he created and marketed chocolate chip cookies under the name "Famous Amos." Wally Amos's meteoric rise was the culmination of years of determination, hard work, and an unwavering belief in himself and his abilities. Amos was never afraid to leave one endeavor to explore another or to face failure on his way to success. His energy, popularity, initiative, discipline, and wish to succeed prompted President Ronald Reagan to present Wally Amos with the 1986 President's Award for Entrepreneurial Excellence. Since then, Amos has distinguished himself for his involvement in literacy campaigns, fundraising, and new product lines.

Before Reading

Building Background

Explain to students that Wally Amos is a real person who started a very successful business selling cookies. His face appeared on the package of his brand, Famous Amos Chocolate Chip Cookies. Ask students to brainstorm ways they would advertise or promote a business they had started.

English Language Learners

Write the word *famous* on the board. Pronounce it and have students say the word after you. Suggest names of famous people students are familiar with, and have them take turns completing the statement *(Name) is a famous ____*.

Vocabulary

manners, reputation, tips, profits

Target Reading Skill: Main Idea and Details

Explain that the main idea is the most important idea in a piece of writing. Details are information that tell more about the main idea. A small piece of writing such as a paragraph may have a sentence that tells the main idea. A longer piece, such as a book, will have several important, or main, ideas about the subject. After students have read the book, work with them to complete the activity on the inside cover of their Readers.

During Reading

Think Critically

1. What things did Amos learn from his parents? (He learned good manners and he learned to work hard.)

2. How did good manners help Amos earn money as a child? (When Amos delivered his mother's food, he talked to customers and was polite to them. They liked him, so they gave him tips.)

3. Why did Amos open a cookie store? (Sample answer: He knew people liked his Aunt Della's chocolate chip cookies. He thought he might be successful at selling them.)

4. Why do you think Amos was successful? (Sample answer: He worked hard. He had good ideas. He tried different things and didn't give up.)

After Reading

Writing

Have students work with a partner to think of an idea for a business they might like to start. Have them create a poster advertising the business.

Answers to Target Reading Skill

There are several main ideas about Amos in the book. Sample Main Idea: Amos worked hard as a child. Details: He shined shoes. He delivered newspapers. He delivered food.

Wally Amos and His Famous Cookies

by Jeri Cipriano

Summary

Wally Amos (born 1936) became a hugely successful entrepreneur in the 1970s, when he created and marketed chocolate chip cookies under the name "Famous Amos." Wally Amos's meteoric rise was the culmination of years of determination, hard work, and an unwavering belief in himself and his abilities. Amos was never afraid to leave one endeavor to explore another or to face failure on his way to success. His energy, popularity, initiative, discipline, and wish to succeed prompted President Ronald Reagan to present Wally Amos with the 1986 President's Award for Entrepreneurial Excellence. Since then, Amos has distinguished himself for his involvement in literacy campaigns, fundraising, and new product lines.

Before Reading

Building Background

Explain to students that Wally Amos started a very successful business selling cookies. Ask students to brainstorm ways they would advertise or promote a business they had started.

English Language Learners

Write the word *famous* on the board. Have children pronounce it. Suggest names of famous people students are familiar with, and have them take turns completing the statement *(Name) is a famous _____*. Write the word *promote*. Discuss with students ways they could promote a business to make it famous. Discuss idioms that appear in the text, such as *paid off, "can-do" attitude,* and [his] *name grew*.

Vocabulary

reputation, tips, agent, promote

Target Reading Skill: Main Idea and Details

Explain that a main idea is the most important idea about a subject in a piece of writing. Details are information that tell more about the main idea. After students read the book, allow students time to complete the Target Reading Skill activity.

During Reading

Think Critically

1. What lessons did Amos learn from his parents? (Sample answer: He learned to work as hard as he could and to believe in himself. He learned good manners and showing respect to adults.)

2. How did Amos's Aunt Della influence him? (She taught Amos how to make chocolate chip cookies. Later in life, he remembered the good times he had with his aunt and how delicious her cookies were. The memories influenced him to create a business selling cookies.)

3. Why do you think Amos's cookies became so popular? (Sample answer: They were tasty. In addition, Amos's personality and people skills made them stand out. He also did a lot to promote them.)

4. How did Amos handle failure? (Amos never gave up. When one business was not successful, he found something else to do.)

After Reading

Writing

Have students pair up and imagine that they work at the Famous Amos Chocolate Chip Cookie store. Have them brainstorm ways to advertise the cookies that they didn't read about in the book (such as billboards, magazine ads, Web sites, etc.). Have students share their lists.

Answers to Target Reading Skill

There are several main ideas in the book. Accept any that can be supported by the text.

Sample Main Idea: Amos was a good businessman.

Details: Amos succeeded at many of his businesses. He worked hard. He had a good reputation. He knew how to be friendly to customers. He did a lot to promote his cookie business.

Wally Amos
Building a Cookie Empire

by Jeri Cipriano

We Are Connected

Chapter: Working in Our Communities

Lexile Measure: 770

Summary

Wally Amos (born 1936) became a hugely successful entrepreneur in the 1970s, when he created and marketed chocolate chip cookies under the name "Famous Amos." Wally Amos's meteoric rise was the culmination of years of determination, hard work, and the unwavering belief in himself and his abilities. President Ronald Reagan presented Wally Amos with the 1986 President's Award for Entrepreneurial Excellence. Since then, Amos has distinguished himself for his involvement in literacy campaigns, fundraising, and new product lines.

Before Reading

Building Background

Tell students that Wally Amos had several jobs as a child, including shining shoes and delivering newspapers. Later, he started his own business. Ask students to suggest ways they would to promote a business. Discuss what qualities they think a person needs to run a successful business.

Vocabulary

founded, empire, reputation, profit, segregation, advertising, promote, entrepreneurial

English Language Learners

Write on the board: *He has a can-do attitude.* Explain *attitude* as the way someone thinks about something. Discuss the idiom, explaining that it means to have the attitude of "I can do this." Another phrase that means the same is to have a *positive attitude.* Tell students to look for things that show Amos had a "can-do" attitude.

Target Reading Skill: Main Idea and Details

Explain that a short piece of writing such as a paragraph may have one main idea. A longer piece, such as a book, has several important, or main, ideas. Details help explain or support the main idea. After students read the book, allow time for them to complete the Target Reading Skill activity on the inside covers of their Readers.

During Reading

Think Critically

1. What lessons did Amos learn as a child? (Sample answer: He learned to work as hard as he could, to believe in himself, to do the best he could with what he had. He learned good manners and to show respect to adults.)

2. In what ways did Amos show that he never gave up? (Even when he failed or discovered that the work he was doing did not suit him, he did not let it get him down. He tried something new.)

3. How did Amos promote his cookies? (He put his own name and face on the bags of cookies that he sold. He sometimes passed out cookies to people on the street. He made television commercials, did interviews, and appeared in a parade.)

4. What does it mean to say Amos was a "people person"? (He was friendly and liked people. He cared about making his customers happy.)

After Reading

Writing

Have students work in small groups to think of an imaginary product they would like to promote. Have them work together to create the script for a television commercial promoting their product. Have them perform their commercial for the class.

Answers to Target Reading Skill

There are several main ideas in the book. Accept any that can be supported by the text.

Sample Main Idea: Amos was a good businessman.

Details: Amos succeeded at many of his businesses. He worked hard. He had a good reputation. He knew how to be friendly to customers. He did a lot to promote his cookie business.

Hawaii's Queen Liliuokalani

by Darleen Ramos

We Are Connected

Chapter: Celebrating Our Communities

Lexile Measure: 400

Summary

Queen Liliuokalani (LIH lee oo oh kuh LAH nee), who was born in 1838 and died in 1917, was Hawaii's first and only ruling queen. She was well educated and became an accomplished musician who wrote over 150 songs and poems. She came into power in 1891, but her reign was short lived. In 1893, American armed forces took over the government. Queen Liliuokalani was tried and convicted of treason and sentenced to five years, but she only served eight months. Five years later, the United States annexed Hawaii as a territory. Liliuokalani fiercely opposed the annexation. She died in 1917 at her home in Honolulu.

Before Reading

Building Background

Show the location of Hawaii on a world map, making sure to note that it is a collection of islands. Point out that even though Hawaii is now a state in the United States, it was once a kingdom.

Vocabulary

kingdom, culture, missionary, outlaw, royal, plantation, port

Target Reading Skill: Compare and Contrast

Explain to students that when we compare and contrast, we look for similarities and differences. Draw a Venn diagram on the board. Title one side *Orange*, the other side *Apple*. Write *Alike* in the intersecting section. Ask students to say how the two objects are different and alike. Answers may include:

Orange: Orange in color. Do not eat the rind, or skin. Has segments inside.

Apple: Red in color. Can eat the skin, and can eat it without peeling. It is crunchy.

Similarities: Both are fruits. Both are round. Both grow on trees.

Distribute the compare-and-contrast graphic organizer, a Venn diagram. Tell students that after reading they will compare and contrast life in Hawaii before and after Americans came.

English Language Learners

Read the first several pages of the book to the class. As you read, identify any vocabulary words or other words that students might find difficult to pronounce, such as Hawaiian names. Write them on the board. Point to each word and say it aloud. Ask students to repeat the words.

During Reading

Think Critically

1. How did early Hawaiians pass on their history? (They sang chants.)

2. What did Liliuokalani do when smallpox started to spread? (She closed the ports.)

3. Why did Liliuokalani give up the throne? (She didn't want anyone to get hurt.)

After Reading

Writing

Ask students to write a few sentences about what they would like to see and do if they visited Hawaii. Have them read their sentences to a partner.

Answers to Target Reading Skill

Possible answers. Hawaii before Americans arrived: kingdom, no written language, chants to tell history

After: not a kingdom, part of U.S.

Before and after: parts of culture such as chants, hula dancing

Liliuokalani Hawaii's Last Queen

by Darleen Ramos

Summary

Queen Liliuokalani (LIH lee oo oh kuh LAH nee), who was born in 1838 was Hawaii's first and only ruling queen. She was well educated and an accomplished musician who wrote over 150 songs and poems. She came into power in 1891, but her reign was short lived. In 1893, American armed forces took over the government. Queen Liliuokalani was tried and convicted of treason and sentenced to five years, but she only served eight months. Five years later, the United States annexed Hawaii as a territory. Liliuokalani fiercely opposed the annexation. She died in 1917 at her home in Honolulu.

Before Reading

Building Background

Show the location of Hawaii on a world map, making sure to note that it is a collection of islands. Point out that even though Hawaii is now a state in the United States, it was once a kingdom.

Vocabulary

reign, culture, royalty, missionary, outlaw, heir, plantation, port, annex

Target Reading Skill: Compare and Contrast

Explain to students that when we compare and contrast, we look for similarities and differences. Draw a Venn diagram on the board. Title one side *Orange*, the other side *Apple*. Write *Alike* in the intersecting section. Ask students to say how the two objects are different and alike. Answers may include:

Orange: Orange in color. You do not eat the outside rind.

Apple: Red in color. You can eat the skin.

Similarities: Both are fruits. Both are round. Both are sweet and grow on trees.

Distribute copies of a diagram. Tell students they will complete it after reading. They will compare and contrast Hawaii before and after Americans arrived.

English Language Learners

Read the first several pages of the book to the class. As you read, identify any vocabulary words or other words that students might find difficult to pronounce, such as Hawaiian names. Write the words on the board. Point to each and say it aloud. Ask students to repeat the words.

During Reading

Think Critically

1. What kind of government did Hawaii have long ago? (It was a kingdom ruled by kings and a queen.)
2. What changes happened when Americans arrived? (They brought their own religion and clothing, they outlawed the hula, and they created a written Hawaiian language.)
3. Why did Queen Liliuokalani write a new constitution? (She wanted to return power to the kingdom.)

After Reading

Writing

Queen Liliuokalani wrote songs and chants about the beauty of her home. Have students write a short paragraph or poem about the ways in which the place where they live is special.

Answers to Target Reading Skill

Possible answers: Hawaii before Americans arrived: kingdom, no written language, chants to tell history.

Hawaii after Americans arrived: written language to tell history, no kingdom

Before and after: chants, hula dancing, surfing

Liliuokalani Queen of the Hawaiian Islands

by Darleen Ramos

We Are Connected

Chapter: Celebrating Our Communities

Lexile Measure: 650

Summary

Queen Liliuokalani (LIH lee oo oh kuh LAH nee), who was born in 1838 and died in 1917, was Hawaii's first and only ruling queen. She was well educated and an accomplished musician. She came into power in 1891, but her reign was short lived. In 1893, American armed forces took over the government of Hawaii. Queen Liliuokalani was tried and convicted of treason and sentenced to five years but only served eight months. Five years later, the U.S. annexed Hawaii as a territory. Liliuokalani fiercely opposed the annexation. She died in 1917.

Before Reading

Building Background

Build background for the book by explaining that the state of Hawaii has a unique history. It was once a kingdom. Locate Hawaii on a world map.

Vocabulary

culture, reign, missionary, royal, heir, plantation, port, annex, reinstate, outlaw, uprising

Target Reading Skill: Compare and Contrast

Explain that when we compare and contrast things, we look for similarities and differences. Describe two scenes: one of surfers riding a wave, the other of skaters on a frozen lake. Draw a Venn diagram on the board. Ask students to tell how the scenes are similar and how they are different.

Place their answers in the Venn diagram. On the left, write ways in which the first scene is different. On the far right, write down the ways in which the second scene is different. In the overlapping area, write down the ways in which they are similar or the same.

Tell students that they will later use a diagram like this to compare and contrast life in Hawaii before and after Americans arrived.

English Language Learners

Read the first several pages to the class. As you read, identify any vocabulary words or other words that students might find difficult to pronounce. Write the words on the board. Point to each word and say it aloud. Ask students to repeat them. Provide meanings in your own words.

During Reading

Think Critically

1. What kind of government did Hawaii have long ago? (It was a kingdom ruled by kings and a queen.)

2. How was Liliuokalani's childhood a mix of American and Hawaiian culture? (She sang Hawaiian chants. She was adopted by other chiefs. In school, she learned about American clothes and behavior. She learned to read and write English.)

3. What were some new things Liliuokalani experienced during her trip to the U.S. and Great Britain? (snow, trees without leaves, castles)

After Reading

Writing

Ask students to write a paragraph as if they are Queen Liliuokalani explaining why Hawaii should remain a kingdom.

Answers to Target Reading Skill

Possible answers: Before Americans arrived: Hawaii was a kingdom, no written language, chants to tell history

After Americans arrived: no longer kingdom, part of United States

Before and after: parts of culture such as chants, dancing, and surfing; always a beautiful place

President Theodore Roosevelt

by Tamara Orr Staats

Summary

Theodore Roosevelt (1858–1919) was the popular twenty-sixth president of the United States. Asthmatic as a child, Roosevelt was able to overcome a sickly childhood as well as the later devastating loss of his mother and wife on the same day. Despite his privileged upbringing, he was an advocate for working men and women. He created laws to improve their quality of life while encouraging policies to help businesses prosper. Roosevelt also helped the United States become a world power. But for many people, his greatest accomplishment was the preservation of millions of acres of wilderness by creating national parks, forests, and preserves.

Before Reading

Building Background

Ask students if they have ever visited a national park or seen photographs of one. Ask why one might want to protect wilderness areas and the animals that live there.

Vocabulary

wilderness, strike, canal, conservation

English Language Learners

Point out the glossary term *conservation*. Explain that the root word, *conserve*, means "to save or protect." The suffix *-ation* changes the meaning to "the action of saving or protecting." Have students search the text to find other words with the same root, such as *conserving* and *conservationist*.

Target Reading Skill: Generalize

Reproduce the graphic organizer on the board. Use this example:

Fact: Janet gets the right amount of sleep every night.

Fact: Janet eats healthy foods.

Fact: Janet exercises often.

Generalization: Janet has healthy habits.

Distribute the Generalize graphic organizer. Allow students time to complete the Reading Skill activity on the inside covers of their Readers.

During Reading

Think Critically

1. What kinds of things did Roosevelt do as a boy? (He exercised in a home gym; he studied nature and collected things.)

2. Why did many people want to build the Panama Canal? (It took too long to travel around the tip of South America.)

3. How would Roosevelt's time as president have been different if he hadn't loved nature? (He might not have been as interested in conservation.)

After Reading

Writing

Teddy Roosevelt was affected by nature. Have students write a short paragraph about how nature affects them.

Answers to Target Reading Skill

Possible facts: As a child, Roosevelt studied nature. He loved nature in the West where he was a rancher.

As president he supported conservation.

Possible generalization: Roosevelt cared deeply about nature.

Theodore Roosevelt
Progressive President

by Tamara Orr Statts

Regions of Our Country

Chapter: Geography of the United States

Lexile Measure: 710

Summary

Theodore Roosevelt (1858–1919) was the popular twenty-sixth president of the United States. Asthmatic as a child, Roosevelt was able to overcome a sickly childhood as well as the later devastating loss of his mother and wife on the same day. Despite his privileged upbringing, he was an advocate for working men and women. He created laws to improve their quality of life while encouraging policies to help businesses prosper. Roosevelt also helped the United States become a world power. But for many people, his greatest accomplishment was the preservation of millions of acres of wilderness by creating national parks, forests, and preserves.

Before Reading

Building Background

Ask students if they have ever visited a national park or seen photographs of one. Ask why they think it might be important to protect wilderness.

Vocabulary

wilderness, politics, progressive, regulation, strike, canal, environment, conservationist

English Language Learners

Point out the glossary term *conservationist*. Explain that the root word, *conserve*, means "to save or protect." The suffix *-ist* changes the meaning to "one who saves or protects something." Have students write a sentence using the word *conserve* or *conservationist*.

Target Reading Skill: Generalize

Reproduce the graphic organizer on the board. Use this example:

Fact: Janet gets the right amount of sleep every night.

Fact: Janet eats healthy foods.

Fact: Jane exercises regularly.

Generalization: (leave blank)

Ask the class to think of a generalization that fits the facts. (Janet has healthy habits.)

Distribute the graphic organizer. Allow students time to complete the Reading Skill activity on the inside covers of their Readers.

During Reading

Think Critically

1. What kinds of things did Roosevelt do as a boy? (He exercised in a home gym; he studied nature and collected things.)

2. Why did many people want to build the Panama Canal? (It took too long to travel around the tip of South America.)

3. What was the "Square Deal"? (Roosevelt's way of saying that the government should be fair to everyone)

4. How would Roosevelt's time as president have been different if he hadn't loved nature? (He might not have been as interested in conservation.)

After Reading

Writing

Teddy Roosevelt was affected by nature. Have students write a paragraph about how nature affects them.

Answers to Target Reading Skill

Possible facts: As a child, Roosevelt studied nature. He loved nature in the West where he was a rancher. As president he supported conservation.

Possible generalization: Roosevelt cared deeply about nature.

Theodore Roosevelt President and Conservationist

by Tamara Orr Staats

Regions of Our Country

Chapter: Geography of the United States

Lexile Measure: 780

Summary

Theodore Roosevelt (1858–1919) was the popular twenty-sixth president of the United States. Asthmatic as a child, Roosevelt was able to overcome a sickly childhood as well as the later devastating loss of his mother and wife on the same day. Despite his privileged upbringing, he was an advocate for working men and women. He created laws to improve their quality of life while encouraging policies to help businesses prosper. Roosevelt also helped the United States become a world power. But for many people, his greatest accomplishment was the preservation of millions of acres of wilderness by creating national parks, forests, and preserves.

Before Reading

Building Background

Encourage students to share what they already know about conservation and geography. Ask students if they have ever visited a national park or seen photographs of one. Ask why they think it might be important to protect wilderness.

Vocabulary

wilderness, politics, progressive, candidate, campaign, regulation, strike, diplomacy, canal, environment, conservationist

English Language Learners

Point out the glossary term *conservationist*. Explain that the root word, *conserve*, means "to save or protect." The suffix *-ist* changes the meaning to "one who saves or protects something." Have students write sentences that use the terms *conserve* and *conservationist* to describe the conservation of natural resources.

Target Reading Skill: Generalize

Reproduce the graphic organizer on the board. Use this example:

Fact: Janet gets the right amount of sleep every night.

Fact: Janet eats healthy foods.

Fact: (leave blank)

Generalization: Janet has healthy habits.

Ask the class to think of another fact that might support the generalization. (Jane exercises regularly.)

Distribute the graphic organizer. Allow students time to complete the Reading Skill activity on the inside covers of their Readers.

During Reading

Think Critically

1. What kinds of things did Roosevelt do as a boy? (He exercised in a home gym. He studied nature.)

2. Why did many people want to build the Panama Canal? (It took too long to travel around the tip of South America.)

3. What was the "Square Deal"? (Roosevelt's way of saying that the government should be fair to everyone)

4. How would Roosevelt's time as president have been different if he hadn't loved nature? (He might not have been as interested in conservation.)

After Reading

Writing

Teddy Roosevelt was affected by nature. Have students write a paragragh about how nature affects them.

Answers to Target Reading Skill

Possible facts: As a child, Roosevelt studied nature. He loved nature in the West, where he was a rancher. As president he supported conservation.

Possible generalization: Roosevelt cared deeply about nature.

Martin Luther King
A Brave Leader

by Dennis Fertig

Regions of Our Country

Chapter: Americans and Their History

Lexile Measure: 600

Summary

Martin Luther King, Jr., was born in 1929, into an America where segregation was common. In 1955, King was pastor of the Dexter Avenue Baptist Church in Montgomery, Alabama, when Rosa Parks was arrested for refusing to give up her seat on a bus to a white passenger. King and other community leaders organized a boycott of Montgomery city buses. After 13 months, it was successful, resulting in a U.S. Supreme Court ruling against bus segregation. During those months, King proved his leadership strengths as he confronted and defeated his own fears. He continued to call for nonviolence, even when his own home was bombed. By the time the boycott ended, King had become a national leader. He was awarded the Nobel Peace Prize in 1964. His efforts in the civil rights movement helped change America.

Before Reading

Building Background

Tell students that this book is a biography. It tells information about the life of Dr. Martin Luther King, Jr. Remind students that Martin Luther King Day is a national holiday. Have students share what they know about King. Point out the photo on page 2, and use it to discuss *segregation* with students.

Vocabulary

segregation, boycott, civil rights, assassin

Target Reading Skill: Sequence

Review the idea of putting events in order, or sequence, by having students tell, in order, three things they did this morning. Point out that biographies are usually written in the order in which things happen in the subject's life. Point out that writers help us follow the sequence of events by using dates. Allow students time to complete the Target Reading Skill activity on the inside cover of their Reader.

English Language Learners

Review the idea of time order with students, introducing the word *sequence*. Read the book aloud to students. As you read, point out and reinforce words that signal the sequence of events, such as dates. Then have students choral-read the book with you.

During Reading

Think Critically

1. What are some ways that African Americans and white Americans were segregated in their daily lives? (They went to different schools, used different seats on buses.)

2. Why was segregation unfair? (Schools for blacks were usually not as good as those for whites. Blacks did not have the same rights as whites.)

3. How did Martin Luther King show he was brave? (He knew he might be killed for what he was doing. It took courage to continue doing what he thought was right even in the face of death threats.)

After Reading

Writing

Have students write a short paragraph that tells how Martin Luther King helped change the United States.

Answers to Target Reading Skill

The completed chart should contain any of the events below, in correct order. Except for the first date, dates are not necessary but are included here.

December 1, 1955: Rosa Parks is arrested.
December 5, 1955: The boycott begins.
Late January 1956: King spends a sleepless night.
January 30, 1956: King's house is bombed.
December 21, 1956: Bus boycott ends.

Martin Luther King Courageous Civil Rights Leader

by Dennis Fertig

Regions of Our Country

Chapter: Americans and Their History

Lexile Measure: 730

Summary

Martin Luther King, Jr., was born in 1929, into an America where segregation was common. In 1955, King was pastor of a church in Montgomery, Alabama, when Rosa Parks was arrested for refusing to give up her bus seat to a white passenger. King and other community leaders organized a boycott of city buses. After 13 months, it was successful, resulting in a U.S. Supreme Court ruling against the bus segregation law. During those months, King proved his leadership. He continued to call for nonviolent methods, even when his own home was bombed. By the time the boycott ended, King was a national leader. He was awarded the Nobel Peace Prize in 1964. His efforts in the civil rights movement helped change America.

Before Reading

Building Background

Remind students that Martin Luther King Day is a national holiday. Ask students to discuss why a day is set aside to honor Dr. King. Have students share what they know about King. Point out the photo on page 2, and use it to discuss *segregation* with students.

Vocabulary

segregation, custom, integrated, society, civil rights, boycott, assassin

Target Reading Skill: Sequence

Review the idea of putting events in order, or sequence, by having students tell, in order, three things they do in the morning before arriving at school. Discuss why understanding sequence is important in reading biography and history. Point out that writers help us follow the sequence of events by using dates and other clues, such as the words *after*, *before*, and *next*. Allow students time to complete the Target Reading Skill activity on the inside cover.

English Language Learners

Review the idea of time order with students, introducing the word *sequence*. Read the selection aloud to students, pausing to point out sequence signals and to clarify the sequence of events. Then have students take turns rereading the book aloud with a partner.

During Reading

Think Critically

1. What are some ways that African Americans and white Americans were segregated in their daily lives? (They lived in different neighborhoods and went to different schools.)

2. Why was segregation unfair? (African Americans didn't have the same rights as whites.)

3. How did Martin Luther King, Jr., show he had courage? (It took courage to do what he thought was right in the face of death threats.)

4. How did Martin Luther King, Jr., help change America? (He helped African Americans gain equal treatment. He showed that nonviolent protest can work. He inspired other people.)

After Reading

Writing

Have students write a short paragraph explaining how Martin Luther King showed courage. Have volunteers share their paragraphs with the class.

Answers to Target Reading Skill

The completed chart should contain any of the events below, in correct order. Dates are not necessary but are included here.

December 1, 1955: Rosa Parks is arrested.
December 5, 1955: The boycott begins.
Late January 1956: King spends a sleepless night.
Late January 1956, a few days later: King's house is bombed.
December 21, 1956: Bus boycott ends.

Martin Luther King and the Struggle for Civil Rights

by Dennis Fertig

Regions of Our Country

Chapter: Americans and Their History

Lexile Measure: 790

Summary

Martin Luther King, Jr., was born in 1929, into an America where segregation was common. In 1955, King was a church pastor in Montgomery, Alabama, when Rosa Parks was arrested for refusing to give up her seat on a bus. King and other community leaders organized a boycott of the city buses. After 13 months, it was successful, resulting in a U.S. Supreme Court ruling against the city's bus segregation law. Afterward, King continued to call for nonviolence, even after his own home was bombed. By the time the boycott ended, King was a national leader. He was awarded the Nobel Peace Prize in 1964. His efforts in the civil rights movement helped change America.

Before Reading

Building Background

Remind students that Martin Luther King Day is a national holiday. Ask students to discuss why a day is set aside, and have them share what they know about him.

Vocabulary

segregation, civil rights, integrated, society, boycott, official, assassin

Target Reading Skill: Sequence

Discuss why understanding sequence is important in reading biography and history. Explain that dates are obvious clues in following sequence, but that other signal words, such as *after* and *next*, help too. Allow students time to complete the Target Reading Skill activity on the inside cover of their reader.

English Language Learners

Review the idea of time order and introduce the word *sequence*. Read the selection aloud to students, pausing to point out sequence signals and to clarify the sequence of events.

During Reading

Think Critically

1. What are some ways that black and white Americans lived segregated lives? (They lived in different neighborhoods and went to different schools.)

2. Why was segregation unfair? (African Americans didn't have civil rights.)

3. How did Martin Luther King, Jr., show he had courage? (It took courage to continue doing what he thought was right even in the face of death threats.)

4. How did Martin Luther King, Jr., help change the country? (He helped African Americans gain equal treatment. He showed that nonviolent protest can work. He inspired other people.)

After Reading

Writing

Have students write a persuasive paragraph explaining why Martin Luther King, Jr., deserves to be remembered. Have volunteers share their paragraphs with the class.

Answers to Target Reading Skill

The completed organizer should contain any of the events below, in correct order. Dates are not necessary but are included here.

December 1, 1955: Rosa Parks is arrested.
December 5, 1955: The boycott begins.
Late January 1956: King spends a sleepless night.
Late January 1956, a few days later: King's house is bombed.
December 21, 1956: Bus boycott ends.

James Madison America's Fourth President

by Tamara Orr Staats

Summary

James Madison (1751–1836) was the fourth president of the United States, serving from 1809 to 1817. He was a frail child, but he had one of the most brilliant minds of the Revolutionary era. He was born into wealth and privilege. He studied at the College of New Jersey (later Princeton University) under John Witherspoon, who taught him the principle that liberty must be guarded from the abuse of power. Madison's major accomplishments include providing the blueprint for the United States Constitution, which included three branches of government and a system of checks and balances. He was also responsible for drafting the Bill of Rights. He is often referred to as the Father of the Constitution.

Before Reading

Building Background

Discuss with students the beginnings of our country, explaining that the colonies were under the rule of Great Britain. Have students tell what they know of this time period and identify leaders they may know of, such as George Washington. Explain that when our country no longer was ruled by Great Britain, one big job our leaders had was to decide what kind of government the country would have.

Vocabulary

colony, tax, independence, revolution, constitution, compromise, amendment

English Language Learners

Write the following sentence on the board: *A baby depends on its parents.* Discuss the meaning of *depend.* Then build a word family by writing and discussing *dependent*, *independent*, and *independence.* Help students use each word in a sentence.

Target Reading Skill: Main Idea and Details

Remind students that the main idea is the most important idea in a piece of writing. Details tell more about the main idea. Explain that a paragraph, a section of a book or chapter, and a book can all have a main idea. After students read the book, guide them as they work through the Target Reading Skill activity.

During Reading

Think Critically

1. What was James Madison like as a child? (He was small and shy and often sick. He was also curious and spent a lot of time reading.)

2. What was going on in the country while Madison was in college? (People were upset about British taxes.)

3. Why do you think some people were afraid of having a strong central government? (They were fighting to get rid of a king. They may have been afraid of letting the government have too much power, the way a king does.)

4. Why did some states refuse to approve the new Constitution? (There was no list of rights.)

After Reading

Writing

Have students think about one of the rights the Bill of Rights protects, such as the right to speak freely. Then have them draw a picture of themselves doing something that is protected by the Bill of Rights. Have them write two or three sentences that explain their drawing.

Answers to Target Reading Skill Activity

Possible main idea: The colonists began a revolution against Great Britain.

Possible details: Colonists were upset about taxes. Colonists and soldiers fought in Lexington.

James Madison Founder and President

by Tamara Orr Staats

Regions of Our Country

Chapter: Government in the United States

Lexile Measure: 680

Summary

James Madison (1751–1836) was the fourth president of the United States, serving from 1809 to 1817. He was a frail child, but he had one of the most brilliant minds of the Revolutionary era. He was born into wealth and privilege. He studied at the College of New Jersey (later Princeton University) under John Witherspoon, who taught him the principle that liberty must be guarded from the abuse of power. Madison's major accomplishments include providing the blueprint for the United States Constitution, which included three branches of government and a system of checks and balances. He was also responsible for drafting the Bill of Rights. He is often referred to as the Father of the Constitution.

Before Reading

Building Background

Discuss with students the beginnings of our country, explaining that the colonies were under the rule of Great Britain. Have students tell what they know of this time period and identify leaders they may know of, such as George Washington. Explain that when our country no longer was ruled by Britain, one big job our leaders had was to decide what kind of government the country would have.

Vocabulary

founder, colony, tax, independence, militia, revolution, constitution, council, delegate, compromise, amendment

English Language Learners

Write the following sentence on the board: *A baby depends on its parents.* Discuss the meaning of *depend*. Then build a word family by writing and discussing *dependent*, *independent*, and *independence*. Help students use each word in a sentence.

Target Reading Skill: Main Idea and Details

Explain that the main idea is the most important idea in a piece of writing. Details tell more about the main idea. Explain that a paragraph, a section of a book or chapter, and a book can each have a main idea. After students have read the book, have them complete the Target Reading Skill activity. Give guidance as needed.

During Reading

Think Critically

1. What was James Madison like as a child? (He was small and shy and often sick. He was also very curious and spent a lot of time reading.)

2. What was happening in the country when Madison was in college? (People were upset about British taxes.)

3. Why was Madison afraid that the Articles of Confederation would not work well? (They were weak and gave the states most of the power. Madison favored a strong central government.)

4. Why did some states refuse to approve the new Constitution? (There was no list of rights.)

After Reading

Writing

Ask students to think about some of the rights the Bill of Rights protects, such as the right to speak freely. Then have them find a picture in a newspaper or magazine that shows people exercising a right protected by the Bill of Rights. Then have them write a paragraph that explains the right the picture shows.

Answers to Target Reading Skill Activity

Sample main idea: Madison worked for Virginia's government.

Sample details: He helped write the Virginia constitution. He made sure there was strong protection of religious freedom in Virginia's constitution. He served on the governor's council.

James Madison
Father of the Constitution

by Tamara Orr Staats

Summary

James Madison (1751–1836) was the fourth president of the United States, serving from 1809 to 1817. He had one of the most brilliant minds of the Revolutionary era. He studied at the College of New Jersey (later Princeton University) under John Witherspoon, who taught him the principle that liberty must be guarded from the abuse of power. Madison's major accomplishments include providing the blueprint for the United States Constitution and drafting the Bill of Rights. He is often referred to as the Father of the Constitution.

Before Reading

Building Background

Have students tell what they know of the time of the Revolutionary War and identify leaders they may know of, such as George Washington. Explain that while the colonies were fighting for independence, people also had to plan the kind of government they would have after the war.

Vocabulary

founder, colony, tax, protest, revolution, militia, independence, constitution, council, delegate, convention, compromise, amendment

English Language Learners

Write *independence* on the board and underline the base word, *depend*. Discuss what it means to depend on someone, the way a baby depends on its parents. Then write and discuss *dependent*, *independent*, and *independence*. Help students use each word in a sentence.

Target Reading Skill: Main Idea and Details

Explain that the main idea is the most important idea in a piece of writing. A paragraph, a section of a book or chapter, and an entire book can each have a main idea. Have students complete the Target Reading Skill activity.

During Reading

Think Critically

1. What was James Madison like as a child? (He was small and shy and often sick. He was also very curious and read lots of books.)

2. What was going on in the country while Madison was in college? (People were upset about and protesting British taxes.)

3. How did Madison feel about religious freedom? (He had strong opinions about it. He thought the government should not tell people what to believe.)

4. Why is Madison called the Father of the Constitution? (It was Madison's Virginia Plan that became the blueprint of the Constitution. Madison also wrote the draft of the Bill of Rights.)

After Reading

Writing

Ask students to think about things they did in the past week. Have them choose one or two things that show rights that are protected by the Bill of Rights. Have students write a paragraph that explains how the Bill of Rights protected those rights.

Answers to Target Reading Skill

Possible main idea: James Madison played a large part in designing the government we have today.

Possible details: Madison's education and early life prepared him to work in government. Madison designed the blueprint for the Constitution. Madison wrote the Bill of Rights.

Cornelius Vanderbilt Builder of Railroads

by Dennis Fertig

Regions of Our Country

Chapter: The Nation's Economy

Lexile Measure: 670

Summary

Cornelius Vanderbilt was born in 1794. As a young man, he learned to handle a sailboat ferry and started a ferry business to carry goods and people from Staten Island to Manhattan. He later learned the steamboat business. He owned and sold several steamship businesses and became wealthy. Later he built a railroad empire. Vanderbilt was a tough, feared competitor. When he died in 1877, he was considered the wealthiest person in the United States. His transportation businesses contributed to the economic development of the United States.

Before Reading

Building Background

Ask students how they got to school. Tell them that whatever way they took—even walking—was a type of transportation. Tell students that when the country was young, there were fewer transportation choices than today. Ask students to suggest a few of them. (walking, riding a horse or other animal, riding in a wagon or stagecoach, using a boat) Explain that in the new country, even these means of travel were hard because there weren't many roads and many river routes were dangerous or unknown.

Vocabulary

profit, invest, monopoly, cargo, competitor

English Language Learners

Explain to students that there are many words in this book that are related to travel. Write these words on the board: *ferry, sail, sailboat, steamship, railroad*. Using illustrations within the story, discuss the meanings each of these words when used as nouns. Help students give examples of sentences using the words.

Target Reading Skill: Summarize

Remind students that *summarize* means to give a brief retelling of the main points of a reading selection. Allow students time to complete the Target Reading Skill activity on the inside cover of their Reader.

During Reading

Think Critically

During Reading

Comprehension and Critical Thinking

1. How did Vanderbilt get started in the transportation business? (His mother lent him $100 and he used it to start a ferryboat business.)

2. How did Vanderbilt make money by investing in other ferry companies? (By investing he bought a part of the other company. If the company made a profit, Vanderbilt did too.)

4. What made Vanderbilt's railroad business successful? (The trains went to many places, they ran on time, and they were comfortable.)

After Reading

Writing

Ask students to write a slogan and draw a poster to convince someone to use Vanderbilt's company to transport them to California during the gold rush.

Answers to Target Reading Skill

Possible main ideas or facts:

Vanderbilt started a ferry business at age 16.

Vanderbilt started several successful steamship companies.

Vanderbilt built a successful railroad empire.

Possible summary:

Vanderbilt built many successful transportation companies.

The Business Empire of Cornelius Vanderbilt

by Dennis Fertig

Regions of Our Country

Chapter: The Nation's Economy

Lexile Measure: 650

Summary

Cornelius Vanderbilt was born in 1794. As a young man, he learned to handle a sailboat ferry and started a ferry business to carry goods and people from Staten Island to Manhattan. Then he learned the steamship business. He owned and sold several steamship businesses and became wealthy. Later he built a railroad empire. Throughout, Vanderbilt was a tough, feared competitor. When he died in 1877, he was considered the wealthiest person in the United States. His transportation businesses also contributed greatly to the economic development of the United States.

Before Reading

Building Background

Ask students what form or forms of transportation they use to get to school. Remind students that when the country was young, there were fewer forms of transportation than today. Ask students to suggest a few of them. (walking, riding horseback, riding in a wagon or stagecoach, sailing in a boat)

Vocabulary

profit, competitor, invest, monopoly, resource, economy

English Language Learners

Explain to students that there are many travel-related words in this book. Write these words on the board: *ferry, boat, sailboat, steamship*. Use images from the book to discuss these kinds of transportation. Ask students to provide words for additional methods of transportation.

Target Reading Skill: Summarize

Remind students that a summary is a short statement that retells the main idea of a reading passage or book. A summary includes the most important ideas of the book. Pause periodically to identify important ideas as you read the book. Allow students time to complete the Target Reading Skill activity on the inside cover of their Reader.

During Reading

Think Critically

Comprehension and Critical Thinking

1. How did Vanderbilt get started in the transportation business? (His mother lent him $100, and he used it to start a ferryboat business.)

2. Explain how Vanderbilt made money by investing in other ferry companies. (By investing he bought a part of the other company. If the company earned a profit, Vanderbilt got part of it.)

3. Describe Vanderbilt's personality. How do you think his personality helped make him a good businessman? (His toughness, bravery, ability to work hard, honesty, and cleverness made him a very successful businessman.)

4. Summarize how Vanderbilt helped make the United States a richer country. (His transportation companies helped carry people and products around the country. The people used the products to create new businesses.)

After Reading

Writing

Ask students to write a speech that Vanderbilt might have made as an older man, talking about the highlights of his life.

Answers to Target Reading Skill

Possible main ideas or facts:

Vanderbilt started a ferry business at age 16.

Vanderbilt started several successful steamboat companies.

Vanderbilt built a successful railroad empire.

Possible summary:

Vanderbilt built many successful transportation companies.

Cornelius Vanderbilt American Entrepreneur

by Dennis Fertig

Regions of Our Country

Chapter: The Nation's Economy

Lexile Measure: 840

Summary

Cornelius Vanderbilt was born in 1794. As a young man, he learned to handle a sailboat ferry and started a ferry business to carry goods and people from Staten Island to Manhattan. He later learned the steamship business. He owned and sold several steamship businesses and became wealthy. Later he built a railroad empire. Vanderbilt was always a tough, feared competitor. When he died in 1877, he was considered the wealthiest person in the United States. His transportation businesses contributed to the economic development of the United States.

Before Reading

Building Background

Ask students what form or forms of transportation they use to get to school or family members use to get to work. Remind students that when the country was young, there weren't as many modes of transportation. Ask students to suggest a few of them, such as walking, riding horseback, riding in a wagon or stagecoach, sailing in a boat)

Vocabulary

entrepreneur, profit, competitor, invest, technology, monopoly, economy

English Language Learners

Explain to students that there are many travel-related words in this book. Write these words on the board: *ferry, boat, sailboat, steamboat*. Use images from the book and supplemental materials to discuss these modes of transportation. Ask students to provide words for additional methods of transportation.

Target Reading Skill: Summarize

Remind students that to *summarize* means to provide a brief overview of what something is about based on a group of main points. Allow students time to complete the Target Reading Skill activity on the inside cover of their Reader.

During Reading

Think Critically

Comprehension and Critical Thinking

1. How do you think young Vanderbilt knew that transportation could be an important business? (His family depended on a ferry to sell its goods and to make a living.)

2. Why did Vanderbilt sell his sailboat company? (He was interested in newer boats powered by steam.)

3. Describe Vanderbilt's personality. How do you think his personality helped make him a good businessman? (His toughness, bravery, honesty, ability to work hard, and cleverness made him a very successful businessman.)

4. Summarize how Vanderbilt helped make the United States a richer country. (His transportation companies helped carry people and products around the country. The people used the products to create new businesses in different places.)

After Reading

Writing

Ask students to write a dialogue between two of Vanderbilt's competitors about why they fear Vanderbilt. They should mention specific details about Vanderbilt's business career.

Answers to Target Reading Skill

Possible main ideas or facts:

Vanderbilt started a ferry business at age 16.

Vanderbilt started several successful steamship companies.

Vanderbilt built a successful railroad empire.

Possible summary:

Vanderbilt built many successful transportation companies.

Abigail Adams
First Lady

by Tamara Orr Staats

Summary

Abigail Adams (1744–1818) was born in Weymouth, Massachusetts, the daughter of the town minister, William Smith. She had little formal education, but read avidly in her father's library. In 1764 she married lawyer John Adams, who became involved in the Revolutionary cause, and later served as second president of the United States. John and Abigail Adams spent many months, sometimes years, apart and during this time kept up a voluminous correspondence. Abigail Adams's letters give us a good idea of life during the Revolutionary War and the early days of our country. They also give us insight into her strong opinions, as well as show the great amount of influence she had in her marriage.

Before Reading

Building Background

Explain that Abigail Adams and her husband, John Adams, were born in Massachusetts during the time that our country was still ruled by Great Britain, and both were very involved in the cause of gaining independence for the colonies. Read the title of the book and explain that *First Lady* is the honorary title given to the wife of a president of the United States.

Vocabulary

influence, colony, independence, delegate, unlimited, slavery

English Language Learners

Preview the book with students. Use the illustrations to help students predict what they think they will learn about Abigail Adams's life. Then read the text aloud, stopping after each page to use the 5 Ws (Who, What, Where, When, Why) to model think-alouds about the page's content.

Target Reading Skill: Draw Conclusions

Explain that writers often present facts about a subject, but expect readers to use these facts and what they already know to draw a conclusion— that is, to form their own opinions about what they read. After students have read the book, work with them to complete the Target Reading Skill activity.

During Reading

Think Critically

1. What kind of education did Abigail get? (She was taught at home. She did not go to school but had access to her father's library and was encouraged to learn as much as possible.)

2. Why was letter writing so important to Abigail Adams? (Abigail and and John Adams were often separated for long periods of time and wrote letters to stay in touch.)

3. What was Abigail Adams's opinion of slavery? (She thought it was wrong.)

4. Name something you admire about Abigail Adams. Tell why you admire her for this. (Answers will vary, but students may say Adams never stopped learning, she took care of her farm, and was a help to John Adams.)

After Reading

Writing

Ask students to draw a picture that shows one strong opinion that Abigail Adams expressed in her life. Have them write a sentence or two about their drawings.

Answers to Reading Skill activity

Possible details: Adams tried to learn as much as she could. She was embarrassed by her poor grammar and spelling. She wished she could have gone to school. She thought it was unfair that girls were not educated the same as boys.

Sample conclusion: Abigail Adams thought education was as important for women as for men.

Abigail Adams From the Revolution to the White House

by Tamara Orr Staats

Regions of Our Country

Chapter: The Northeast

Lexile Measure: 800

Summary

Abigail Adams (1744–1818) was born in Weymouth, Massachusetts, the daughter of the town minister, William Smith. She had little formal education, but read avidly in her father's library. In 1764 she married lawyer John Adams, who became involved in the Revolutionary cause, and who later served as second president of the United States. John and Abigail Adams spent many months, sometimes years, apart and during this time kept up a voluminous correspondence. Abigail Adams's letters give us insight into her strong and progressive opinions.

Before Reading

Building Background

Explain that Abigail Adams and her husband, John Adams, were born during the time when our country was still ruled by Great Britain, and both were very involved in the cause of gaining independence for the colonies.

Vocabulary

influence, colony, independence, delegate, boycott, slavery, treason, sacrifice

English Language Learners

Read the text aloud as students follow along. Stop after each section and use the 5 Ws (Who, What, Where, When, Why) to ask questions.

Target Reading Skill: Draw Conclusions

Explain that writers often present facts about a subject but expect readers to use these facts and what they already know to draw conclusions and form opinions about what they read.

After students have read the book, have them work with a partner to complete the Target Reading Skill activity. Give assistance as needed.

During Reading

Think Critically

1. What kind of education did Abigail Adams have? (She was taught at home and read in her father's library.)

2. Why was letter writing so important to Abigail? (The Adamses were often separated for long periods of time. Writing kept them in touch.)

3. What important historical events happened during Abigail Adams's life? (Possible answers include the Boston Massacre, Continental Congress, signing of the Declaration of Independence, and the American Revolution.)

4. Why is Abigail Adams remembered today? (Her letters tell us a great deal about her life and the times she lived in, and tell us that she was a strong and intelligent woman.)

After Reading

Writing

Ask students to write a letter that Abigail Adams might write to her grandchildren encouraging them to learn as much as they can. They should use her life as an example.

Answers to Target Reading Skill

Possible details: Adams tried to learn as much as she could. She was embarrassed by her poor grammar and spelling. She wished she could have gone to school. She thought it was unfair that girls were not educated the same as boys.

Sample conclusion: Abigail Adams thought a good education was as important for women as for men.

Abigail Adams Advocate for Women

by Tamara Orr Staats

Regions of Our Country

Chapter: The Northeast

Lexile Measure: 800

Summary

Abigail Adams (1744–1818) was born in Weymouth, Massachusetts, the daughter of the minister William Smith. In 1764 she married John Adams, who became involved in the Revolutionary cause, and who later served as second president of the United States. John and Abigail Adams spent many months, sometimes years, apart and during this time kept up a voluminous correspondence. Abigail Adams's letters give us insight into her strong and progressive opinions, as well as show the great amount of influence she had in her marriage.

Before Reading

Building Background

Explain that Abigail Adams and her husband John Adams were born in Massachusetts during the time that our country was still ruled by Great Britain. Both were very involved in the cause of gaining independence for the colonies. Read the title and explain that *advocate* means "someone who speaks up for, or who argues for some point of view."

Vocabulary

influence, advocate, neglect, colony, delegate, independence, sacrifice, boycott, scarce, tyrant, slavery, treason

English Language Learners

Read the text aloud as students follow along in their Readers. Stop after each section and use the 5 Ws (Who, What, Where, When, Why) to ask questions.

Target Reading Skill: Draw Conclusions

Explain that writers often present facts about a subject but expect readers to use these facts and what they already know to draw conclusions about what they read. After students have read the book, have them work with a partner to complete the Target Reading Skill activity.

During Reading

Think Critically

1. What kind of education did Abigail Adams have? (She was taught at home and never went to school, but she read all she could in her father's library.)

2. Why was letter writing so important to Abigail? (Abigail and her husband were often separated for long periods of time and had to write letters to stay in touch. She also felt she could express herself better in letters.)

3. What important historical events happened during Abigail's life? (Possible answers include the Boston Massacre, signing of the Declaration of Independence, and the American Revolution.)

4. What conclusion can you draw about the kind of person Abigail Adams was? (Sample conclusions: She was smart and interested in learning; She thought for herself and was not afraid to express her opinions; She was willing to make sacrifices for something important.)

After Reading

Writing

Ask students to write a letter that Abigail Adams might write to a young girl who is in school today, telling her why education is important.

Answers to Target Reading Skill

Possible details: Adams believed women should receive the same education as men. She thought women should have opinions about government.

Possible conclusion: Abigail Adams thought women should be treated equally to men.

Mary McLeod Bethune Fights for Justice

by Kate Broad

Regions of Our Country

Chapter: The Southeast

Lexile Measure: 560

Summary

Mary McLeod Bethune was an African American educator and civil rights leader. Although she was born ten years after the Civil War ended, her early life was shaped by the effects of slavery and the war. She was the first in her family to be born free and to attend school. In 1904, she started a school in Daytona Beach, Florida, for African American girls, which grew into Bethune-Cookman University. She became nationally known and respected, serving as leader of several organizations and as an advisor to several presidents. Today Bethune is remembered for her tireless fight to advance equality.

Before Reading

Building Background

Using the illustration on page 2 of separate drinking facilities, discuss the term *segregation* and have students share what they already know about segregation. Be sure students understand that because of segregation, African Americans were often treated unjustly.

Vocabulary

segregation, equality, poll tax, civil rights, advisor, federal agency

English Language Learners

Write the word *segregation* and the base word, *segregate*. Explain that *segregate* means to keep separate or apart. Tell students that during segregation, blacks and whites were kept separated in many parts of their daily lives.

Target Reading Skill: Categorize

Explain that one way to organize information that we read is to categorize it. To *categorize* is to sort things into groups that are alike in some way. Tell students that they will read facts about the life of Mary McLeod Bethune. Later, they will categorize things they read about. After students read the book, allow them time to complete the activity.

During Reading

Think Critically

1. Why didn't Mary McLeod's parents or her older brothers or sisters know how to read? (They had been enslaved, and it was against the law to teach enslaved people how to read.)

2. How do you think Mary McLeod felt when the girl told her she couldn't read? (Sample answer: Her pride was hurt. She probably felt embarrassed and ashamed.)

3. Why did Mary McLeod Bethune want to start a school in Florida for African American girls? (There were no schools there for African Americans at the time. She wanted to go where she would do the most good.)

4. What laws made it difficult for African Americans to vote? (They often had to pay a poll tax and pass a test to show they could read.)

After Reading

Writing

Ask students to write a letter that Mary McLeod Bethune might write to her grandchildren telling them how she fought for justice. Students should use events in her life as examples.

Answers to Target Reading Skill

Accept any answers that can be supported by the text. Sample answers are given below.

People: Mary McLeod Bethune; Patsy McLeod; Samuel McLeod; Eleanor Roosevelt; Franklin Delano Roosevelt

Places: Mayesville, Florida; South Carolina; Daytona Beach, Florida; Washington, D.C.

Events: Mary McLeod is born; starts school; meets Albertus Bethune; gets married; starts her own school; becomes an advisor to the president; Supreme Court makes school segregation illegal

Mary McLeod Bethune Works for Civil Rights

by Kate Broad

Regions of Our Country

Chapter: The Southeast

Lexile Measure: 770

Summary

Mary McLeod Bethune was an African American educator and civil rights leader. Born in South Carolina in 1875, she was the first in her family to be born free and to attend school. In 1904, she started a school in Daytona Beach, Florida, for African American girls, which grew into Bethune-Cookman University. She became nationally known and respected, serving as leader of several organizations, and as an advisor to several presidents. Today, Bethune is remembered for her tireless work to advance equality.

Before Reading

Building Background

Using the illustration on page 2 of separate drinking facilities, discuss the term *segregation* with students and have students share what they already know about segregation. Discuss the term *civil rights* and help students understand its meaning as "the rights citizens all have," such as the right to equal treatment under the law.

Vocabulary

segregated, equality, poll tax, literate, civil rights

English Language Learners

Read the vocabulary words aloud and have students repeat them after you. Write the word *segregated* and underline the base word, *segregate*. Explain that to segregate means to keep separate or apart. Then write *segregation*. Tell students that the word usually means the way blacks and whites were kept separate in this country until the late 1950s.

Target Reading Skill: Categorize

Explain that one way to organize information that we read is to categorize it. To *categorize* means to sort things into groups that are alike in some way. Tell students that they will read facts about the life of Mary McLeod Bethune. Later, they will categorize things they read about. After students read the book, allow them time to complete the activity.

During Reading

Think Critically

1. Why didn't Mary McLeod's parents or her older brothers or sisters know how to read? (They had been enslaved, and it was against the law to teach enslaved people how to read.)

2. Why did Mary McLeod Bethune want to start a school in Daytona, Florida for African American girls? (There were no schools there for African Americans at the time. She wanted to go where she would do the most good.)

3. What laws made it harder for African Americans to vote? (They often had to pay a tax and pass a reading test.)

4. Which accomplishment of Bethune's do you think was the most important? Give a reason. (Answers will vary, but students should support their answers.)

After Reading

Writing

Think about the things that were important to Mary McLeod Bethune. Choose one way she worked to help African Americans have equal civil rights. Write a paragraph about what she did and why you think it is important.

Answers to Target Reading Skill

Accept any answers that can be supported by the text. Sample answers are given below.

People: Mary McLeod Bethune; Patsy McLeod; Samuel McLeod; Eleanor Roosevelt; Franklin Delano Roosevelt
Places: Mayesville, Florida; Scotia Seminary, North Carolina; Chicago, Illinois; South Carolina; Daytona Beach, Florida; Washington, D.C.
Events: Mary McLeod is born; goes to school; meets Albertus Bethune; gets married; starts her own school; becomes an advisor to the president; Supreme Court makes school segregation illegal

Mary McLeod Bethune's Many Achievements

by Kate Broad

Regions of Our Country

Chapter: The Southeast

Lexile Measure: 810

Summary

Mary McLeod Bethune was an African American educator and civil rights leader. Born in South Carolina in 1875, she was the first in her family to be born free and to attend school. In 1904, she started a school in Daytona Beach, Florida, for African American girls, which grew into Bethune-Cookman University. She became nationally known and respected, serving as leader of several organizations, and as an advisor to several presidents. Today Bethune is remembered for her tireless work to advance equality.

Before Reading

Building Background

Discuss the term *civil rights* and help students understand its meaning as "the rights citizens all have," such as the right to equal treatment under the law. Using the illustration on page 2 of separate drinking facilities as a discussion starter, discuss the term *segregation* with students and have students share what they know about it.

Vocabulary

segregated, discrimination, literate, philanthropist, poll tax

English Language Learners

Read the vocabulary words aloud and have students repeat them after you. Write the word *segregated* and underline the base word, *segregate*. Explain that to *segregate* means to keep separate or apart. Then write *segregation*. Tell students that the word usually means the way blacks and whites were kept separate in this country until the late 1950s.

Target Reading Skill: Categorize

Explain that to *categorize* means to sort things into groups that are alike in some way. Tell students that they will read facts about the life of Mary McLeod Bethune. Later, they will categorize these facts. After students read the book, allow them time to complete the activity.

During Reading

Think Critically

1. Why didn't Mary McLeod's parents or siblings know how to read? (They had been enslaved, and it was against the law to teach enslaved people how to read.)

2. How was Mary McLeod affected by the incident of the child telling her to put the book down? (Her pride was hurt. She made up her mind to learn to read.)

3. Why did Mary McLeod Bethune want to start a school in Daytona, Florida for African American girls? (There were no schools there for African Americans at the time. She wanted to go where she would do the most good.)

4. What laws made it harder for African Americans to vote? (They often had to pay a poll tax and pass a test to show they could read.)

5. Which accomplishment of Bethune's do you think was the most important? Give your reason. (Answers will vary but students should support their answers.)

After Reading

Writing

Think about all that Mary McLeod Bethune did in her life. Write a paragraph explaining which achievement of Bethune's you think was the most important. Give reasons for your choice.

Answers to Target Reading Skill

Accept any answers that can be supported by the text. Sample answers are given below.

People: Mary McLeod Bethune; Patsy McLeod; Samuel McLeod; Albertus Bethune; Eleanor Roosevelt; Franklin Delano Roosevelt

Places: Mayesville, Florida; Scotia Seminary, North Carolina; Chicago, Illinois; South Carolina; Daytona Beach, Florida; Washington, D.C.

Events: Mary McLeod is born; goes to school; meets Albertus Bethune; gets married; starts her own school; becomes an advisor to the president; Supreme Court makes school segregation illegal

Willa Cather
Writer of Pioneer Stories

by Tammy Orr Staats

Summary

Willa Cather (1873–1947) was nine when her family moved from Virginia's Shenandoah Valley to the Nebraska prairie. Cather was affected by pioneer and immigrant families as she listened to them talk about their struggle adjusting to life on the prairie. For several decades, Cather was a writer and editor for newspapers and magazines and then a high school teacher. Ultimately, she focused on writing, producing many well-known novels about the pioneer experience. Many people consider *My Ántonia* her best novel. Cather later won a Pulitzer Prize for her novel *One of Ours*. Today, Willa Cather is considered one of America's great writers.

Before Reading

Building Background

Use a map of the United States to show the location of Nebraska, one of the Great Plains states. Explain that in the 1800s, many families moved to the prairies of the Midwest from other places in the United States and from other countries. Use images of pioneers from the book and other resources to demonstrate that life on the prairie was challenging.

Vocabulary

prairie, sod, pioneer, immigrant, essay, novel

English Language Learners

Read the text aloud, modeling think-aloud strategies to aid comprehension, and identify facts and opinions about Willa Cather. Have students work with partners to read the text to one another.

Target Reading Skill: Fact and Opinion

Provide students with this example a fact and opinion: *Willa Cather was an American writer. Willa Cather was America's greatest writer.* As a class, think of more facts and opinions. Distribute the Fact and Opinion graphic organizer. Allow students time to complete the Reading Skill activity on the inside cover of their Readers.

During Reading

Think Critically

1. How did Willa Cather feel when she moved to Nebraska? (She felt startled by how different it was from Virginia, where she had lived before. Over time, she came to love it.)

2. What did Cather learn from the immigrants she met? (She learned about their ways of life.)

3. How did Cather's childhood have an effect on the stories she wrote? (She wrote about pioneers on the prairie where she had lived. Her characters were often based on people she had known.)

After Reading

Writing

Ask students to write a short letter to a person who is thinking about moving to a place the students love. Have students explain why this person should make the move. Encourage students to use both facts and opinions in the brief letter.

Answers to Target Reading Skill

Possible Facts: Willa Cather's family came to Nebraska in 1883 when she was nine.

Many immigrants lived there.

She became a writer.

Possible Opinions: *My Ántonia* is her best book.

Her writing was unusual.

Telling the stories of pioneers was a great gift to her readers.

Willa Cather
American Novelist

by Tammy Orr Staats

Regions of Our Country

Chapter: The Midwest

Lexile Measure: 720

Summary

Willa Cather (1873–1947) was nine when her family moved from Virginia's Shenandoah Valley to the Nebraska prairie. Cather was affected by pioneer and immigrant families as she listened to them talk about the struggle to adjust to life on the prairie. For several decades, Cather was a writer and editor for newspapers and magazines and then a high school teacher. Ultimately, she focused on writing, producing many well-known novels about the pioneer experience and the prairie that so moved her. Many people consider *My Ántonia* her best novel. Cather later won a Pulitzer Prize for her novel *One of Ours*. Today, Willa Cather is considered one of America's great writers.

Before Reading

Building Background

Use a map of the United States to show the location of Nebraska, one of the Great Plains states. Explain that in the 1800s, many families moved to the prairies of the Midwest from other places in the United States and from other countries. Use images of pioneers from the book and other resources to demonstrate that life on the prairie was challenging.

Vocabulary

pioneer, prairie, immigrant, sod, culture, essay, novel, novelist

English Language Learners

Read the text aloud, modeling think-aloud strategies to aid comprehension and identify facts and opinions about Willa Cather. Have students work with partners to read the text to one another.

Target Reading Skill: Fact and Opinion

Provide students with an example of a fact and an opinion. (Willa Cather was an American writer. Willa Cather was America's greatest writer.) Ask the class to think of other examples. Distribute the Fact and Opinion graphic organizer. Allow students time to complete the Reading Skill activity on the inside cover of their Readers.

During Reading

Think Critically

1. What did Willa Cather think of Nebraska when she first moved there? (She thought it was flat and empty. She felt lonely and homesick.)

2. What did Cather learn from the immigrants she met? (She learned about other cultures.)

3. How did Cather's childhood influence her stories? (She wrote about pioneers on the prairie where she had lived. Her characters were often based on people she had known.)

After Reading

Writing

Ask students to write a letter to a person who is thinking about moving to a place the students love. Have students explain why this person should make the move. Encourage students to use both facts and opinions in the letter.

Answers to Target Reading Skill

Possible facts: Many people were moving west.

A fire destroyed the sheep barn at Willow Shade.

Willa Cather died on April 24, 1947.

Possible opinions: Willa Cather's life was an adventure.

Willa Cather is considered one of America's great writers.

Willa Cather had a long and successful career.

Willa Cather Writing about the American Frontier

by Tammy Orr Staats

Regions of Our Country

Chapter: The Midwest

Lexile Measure: 800

Summary

Willa Cather (1873–1947) was nine when her family moved from Virginia's Shenandoah Valley to the Nebraska prairie. Cather was affected by pioneer and immigrant families as she listened to them talk about the struggle to adjust to life on the prairie. For several decades, Cather was a writer and editor for newspapers and magazines and then a high school teacher. Ultimately, she focused on writing, producing many well-known novels about the pioneer experience. Many people consider *My Ántonia* her best novel. Cather later won a Pulitzer Prize for her novel *One of Ours*. Today, Willa Cather is considered one of America's great writers.

Before Reading

Building Background

Use a map of the United States to show the location of Nebraska, one of the Great Plains states. Explain that in the 1800s, many families moved to the prairies of the Midwest from other places in the United States and from other countries. Use images of pioneers from the book and other resources to demonstrate that life on the prairie was challenging.

Vocabulary

pioneer, prairie, immigrant, frontier, homestead, sod, custom, culture, essay, novel

English Language Learners

Read the text aloud, modeling think-aloud strategies to aid comprehension and identify facts and opinions about Willa Cather. Have students work with partners to read the text to one another.

Target Reading Skill: Fact and Opinion

Provide students with an example of a fact and an opinion. (Willa Cather was an American writer. Willa Cather was America's greatest writer.) Ask the class to think of other examples. Distribute the Fact and Opinion graphic organizer. Allow students time to complete the Reading Skill activity on the inside cover of their Readers.

During Reading

Think Critically

1. What did Willa Cather think of Nebraska when she first moved there? (Sample answers: She felt it was flat and empty. She felt homesick.)

2. What did Cather learn from immigrants she met? (Sample answer: She learned about other cultures.)

3. How did Cather's childhood influence her stories? (Sample answer: She wrote about pioneers on the frontier. Her characters were often based on people she had known. She wrote about the land on the Great Plains.)

After Reading

Writing

Ask students to write a letter to a person who is thinking about moving to a place the students love. Have students explain what why this person should make the move. Encourage students to use both facts and opinions in the letter.

Answers to Target Reading Skill

Possible facts: In 1883 Cather's family left Virginia and moved to Nebraska. Cather studied at the University of Nebraska. Willa Cather died on April 27, 1947.

Possible opinions: Willa Cather's life was an adventure. She was determined to succeed. Her fourth novel is her best.

Fred Begay, Scientist

by Dennis Fertig

Summary

Fred Begay (1932–) was born on a Ute reservation to parents who were Navajo and Ute. Both parents were healers who traveled around reservation lands. When Begay was ten, he was sent to a Bureau of Indian Affairs boarding school where he lived for eight years. He resented the school and felt he was being stripped of his Navajo culture. After he left, he served in the U.S. Air Force during the Korean War. Thanks to a scholarship for Native American veterans, he was able to attend the University of New Mexico, even though he did not have a high school diploma and could barely read English. He struggled at first but eventually earned a doctorate in physics. He has credited much of his success to his Navajo culture. He has since worked to see that other Navajo benefit from his knowledge.

Before Reading

Building Background

Display a map of the United States and locate the Four Corners area of New Mexico, Arizona, Utah, and Colorado. Explain that the Four Corners area is the home to several Native American groups. Begay was born in southwestern Colorado on the Ute reservation.

Vocabulary

reservation, mesa, scarce, agriculture, scholarship, physics, atom, elder

English Language Learners

Point out that Begay's story mentions the problems he had learning English. It also points out some positive effects of being able to think in more than one language. Discuss with students what advantages they might have by knowing more than one language.

Target Reading Skill: Cause and Effect

Review cause-and-effect relationships with students, giving some examples. Explain that an effect is something that happens. A cause is what makes the effect happen. Remind students that as they read, they should look for causes and effects. Allow time to complete the skill activity.

During Reading

Think Critically

1. What was Fred Begay's early life like? (His family traveled from place to place. His parents taught him about Navajo culture. Begay hunted for food. He moved to a boarding school at a young age.)

2. Why didn't Fred Begay like the school he was sent to? (It seemed to be trying to separate him from his Navajo culture. He had to speak only English.)

3. What was one effect of Begay's decision to accept a scholarship and go to college? (He became a scientist.)

4. How does Begay use his knowledge of science to help Navajo people? (He visits Navajo schools to help students.)

After Reading

Writing

Remind students that Fred Begay closely watched nature. Ask students to spend time gazing out of a classroom window or sitting outside. Have them write notes about what they see. Then have them repeat the observation a few days later. Have them draw a picture or write a paragraph that explains how things have changed in what they observed.

Answers to Target Reading Skill

Possible causes and effects:

Cause: Food was scarce.

Effect: Begay's mother sent him away to school.

Cause: As a boy, Begay learned to observe nature.

Effect: Being a good observer helped him with physics.

Cause: Begay went to college on a scholarship.

Effect: Begay became a respected scientist.

Fred Begay, Physicist

by Dennis Fertig

Summary

Fred Begay (1932–) was born on a Ute reservation to parents who were Navajo and Ute. Both parents were healers who traveled around reservation lands. When Begay was ten, he was sent to a Bureau of Indian Affairs boarding school where he lived for eight years. He resented the school and felt he was being stripped of his Navajo culture. After he left, he served in the U.S. Air Force during the Korean War. Thanks to a scholarship for Native American veterans, he was able to attend the University of New Mexico, even though he did not have a high school diploma and could barely read English. He struggled at first, but eventually earned a doctorate in physics. He has credited much of his success to his Navajo culture. He has since worked to see that other Navajo benefit from his knowledge.

Before Reading

Building Background

Remind students that many Native American groups live on reservations. Display a map of the United States and locate the Four Corners area of New Mexico, Arizona, Utah, and Colorado. Point out that this is the area of the Navajo and Ute reservations.

Vocabulary

reservation, mesa, legend, scarce, agriculture, scholarship, physics, atom, elder

English Language Learners

Write the word *physics* and point out that *ph* stands for the sound usually written with *f.* Compare the spelling of /f/ in *physics* to that of /f/ in the words *photo* and *phone*. Explain that Fred Begay learned English as his third language, and that his story points out some of the advantages of having more than one language.

Target Reading Skill: Cause and Effect

Remind students that an effect is something that happens. A cause is what makes the effect happen. Discuss why identifying cause and effect is important in understanding a person's life.

During Reading

Think Critically

1. What was Fred Begay's early life like? (His family traveled from place to place. He learned about Navajo culture. He hunted for food. He moved to a boarding school at a young age.)

2. Why didn't Fred Begay like the school he was sent to? (It seemed to be trying to separate students from their Native American cultures. They had to speak only English.)

3. What was one effect of Begay's decision to join the Air Force? (It led to an offer of a scholarship to college, and college changed his life.)

4. How does Begay use his knowledge of science to help Navajo people? (He shares his knowledge with Navajo people, he tries to use scientific discoveries to improve their lives, and he visits Navajo schools to help students.)

After Reading

Writing

Remind students that young Fred Begay was a careful observer of nature. Ask students to spend time gazing out a classroom window or sitting outside. Have them write notes about what they see in nature. Ask them do the same thing several days later. Have them draw a picture or write a paragraph about their observations.

Answers to Target Reading Skill

Possible causes and effects:

Cause: Food was scarce.

Effect: Begay's mother sent him away to school.

Cause: As a boy, Begay studied the world.

Effect: Being a good observer helped him with physics.

Cause: Begay went to college on a scholarship.

Effect: Begay became a respected scientist.

Fred Begay Connecting Physics and Navajo Culture

by Dennis Fertig

Regions of Our Country

Chapter: The Southwest

Lexile Measure: 690

Summary

Fred Begay (1932–) was born to parents who were Navajo and Ute. Both parents were healers who traveled around reservation lands. When Begay was ten, he was sent to a Bureau of Indian Affairs boarding school. He resented the school and felt he was being stripped of his Navajo culture. After he left, he served in the U.S. Air Force during the Korean War. Thanks to a scholarship for Native American veterans, he was able to attend the University of New Mexico, even though he did not have a high school diploma. He struggled at first but eventually earned a doctorate in physics. He has credited much of his success to his Navajo culture. He has since worked to see that other Navajo benefit from his knowledge.

Before Reading

Building Background

Display a map of the United States and locate the Four Corners area of New Mexico, Arizona, Utah, and Colorado. Point out that this is the area of the Navajo and Ute reservations.

Vocabulary

reservation, mesa, culture, legend, scarce, agriculture, scholarship, physics, agency, atom, elder

English Language Learners

Write the word *physics*. Point out that *ph* stands for the sound usually written with *f*. Compare the spelling of /f/ in *physics* to that of /f/ in *photo* and *phone*. Explain that Begay knows three languages, and that his story points out some of the advantages of having more than one language.

Target Reading Skill: Cause and Effect

Remind students that an effect is something that happens. A cause is what makes the effect happen. Discuss why identifying cause and effect is important in understanding a biography.

During Reading

Think Critically

1. What was Fred Begay's early life like? (His family traveled from place to place. His parents taught him about Navajo culture. Begay hunted for food. He moved to a boarding school at a young age.)

2. Why didn't Begay like the school he was sent to? (The school seemed to be trying to separate students from their Native American cultures. He wasn't allowed to speak his language.)

3. What was one effect of Begay's decision to join the Air Force? (It led to an offer of a scholarship to college, and college changed his life.)

4. How does Begay use his knowledge of science to help Navajo people? (He shares his knowledge, he tries to use scientific discoveries to improve lives, and he visits Navajo schools.)

After Reading

Writing

Remind students that Fred Begay closely watched nature. Ask students to spend time gazing out a classroom window or sitting on a playground. Have them write notes about what they see. Ask them to do this again several days later and write a paragraph about their observations.

Answers to Target Reading Skill

Possible causes and effects:

Cause: Food was scarce.

Effect: Begay's mother sent him away to school.

Cause: As a boy, Begay studied the world.

Effect: Being a good observer helped him with physics.

Cause: Begay went to college on a scholarship.

Effect: Begay became a respected scientist.

Jedediah Smith, Mountain Man

by Dennis Fertig

Summary

As a youth, Jedediah Smith (1799–1831) was inspired by Lewis and Clark's journals. He set out to earn a living as a trapper, and his reputation as an explorer quickly grew as he blazed trails westward. He was responsible for the rediscovery of the South Pass over the Rockies, which became part of the Oregon Trail. He was the first American to cross the Mojave Desert, use a land route to California, and blaze trails from California into Oregon. His exploration paved the way for the many pioneers who traveled west.

Before Reading

Building Background

Tell students that when Jedediah Smith began to explore, our country had only 24 states. Use a map of the United States to show them the one state, Missouri, that was west of the Mississippi River. Most of the West was largely unknown to Americans. Although Native American people lived in much of that land, the only other Americans who knew it were explorers and trappers who explored at great personal risk.

Vocabulary

trapper, explorer, arid, pioneer, rendezvous, desert

English Language Learners

Model using adjectives to describe the land that Jedediah Smith explored. For example: *The desert was dry and hot.* Have students work together to describe other locations mentioned in the book.

Target Reading Skill: Compare and Contrast

Display two objects, such as a banana and an apple. Compare and contrast them by explaining that they are similar because you can eat them and they are both fruit. They are different in color, taste, and shape. Remind students to think about Jedediah Smith and other mountain men as they read. Explain that after reading, they will compare and contrast Smith and other mountain men and fill in the graphic organizer they have created.

During Reading

Think Critically

1. Why were beavers called "brown gold?" (They were valuable, and trappers could make a lot of money by selling them.)

2. Why do you think Smith wanted the job that William Ashley was offering? (He had been inspired by the explorers Lewis and Clark and wanted to go west. He also wanted to make a living trapping animals for fur.)

3. Give examples of Smith's leadership. (After the bear attacked, he asked someone to stitch up his wounds; he fought hard to protect the men when they were attacked; he led two men over the Sierra Nevada)

4. How did nature challenge Smith? How did it help him? (Smith had to overcome challenges such as heat, lack of water, cold winters, and grizzly bears. He benefited by making a good living trapping beavers.)

After Reading

Writing

Have students imagine that they are mountain men or mountain women. Using the images in their book as a model, have them draw a picture of what their life might be like. For example, they could show trapping, setting up camp, or trading at a rendezvous. Have them write a sentence describing their picture.

Answers to Target Reading Skill

Alike: All mountain men were brave, risked their lives, trapped animals to earn money, and traveled for a long time.

Different: Smith was different from most other mountain men in these ways: he saved his money, he could read and write, and he made maps.

Jedediah Smith Explorer in the American West

by Dennis Fertig

Summary

As a youth, Jedediah Smith (1799–1831) was inspired by Lewis and Clark's journals. Later, he set out to earn a living as trapper, and his reputation as an explorer quickly grew as he blazed trails westward. He was responsible for the rediscovery of the South Pass over the Rockies, which became part of the Oregon Trail. He was the first American to cross the Mojave Desert, use a land route to California, and blaze trails from California into Oregon. His efforts paved the way for the many pioneers who traveled west.

Before Reading

Building Background

Tell students that when Jedediah Smith began to explore, our country had only 24 states. Use a map of the United States to show them the one state, Missouri, that was west of the Mississippi River. Most of the West was unknown to Americans. Although Native American people lived in much of that land, the only other Americans who knew it were explorers and trappers who explored at great personal risk.

Vocabulary

trapper, explore, enterprising, arid, pioneer, rendezvous, expedition, desert, blaze

English Language Learners

The compare and contrast skill in this lesson provides students with opportunities to use descriptive language. Pair English learners with English-proficient speakers and have them discuss how Jedediah Smith is both like and different from other mountain men.

Target Reading Skill: Compare and Contrast

Remind students that, as they read, they should be alert for how an author compares and contrasts people or things. They should pay attention to see how things are alike or different. Discuss why it is valuable to identify both.

During Reading

Think Critically

1. Why were beavers called "brown gold"? (They were valuable and trappers could make a lot of money by selling them.)

2. Why do you think Smith wanted the job that William Ashley was offering? (He had been inspired by the explorers Lewis and Clark and wanted to go west. He also wanted to make a living trapping animals for fur.)

3. Give examples of Smith's leadership. (After the bear attacked, he asked a man to sew up his wounds. He made a camp for his men and then came back to get them.)

4. How did nature challenge Smith? How did it benefit him? (Smith had to overcome heat, lack of water, snow, and grizzly bears. He benefited by making a good living trapping beavers.)

After Reading

Writing

Have students imagine that they are mountain men or mountain women. Using the images in their book as a model, have them draw a picture of what their life might be like. For example, they could show trapping, setting up camp, or trading at a rendezvous. Have them write a paragraph describing their picture.

Answers to Target Reading Skill

Alike: All mountain men were brave, risked their lives, trapped animals to earn money, traveled for months and years at a time, and traded for other goods.

Different: Smith was different from most other mountain men in these ways: he saved his money, he was able to read and write, and he made maps.

Jedediah Smith
American Trailblazer

by Dennis Fertig

Regions of Our Country

Chapter: The West

Lexile Measure: 820

Summary

As a youth, Jedediah Smith (1799–1831) was inspired by Lewis and Clark's journals. He set out to earn a living as a trapper, and his reputation as an explorer quickly grew as he blazed trails westward. He was responsible for the rediscovery of the South Pass over the Rockies, which became part of the Oregon Trail. He was the first non–Native American to cross the Mojave Desert, use a land route to California, and blaze trails from California into Oregon. His efforts paved the way for the many pioneers who traveled west.

Before Reading

Building Background

Tell students that in 1822, when Jedediah Smith began to trap in the West, the country had only 24 states. Only one, Missouri, was west of the Mississippi River. Most of the West was unknown except to the Native American people who populated much of it and the explorers and mountain men who explored it at great risk.

Vocabulary

trapper, explore, blaze, expedition, enterprising, arid, pioneer, rendezvous, desert

English Language Learners

The compare and contrast skill in this lesson provides students with opportunities to use descriptive language. Pair English learners with English-proficient speakers and have them discuss how Jedediah Smith was both like and different from other mountain men.

Target Reading Skill: Compare and Contrast

Discuss how, when we compare and contrast two or more things, we look to see how they are the same and different.

Remind students that, as they read, they should be alert for how an author compares and contrasts people or things. They should pay attention to how things or people are similar or different. Discuss why it is valuable to identify both.

During Reading

Think Critically

1. How did Smith's skills and interests prepare him to be an explorer? (He liked to read, and he read the journals of the explorers Lewis and Clark, which inspired him.)

2. Why do you think most people would not want the jobs that William Ashley was offering? (Life as a trapper was dangerous. You had to be away from home for long periods of time.)

3. Give examples of Smith's leadership. (After the grizzly attack, he directed another trapper to sew up his wounds. He stayed in his first battle and protected survivors.)

4. How did nature challenge Smith? How did it benefit him? (Smith had to overcome natural challenges such as heat, lack of water, snow, and grizzly bears. He benefited by making a good living trapping beavers in the wild.)

After Reading

Writing

Much of Smith's writing has been lost. Have students write a journal entry as if they were Smith on one of his expeditions. They should use some of the glossary words in their journal entry.

Answers to Target Reading Skill

Alike: All mountain men were brave, risked their lives, trapped animals to earn money, traveled for months and years at a time, and traded for other goods.

Different: Smith was different from most other mountain men in these ways: he saved his money, he was able to read and write, and he made maps.

Chief Joseph Defends His People

by Bruce T. Paddock

Building Our Country

Chapter: The First Americans

Lexile Measure: 650

Summary

In 1863, the U.S. government forced the Nez Percé people onto a tiny reservation in Idaho. Chief Joseph was one of the leaders of a group of Nez Percé who refused to relocate. In 1877, the U.S. Army forced them off their land. These Nez Percé set out on what would become a 4-month, 1200-mile tactical retreat. They fought four major battles and many more skirmishes, winning them all, while heading for what they hoped would be sanctuary. Chief Joseph, who was not a war chief, kept the noncombatants moving, supplied, and safe. Battles and harsh conditions took their toll. Forty miles from the Canadian border, Chief Joseph surrendered. He spent the rest of his life trying to win justice for his people.

Before Reading

Building Background

Locate northeastern Oregon and the Wallowa Valley. Discuss with students what they already know about the forced removal of Native American groups, such as the Cherokee Trail of Tears. Explain that in the 1850s and 1860s more and more white people moved onto the Great Plains and further west. This brought them into conflict with Native American groups already living there. Write *Nez Percé* on the board and tell students that in English, *Nez Percé* is pronounced "nez purs."

Vocabulary

canyon, treaty, reservation, livestock

English Language Learners

Write *reservation* on the board. Underline *reserve*. Explain that *reserve* means to save, or to set aside. For instance, a restaurant could reserve a table for someone. Explain that the government set aside certain lands for Native Americans. These lands are called reservations. Explain the meaning of *treaty* and point out that many reservations were created as part of treaties.

Target Reading Skill: Compare and Contrast

Comparing and contrasting two things can help us understand them better. To compare is to find how two or more things are alike. To contrast is to find differences between two or more things. Sometimes clue words and phrases such as *as well as, also, instead, and on the other hand,* help you recognize similarities and differences. As you read, look for similarities and differences between Nez Percé life before and after the Nez Percé War.

Allow students time to complete the Reading Skill activity on the inside cover of their readers individually and then with a partner.

During Reading

Comprehension and Critical Thinking

1. Why did Chief Joseph and the Wallowa Valley Nez Percé refuse to move onto the smaller reservation in 1863? (They felt the new treaty was unfair, and they had never signed it.)

2. What two places did Chief Joseph's people try to get to? (Crow lands and Canada)

3. How were the living conditions in Fort Leavenworth like those in Oklahoma? (Both were unhealthy.)

4. What did Chief Joseph want for his people? (He wanted them to be treated fairly and given the same rights as other people in the United States.)

After Reading

Speaking

Have volunteers present their compare-and-contrast charts to the class.

Answers to the Target Reading Skill

Similar: They lived in the Pacific Northwest. They hunted, fished, and gathered plants for food.

Different: Before, they could go wherever they wanted. After, they were forced to stay in a small area. Before, they were at peace. After, they were at war with the United States government.

Chief Joseph
Leader of the Nez Percé

by Bruce T. Paddock

Summary

In 1863, the U.S. government forced the Nez Percé people onto a tiny reservation in Idaho. Chief Joseph was one of the leaders of a group of Nez Percé who refused to relocate. In 1877, the U.S. Army forced them off their land. These Nez Percé set out on what would become a 4-month, 1200-mile tactical retreat. They fought four major battles and many more skirmishes, winning them all, while heading for what they hoped would be sanctuary. Chief Joseph, who was not a war chief, kept the noncombatants moving, supplied, and safe. Battles and harsh conditions took their toll. Forty miles from the Canadian border, Chief Joseph surrendered. He spent the rest of his life trying to win justice for his people.

Before Reading

Building Background

Locate northeastern Oregon and the Wallowa Valley. Discuss with students what they already know about the forced removal of Native American groups, such as the Cherokee Trail of Tears. Explain that in the 1850s and 1860s more and more white people moved onto the Great Plains and further west. This brought them into conflict with Native American groups already living there. Write *Nez Percé* on the board and tell students that in English, *Nez Percé* is pronounced "nez purs."

Vocabulary

treaty, reservation, captivity

English Language Learners

Write *reservation* on the board. Underline *reserve*. Explain that *reserve* means to save, or to set aside. For instance, a restaurant could reserve a table for someone. Explain that the government set aside certain lands for Native Americans. These lands are called reservations. Explain the meaning of *treaty* and point out that many reservations were created as part of treaties.

Target Reading Skill: Compare and Contrast

Tell students that clue words and phrases such as *similarly, also, instead,* and *on the other hand* can help readers recognize similarities and differences. Allow students time to complete the Reading Skill activity on the inside cover of their Readers individually or with a partner.

During Reading

Comprehension and Critical Thinking

1. Why did Chief Joseph and the Wallowa Valley Nez Percé refuse to move onto the smaller reservation in 1863? (They felt the new treaty was unfair, and they had never signed it.)

2. How were the living conditions at Fort Leavenworth different from those in Oregon? (At Fort Leavenworth the Nez Percé lived in unhealthy conditions; in Oregon they lived in mountains and valleys and had clean water.)

3. Why do you think Chief Joseph is still remembered and admired? (Answers will vary, but students may say that he was a great leader who showed great courage in working to keep his people safe and to defend their rights. He worked for peace and spoke in favor of equal rights for all.)

After Reading

Speaking

Have students prepare a brief talk on what they found out about Chief Joseph's life. They may present their talk in front of the class.

Answers to the Target Reading Skill

Similar: They lived in the Pacific Northwest. They hunted, fished, and gathered plants for food.

Different: Before, they could go wherever they wanted. After, they were forced to stay in a small area. Before, they were at peace. After, they were at war with the government.

Chief Joseph
I Will Fight No More
Forever

by Bruce T. Paddock

Building Our Country

Chapter: The First Americans

Lexile Measure: 840

Summary

In 1863, the U.S. government forced the Nez Percé people onto a tiny reservation in Idaho. Chief Joseph was one of the leaders of a group of Nez Percé who refused to relocate. In 1877, the U.S. Army forced them off their land. These Nez Percé set out on what would become a 4-month, 1200-mile tactical retreat. They fought four major battles and many more skirmishes, winning them all, while heading for what they hoped would be sanctuary. Chief Joseph, who was not a war chief, kept the noncombatants moving, supplied, and safe. Battles and harsh conditions took their toll. Forty miles from the Canadian border, Chief Joseph surrendered. He spent the rest of his life trying to win justice for his people.

Before Reading

Building Background

Discuss with students what they already know about the treatment of Native Americans by the U.S. government. Explain that as white people moved west they came into conflict with Native American groups. Write Nez Percé on the board and help students pronounce it as "nez purs."

Vocabulary

treaty, reservation, petition, captivity, appeal

English Language Learners

Write reservation on the board. Underline reserve. Explain that reserve means to save, or to set aside. For instance, a restaurant could reserve a table for someone. Explain that the government set aside certain lands for Native Americans. These lands are called reservations. Explain the meaning of treaty and point out that many reservations were created as part of treaties.

Target Reading Skill: Compare and Contrast

Use the inside cover activity to review the meaning of compare and contrast. As they read, have students look for similarities and differences between Nez Percé life before and after the Nez Percé War.

During Reading

Comprehension and Critical Thinking

1. Why did Chief Joseph and his group refuse to move onto the smaller reservation in 1863? (They felt the new treaty was unfair, and they had never signed it.)

2. How were the living conditions at Fort Leavenworth different from those in Oregon? (At Fort Leavenworth the Nez Percé lived in unhealthy conditions; in Oregon they lived in mountains and valleys and had clean water.)

3. What did Chief Joseph want white people to do for Native Americans? (Possible answers: to treat all people alike; to give all people the same laws; to treat Native Americans fairly; to honor promises made to them.)

4. Why do you think Chief Joseph is still remembered and admired? (Answers will vary, but students may say that he was a great leader who showed great courage. He worked for peace and spoke in favor of equal rights for all.)

After Reading

Speaking

Have students prepare a oral presentation of one of the speeches or writings of Chief Joseph given in this book. They may present their speech in front of the class.

Answers to the Target Reading Skill

Similar: They lived in the Pacific Northwest. They hunted, fished, and gathered plants for food.

Different: Before, they could go wherever they wanted. After, they were forced to stay in a small area. Before, they were at peace. After, they were at war with the government.

Isabella, Queen of Spain

by Catherine Eden Brissette

Summary

In the 1400s, Spain was not one country, but was divided into separate kingdoms. When Isabella of Castile married Ferdinand, king of Aragon, the two kingdoms were united to form Spain. The decisions the two monarchs made, including sponsoring the voyages of Columbus, helped make Spain a world power and create the Spanish empire.

Before Reading

Building Background

Write the date 1492 on the board and ask students what the date makes them think of. Explain that Isabella was the queen who sponsored Columbus to make his voyages to North America.

Explain that at the time, the map of Europe looked very different. Instead of the countries we now have, there were many small kingdoms. Isabella was responsible for uniting several small kingdoms into the country of Spain.

Vocabulary

empire, lord, civil war, conquer

English Language Learners

Read the text aloud to students one page at a time. Then use the five Ws (Who, What, When, Where, Why) to help students to understand the content. Write students' responses on the board, then guide them in using the responses to summarize each page as you read.

Target Reading Skill: Draw Conclusions

Explain that writers do not always tell readers everything. They often include information and let readers form their own opinions, or conclusions, about what they have read.

After students have read the book, work with them to do the Target Reading Skill activity. Draw a graphic organizer on the board like the one on the inside cover of the Reader. Help students find information in the text about Isabella's influence on the world and write them in the small boxes. For instance: *Isabella unified Spain. She sponsored Columbus's voyages. She tried to spread her Catholic faith.* Allow students time to complete the Target Reading Skill activity with a partner.

During Reading

Comprehension and Critical Thinking

1. What was Spain like when Isabella was born? (Sample answer: Spain was not one country, but several smaller kingdoms. The king and lords struggled for power.)

2. Why was Isabella's marriage to Ferdinand important? (Sample answer: Their marriage joined Isabella's kingdom of Castile with Ferdinand's kingdom of Aragon, which helped unite Spain.)

3. What was Columbus's idea? (Sample answer: He thought that by sailing west he could find a new route to Asia.)

4. What did Isabella hope to gain from Columbus's voyages? (Sample answer: She hoped Spain would get rich and become more powerful. She also wanted to spread her Catholic faith overseas.)

5. Why was Isabella important? (Sample answers: She helped unite Spain and make it into an empire.)

After Reading

Writing

Have students write a short paragraph telling how the actions of Isabella had a great influence on the Americas, even though Isabella herself never set foot there.

Answers to Target Reading Skill

Facts: Isabella unified Spain. She sponsored Columbus's voyages. She tried to spread her Catholic faith.

Possible conclusions: By unifying Spain and then sponsoring Columbus, Isabella helped Spain become a great empire. She changed the world.

Isabella
Queen of Two Kingdoms

by Catherine Eden Brissette

Building Our Country

Chapter: Age of Exploration

Lexile Measure: 710

Summary

In the 1400s, Spain was not one country, but was divided into separate kingdoms. When Isabella of Castile married Ferdinand, king of Aragon, the two kingdoms were united to form Spain. The decisions the two monarchs made, including sponsoring the voyages of Columbus, helped make Spain a world power and create the Spanish empire.

Before Reading

Building Background

Write the date 1492 on the board and ask students what the date makes them think of. Explain that Isabella was the queen who sponsored Columbus to make his voyages to North America.

Explain that at the time, the map of Europe looked very different. Instead of the countries we now have, there were many small kingdoms. Isabella was responsible for uniting several small kingdoms into the country of Spain.

Vocabulary

empire, lord, Renaissance, execute, civil war, conquer

English Language Learners

Read the text aloud to students one page at a time. Then use the five Ws (Who, What, When, Where, Why) to help students to understand the content. Write students responses on the board, then guide them to use the responses to summarize each page as you read.

Target Reading Skill: Draw Conclusions

Tell students that to draw conclusions means to form an opinion based on information from their reading. Explain that writers do not tell readers everything. Instead they expect readers to use what they read and what they already know to form their own opinions.

After students have read the book, work with them to do the Target Reading Skill activity. Draw a graphic organizer on the board like the one on the inside cover of the Reader. Help students find information in the text about Isabella's influence on the world and write them in the small boxes. Allow students time to complete the Target Reading Skill activity with a partner. Provide guidance as necessary.

During Reading

Comprehension and Critical Thinking

1. How was Spain different at the time of Isabella's birth than it is now? (Spain was not one country. It was divided into several kingdoms.)

2. Why was the result of Isabella's marriage to Ferdinand? (Their marriage joined Isabella's kingdom of Castile with Ferdinand's kingdom of Aragon, which helped unite Spain.)

3. Why did Isabella become upset with Columbus? (She did not like how Columbus treated the native people he met. She wanted them treated with respect, so they would become Catholic.)

4. What kind of ruler do you think Isabella was? Support your answer with details from the book. (Sample answers: A good ruler—Isabella helped unite Spain and make it into an empire. A poor ruler—Isabella did not treat everyone in her kingdom fairly. As a leader, she should have made sure Columbus treated the native people fairly.)

After Reading

Have students work in small groups to write and act out a play based on scenes from Isabella's life. Suggest they include a narrator who can give historical background for each scene. Have students perform their play for another class.

Answers to Target Reading Skill

Answers will vary. Possible facts include: Isabella unified Spain. She sponsored Columbus's voyages. She tried to spread her Catholic faith.

Possible conclusion: Isabella's life had an influence on both Europe and on the rest of the world.

Queen Isabella and the Exploration of the Americas

by Catherine Eden Brissette

Summary

In the 1400s, Spain was not one country, but was divided into separate kingdoms. When Isabella of Castile married Ferdinand, king of Aragon, the two kingdoms were united to form Spain. The decisions the two monarchs made, including sponsoring the voyages of Columbus, helped make Spain a world power and create the Spanish empire.

Before Reading

Building Background

Write the date 1492 on the board and ask students what the date makes them think of. Explain that Isabella was the queen who sponsored Columbus to make his voyages to North America.

Explain that at the time, Europe was divided into many small kingdoms. Isabella united several small kingdoms into the country of Spain.

Vocabulary

empire, lord, Renaissance, devoted, execute, civil war, tolerance, convert, will

English Language Learners

Read the text aloud to students one page at a time. Then use the five Ws (Who, What, When, Where, Why) to help students to understand the content. Write students responses on the board, then guide them to use the responses to summarize each page orally as you read.

Target Reading Skill: Draw Conclusions

Tell students that to draw conclusions means to form an opinion based on information from their reading. Explain that writers expect readers to use what they read and what they already know to form their own opinions.

After students have read the book, assign the Target Reading Skill activity. Have students find facts in the text about Isabella. Suggest they group the facts by topic, such as facts about Isabella's childhood, influence on the world, or attitude toward native peoples. Provide guidance as necessary.

During Reading

Comprehension and Critical Thinking

1. Why did Isabella wait until after King Henry died to insist she was the rightful queen? (Isabella did not want to cause a civil war.)

2. How did Isabella's marriage to Ferdinand unite Spain? (Their marriage joined Isabella's kingdom of Castile with Ferdinand's kingdom of Aragon, which helped form the nation of Spain.)

3. Why did Isabella and Ferdinand support Columbus's voyages? (They hoped to gain new riches for Spain and increase its power in the world. Isabella also wanted to spread her Catholic faith to new lands.)

4. Was Isabella a good ruler? Support your answer with details from the book. (Answers will vary. Yes—She helped unite a divided land into one country. She also helped make Spain into an empire. No—Isabella's desire to have one religion in Spain resulted in the deaths of many non-Catholics.)

After Reading

Have students work in small groups to write a play based on scenes from Isabella's life. Suggest they include a narrator who can give historical background for each scene. Have students perform their play for another class.

Answers to Target Reading Skill Activity

Possible facts: Isabella unified Spain, sponsored Columbus's voyages, tried to spread her faith.

Possible conclusion: Isabella's life had an influence on both Europe and on the rest of the world.

Chief Powhatan

by Susan Bachner

Building Our Country

Chapter: Settlements Take Root

Lexile Measure: 600

Summary

Chief Powhatan ruled over a confederacy made up of about 30 Native American groups. His people's homeland stretched from what is today southern Maryland to northern North Carolina. In 1607, English settlers established the first permanent English colony at Jamestown, in the Powhatan homeland. Chief Powhatan tried to maintain peaceful relationships between the two sides. He often gave the settlers food or traded food for English goods. The marriage of Powhatan's daughter Pocahontas to the settler John Rolfe brought a time of peace to the region. However, not long after the marriage, Powhatan and his daughter both died and the English settlers pushed the Powhatan people off much of their land to grow tobacco. Today, descendants of the Powhatan people help keep the memory of Chief Powhatan alive as a vital part of American history.

Before Reading

Building Background

Encourage students to share what they may know about the cultures of the early Native Americans and those of the early European settlers.

Vocabulary

lodge, confederacy, wilderness, gentlemen, siege

English Language Learners

Have students turn to the glossary page. Model reading each word and its meaning. Then use the word in a sentence. Write them on the board. Have volunteers use one word in a sentence.

Target Reading Skill: Categorize

Tell students that categorizing helps organize information into categories, or different groups, to help them better understand what they are reading. Provide examples of categories for topics that students are familiar with, such as sports or movie genres. Then tell students that this book includes information about how two groups, the Powhatan and the English, got along. One way to categorize relations between the two groups is to say that relations were friendly or tense.

Distribute the T-chart or have students create one to use themselves. Have students write two categories on their charts—*Friendly Relations* on the left side and *Tense Relations* on the right side. Help them record details to go in the T-chart.

During Reading

Think Critically

1. At first, why did Chief Powhatan trade with the English settlers? (Powhatan wanted the metal weapons and bowls that the English settlers had.)

2. What happened after Pocahontas and John Rolfe married? (There was a time of peace.)

3. What happened to the Powhatan people after Chief Powhatan died? (The English took over more of their lands. Many of the Powhatan people died in wars or from disease.)

After Reading

Writing

Have students write a first-person account of Powhatan's life as if he were writing, shortly before he died.

Answers to Target Reading Skill

Examples of Friendly Relations (Possible answers: Trading for food, Powhatan adopting John Smith, Pocahontas "saving" Smith, Pocahontas's marriage to John Rolfe leading to the Peace of Pocahontas.)

Examples of Tense Relations (Powhatans forcing English back to their ships, English refusing to trade weapons, Powhatans capturing John Smith, Powhatan laying siege to starve Jamestown.)

Powhatan, Native American Leader

by Susan Bachner

Building Our Country

Chapter: Settlements
Take Root

Lexile Measure: 760

Summary

Chief Powhatan ruled over a confederacy of about 30 Native American groups. His people's homeland stretched from what is today southern Maryland to northern North Carolina. In 1607, English settlers established the first permanent English colony at Jamestown there. Chief Powhatan tried to maintain peaceful relations between the sides. He often gave the settlers food or traded food for English goods. After a series of attacks by both sides, the marriage of Powhatan's daughter Pocahontas to the settler John Rolfe brought about a time of peace. However, not long after, Powhatan and his daughter both died and the English settlers pushed the Powhatan people off much of their land to grow tobacco. Today, descendants of the Powhatan people help keep the memory of Chief Powhatan alive as a vital part of American history.

Before Reading

Building Background

Encourage students to share what they may already know about the cultures of the early Native Americans and early European settlers.

Vocabulary

lodge, permanent, confederacy, authority, gentleman, intervene, ceremony, siege

English Language Learners

Have students turn to the glossary. Model reading each word and its meaning. Then use the word in a sentence. Write your sentences on the board. Then ask volunteers to make sentences.

Target Reading Skill: Categorize

Tell students that categorizing helps them organize information into different groups, to better understand what they're reading. Provide examples of categories for topics that students are familiar with, such as sports or movie genres. Then tell students that this book includes information about how the Powhatan and the English got along. One way to categorize relations between the two groups is to say that relations were friendly or tense.

Distribute the T-chart or have students create one to use themselves. Have students write two categories on their charts—*Friendly Relations* on the left side and *Tense Relations* on the right side. Help them to record details to go in the T-chart.

During Reading

Think Critically

1. At first, why did Chief Powhatan trade with the English settlers? (Powhatan wanted their metal weapons and bowls.)

2. What happened after Pocahontas and John Rolfe married? (There was peace.)

3. What happened to the Powhatan people after Powhatan died? (The English took over more of their lands. Many Powhatan people died.)

After Reading

Writing

Have students write a first-person account of Powhatan's life as if he were writing in 1617, shortly before he died.

Answers to Target Reading Skill

Friendly Relations (Trading for food, Powhatan adopting John Smith, Pocahontas "saving" Smith, Pocahontas marrying John Rolfe.)

Tense Relations (Powhatans forcing English back to their ships, English refusing to trade, Powhatans capturing John Smith, Powhatan laying siege.)

Chief Powhatan
Leader of His People

by Susan Bachner

Building Our Country

Chapter: Settlements
Take Root

Lexile Measure: 860

Summary

Chief Powhatan ruled over a confederacy of approximately 30 Native American groups. His people's homeland stretched from what is today southern Maryland to northern North Carolina. In 1607, English settlers established the first permanent English colony at Jamestown in the Powhatan homeland. Chief Powhatan tried to maintain peaceful relationships. He often gave the settlers food or traded food for English goods. After a series of attacks by both sides, the marriage of Powhatan's daughter Pocahontas to the settler John Rolfe brought about a time of peace. However, not long after, Powhatan and his daughter both died and the English settlers pushed the Powhatan people off much of their land to grow tobacco. Today, descendants of the Powhatan people keep the memory of Chief Powhatan alive as a vital part of American history.

Before Reading

Building Background

Encourage students to share what they may already know about the cultures of the early Native Americans and early European settlers.

Vocabulary

lodge, confederacy, fertile, authority, intervene, ceremony, gentlemen, siege, export

English Language Learners

Have students turn to the glossary page. Model reading each word and its meaning. Then use the word in a sentence and write them on the board. Ask volunteers to make sentences.

Target Reading Skill: Categorize

Tell students that the skill of categorizing helps them organize information into categories, or different groups, to help them better understand what they are reading. Provide examples of categories for topics that students are familiar with, such as sports or book and movie genres. Then tell students that this book includes information about how two groups, the Powhatan people and the English, got along. One way to categorize relations between the two groups is to say that relations were friendly or tense.

Distribute the T-chart or have students create one to use themselves. Have students write two categories on their charts—*Friendly Relations* on the left side, and *Tense Relations* on the right side. Help them to record details to go in the T-chart as they read.

During Reading

Think Critically

1. What did the Powhatan people grow for food? (The Powhatans grew corn.)

2. At first, why did Chief Powhatan trade with the English settlers? (Powhatan wanted their metal weapons and bowls.)

3. What happened after Pocahontas and John Rolfe married? (There was a time of peace.)

4. What happened to the Powhatan people after Chief Powhatan died? (The English took over more of their lands. Many of the Powhatan people died in wars or from disease.)

After Reading

Writing

Have students write a first-person account of Powhatan's life as if Powhatan were writing in 1617.

Answers to Target Reading Skill

Friendly Relations (Trading for food, Powhatan adopting John Smith, Pocahontas "saving" Smith, Pocahontas marrying John Rolfe.)

Tense Relations (Powhatans forcing English back to their ships, English refusing to trade, Powhatan people capturing John Smith, Powhatan laying siege.)

Anne Hutchinson Colonial Rebel

by Bruce T. Paddock

Summary

Anne Hutchinson was a Puritan who came with others to Boston in 1634 seeking religious freedom. She was well educated in theology and held regular meetings at which she discussed the ministers' sermons. Hutchinson began to criticize the ministers, saying they were teaching false ideas. This was a threat to both the Puritan church and the civil authority, which were closely intertwined. Hutchinson was placed on trial. When she said God had spoken directly to her, she was convicted and banished from the colony. Later, the right of individual conscience in respect to religious freedom became part of the United States' most cherished ideals.

Before Reading

Building Background

Discuss with students what they have learned about why English colonists came to North America. For Puritans, the motivation was primarily to be free to worship in the way they thought right. Remind students that there was no separation then between the government and the church. To criticize the ministers was to criticize the government.

Vocabulary

official, society, banish

English Language Learners

Do a walk-through of the book with students, having them read aloud the heads. Tell students that the head often provides a clue to the main idea of the section. Read the book aloud to students, asking questions after each selection to elicit the main idea.

Target Reading Skill: Main Idea and Details

Review with students that a main idea tells the most important idea in a piece of writing. Be sure they understand that a paragrah, a section (as under a head), a chapter, and an entire book may all have a main idea. In the Target Reading Skill activity, they will be asked to find the main idea and details of a section under a blue head.

During Reading

Think Critically

1. What was the Massachusetts Bay Colony based on? (the Puritan religion and the Bible)

2. Why were ministers so important in the Puritan system? (They interpreted the Bible.)

3. Why did Hutchinson's ideas get her into trouble? (She thought that the ministers were teaching wrong ideas. She felt she could interpret for herself what the Bible said and that God had spoken to her directly.)

4. Why were people not allowed to criticize the ministers? (The government was based on the ministers' teaching. Attacking the ministers' teachings was like attacking the colony itself.)

After Reading

Writing

Have students write a letter that Anne Hutchinson may have written from Providence to her father in England, explaining what had happened to her in Massachusetts Bay Colony.

Answers to Target Reading Skill

Answers will vary depending on which section students choose to analyze. Sample answer for The Massachusetts Bay Colony (page 4) is shown below.

Main idea: The government of Massachusetts Bay Colony was based on Puritan religion and the Bible.

Details: Only members of the Puritan churches could be government leaders or vote. Ministers were important because they read the Bible and interpreted it for people.

Anne Hutchinson Struggle for Religious Freedom

by Bruce T. Paddock

Summary

Anne Hutchinson was a Puritan who came with others to Boston in 1634 seeking religious freedom. She was well educated in theology and held regular meetings at which she discussed the ministers' sermons. Hutchinson began to criticize the ministers, saying they were teaching false ideas. This was a threat to both the Puritan church and the civil authority, which were closely intertwined. Hutchinson was placed on trial and eventually convicted of "traducing," or badmouthing, the ministers. She was banished from the colony and fled to Rhode Island where she helped found the community that became Portsmouth. Later, the right of individual conscience in respect to religious freedom became part of the United States' most cherished ideals.

Before Reading

Building Background

Discuss with students the reasons the Puritans came to Massachusetts. Remind students that there was little separation then between the government and the church, and that there was no such thing as religious freedom. Point out that women had few rights.

Vocabulary

official, persecute, devout, society, defendant, banish

English Language Learners

Tell students that section heads often provide clues to the main idea of the section. Read the book aloud to students, asking questions after each selection to elicit the main idea.

Target Reading Skill: Main Idea and Details

Review with students that a main idea tells the most important idea in a piece of writing. Be sure they understand that a paragraph, a section, and an entire book may all have a main idea. Have students complete the Target Reading Skill activity.

During Reading

Think Critically

1. What was the Massachusetts Bay Colony based on? (the Puritan religion and the Bible)

2. Why did Anne Hutchinson hold meetings at her home? (She and other women would discuss the week's sermons and the Bible.)

3. Why did Hutchinson's ideas get her into trouble? (She thought that most of the ministers were teaching wrong ideas. She said she doubted they would go to heaven.)

4. Why did Governor Winthrop disapprove of Hutchinson? (She was dividing the colony. She was not acting as a woman was supposed to.)

5. What are some rights people in the United States have today that Anne Hutchinson did not have in Massachusetts Bay Colony? (the right to free speech, religious freedom, right to free assembly, freedom of conscience)

After Reading

Writing

Have students write a letter that Governor John Winthrop might have written, explaining why Hutchinson had to leave the colony.

Answers to Target Reading Skill

Answers will vary depending on which section students choose to analyze. Sample answer for The Massachusetts Bay Colony (page 4) is shown below.

Main idea: The Massachusetts Bay Colony was established as a place where the Puritans could practice their Puritan religion and set an example for the world.

Details: The colony was based on the Bible. Everyone promised to obey the laws. If they did this, God would bless them.

Anne Hutchinson and Religious Freedom in the Colonies

by Bruce T. Paddock

Building Our Country

Chapter: Life in the Colonies

Lexile Measure: 860

Summary

Anne Hutchinson was a Puritan who came with others to Boston in 1634 seeking religious freedom. She was well educated in theology and held regular meetings at which she discussed the ministers' sermons. Hutchinson began to criticize the ministers, saying they were teaching false ideas. This was a threat to both the Puritan church and the civil authority, which were closely intertwined. Hutchinson was placed on trial and eventually convicted of "traducing," or badmouthing, the ministers. She was banished from the colony and fled to Rhode Island. Later, the right of individual conscience in respect to religious freedom became part of the United States' most cherished ideals.

Before Reading

Building Background

Discuss with students the reasons the Puritans came to Massachusetts. Remind students that there was little separation then between the government and the church, and no such thing as religious freedom.

Vocabulary

official, persecute, covenant, devout, denounce, society, defendant, banish

English Language Learners

Do a walk-through of the book with students, having them read aloud the heads. Then read the book aloud to students, asking questions after each selection to elicit the main idea.

Target Reading Skill: Main Idea and Details

Review with students that a main idea tells the most important idea in a piece of writing. Allow time for students to complete the Target Reading Skill activity. Afterward, call the group together and have students discuss the main idea of the book.

During Reading

Think Critically

1. Why was the Massachusetts Bay Colony founded? (The Puritans wanted a place to practice their religion.)

2. What did the male members of the colony promise? (They promised that their families would live by the rules of the Puritan church.)

3. How did Hutchinson's ideas get her into trouble? (She thought that the ministers were teaching wrong ideas.)

4. Why do you think Governor Winthrop was opposed to Hutchinson? (She was causing the colony to become divided. This could destroy Winthrop's idea of an ideal city. Also, she was a woman who was stepping out of her role.)

After Reading

Writing

Have students write a letter that Anne Hutchinson may have written from Rhode Island to her father back in England, explaining what had happened to her in Massachusetts Bay Colony.

Answers to Target Reading Skill

Answers will vary depending on which section students choose to analyze. Sample answer for The Massachusetts Bay Colony (page 4) is shown below.

Main idea: The Massachusetts Bay Colony was established as a place where the Puritans could practice their Puritan religion and set an example for the world.

Details: The colony was based on the Bible. Each male member signed an agreement to live by the church's laws. If they did this, God would bless them.

America's Ben Franklin

by Steven Jay Griffel

Summary

Benjamin Franklin was born in 1706 to a poor family in Boston. He learned the printing trade as an apprentice. In 1723, Franklin went to Philadelphia. He wrote and published *Poor Richard's Almanack,* which helped him become wealthy and famous. Franklin turned to inventing practical things, such as a better stove and lightning rods. During the 1750s and 1760s, he went to Britain to speak up for American rights. When he returned home, Franklin helped write the Declaration of Independence. During the Revolutionary War, Franklin went to France, where he persuaded the French king to give aid to America. Franklin also helped draft the U.S. Constitution before he died in 1790.

Before Reading

Building Background

Encourage students to share what they know about Benjamin Franklin and the American Revolution. Use a map of colonial America to reinforce students' understanding that the thirteen colonies became the first states of the United States.

Vocabulary

diplomat, apprentice, civic, delegate

English Language Learners

To help communicate content, have students work in small groups to paraphrase key ideas and vocabulary in simpler words and phrases. Model how to do this by paraphrasing difficult concepts to students. Read selected passages aloud and restate them in your own words.

Target Reading Skill: Cause and Effect

Draw a cause-and-effect graphic organizer on the board or provide copies to students. Model how to identify an event, and then list one cause and one effect in the graphic organizer. Next, guide a volunteer in doing the same for another event. Repeat this procedure for other causes and effects. Sample responses are shown below. Allow students time to complete the Reading Skill activity on the inside cover of their Readers in small groups.

During Reading

Comprehension and Critical Thinking

1. What was Franklin's first business? Was he a success at it? (Franklin set up his own print shop. Yes, he was successful.)

2. How did Franklin's inventions help people? (His stove helped people stay warmer and burn less wood. His bifocals helped people see better. His lightning rods help protect homes from fires caused by lightning.)

3. What is one way that Franklin helped the colonists win? (Franklin helped write the Declaration of Independence. He went to France and convinced the king to provide America with supplies and weapons.)

4. Why do you think Franklin was a great American leader? (Students should provide specific details from the book to support their answer, such as his efforts in France to help America win the war.)

After Reading

Writing

Have students work with a partner and write what they learned about another person who helped shape our nation's early history. If they need additional research they may use the Internet. Invite students to share their writing with the class.

Answers to Target Reading Skill

Cause: Philadelphia streets were dark and muddy. Effect: Franklin helped get the streets paved and lighted.

Cause: Books were hard to get. Effect: Franklin set up a library.

Cause: Houses were poorly heated. Effect: Franklin invented new stove.

Cause: Parliament passed the Stamp Act. Effect: Franklin persuaded Parliament to repeal the act.

Ben Franklin
Inventor, Leader, Patriot

by Steven Jay Griffel

Summary

Benjamin Franklin was born in 1706 to a poor family in Boston. In 1723, Franklin went to Philadelphia. He wrote and published *Poor Richard's Almanack*, which helped him become wealthy and famous. Franklin turned to inventing practical things, such as a better stove and lightning rods. Franklin also helped people through public service. During the 1750s and 1760s, he went to Britain to speak for American rights. When he returned home, Franklin helped write the Declaration of Independence. During the Revolutionary War, Franklin went to France, where he persuaded the French king to give aid to America. Franklin also helped draft the U.S. Constitution. Through his many writings and famous deeds, Franklin has inspired future generations of Americans.

Before Reading

Building Background

Use a map of colonial America to reinforce students' understanding that the thirteen colonies became the first states of the United States.

Vocabulary

diplomat, apprentice, proverb, civic, theory, delegate, treaty

English Language Learners

To help communicate content, have students work in pairs to paraphrase key ideas and vocabulary in simpler words and phrases. Model how to do this by paraphrasing difficult concepts to students. For example, read selected passages aloud and restate them in your own words.

Target Reading Skill: Cause and Effect

Reinforce students' understanding of cause and effect by providing a few examples from the book:

Cause: *The British passed unjust laws.*
Effect: *The colonists protested these laws.*

Allow students time to complete the Reading Skill activity on the inside cover of their Readers with a partner or in small groups.

During Reading

Comprehension and Critical Thinking

1. Which are your favorite of Franklin's inventions? (Make sure students provide reasons for their choice.)

2. Why was Franklin sent to Britain? (to share the American point of view with the British)

3. What are some of the ways Franklin helped the colonists win independence? (represented America in Britain and France, helped to write the Declaration of Independence)

4. What do you think Franklin should be remembered for today? (Students may note his accomplishments as an inventor, public servant, diplomat, or Patriot leader.)

After Reading

Writing

Have students write what they learned about another person who helped shape our nation's early history. They might need to do additional research on the Internet.

Answers to the Target Reading Skill

Sample Answers:

Cause: Franklin and his brother argue a lot. Effect: Franklin goes to Philadelphia and becomes a printer.

Cause: Houses are poorly heated. Effect: Franklin invents a new stove.

Cause: Parliament passes the Stamp Act. Effect: Colonists are upset. Franklin persuades Parliament to repeal the act.

Cause: War goes badly for the Americans. Effect: Franklin goes to France and persuades the king to aid Americans.

Benjamin Franklin
A Life of Science and Service

by Steven Jay Griffel

Summary

Benjamin Franklin was born in 1706 to a poor family in Boston. He learned the printing trade as an apprentice. In 1723, Franklin went to Philadelphia. He wrote and published *Poor Richard's Almanack*, which helped him become wealthy and famous. During the 1750s and 1760s, he went to Britain to speak up for American rights. When he returned home, Franklin helped write the Declaration of Independence. During the Revolutionary War, Franklin went to France. There, he persuaded the French king to give aid to America. Franklin also helped draft the U.S. Constitution before he died in 1790.

Before Reading

Building Background

Use a map of colonial America to reinforce students' understanding that the thirteen colonies became the first thirteen states of the United States.

Vocabulary

diplomat, apprentice, proverb, institution, civic, theory, mission, delegate, treaty

English Language Learners

Ask students to work in pairs to restate content. Have each pair choose a page or paragraph in the book.

Target Reading Skill: Cause and Effect

Draw a cause-and-effect graphic organizer on the board or provide copies to the students. Reinforce students' understanding of cause and effect by providing one example from the book. Then, fill in one cause and ask a a volunteer to complete its effect, or result. Repeat this procedure for other causes and effects to reinforce the skill. Sample responses are shown below.

During Reading

Comprehension and Critical Thinking

1. How did Franklin's skills as a writer help his career? (Students should note that Franklin first became a published author with his Silence Dogood letters. Later, as the author and publisher of *Poor Richard's Almanack*, Franklin became wealthy and famous.)

2. Why was Franklin sent to France? (The American colonies were in need of an ally. Franklin was experienced in diplomacy, having been in Britain before the war.)

3. What qualities made Franklin an effective diplomat? (Students should include the definition of *diplomat* in their answers.)

4. What do you think Franklin thought was worth fighting for? Support your answer with details from the book. (Sample answer: Franklin tried to reach a peaceful solution between the colonies and Great Britain. When he saw that he could not convince Britain to treat the colonies justly, Franklin decided that fighting for independence was just.)

After Reading

Writing

Have students write what they learned about one event that helped shape our nation's early history, such as the Stamp Act. They might do additional research on the Internet. What were the causes and effects of this event?

Answers to the Target Reading Skill

Sample answers:

Cause: Franklin and his brother argued a lot. Effect: Franklin went to Philadelphia and became a printer.

Cause: Philadelphia streets were dark and muddy. Effect: Franklin helped get the streets paved and lighted.

Cause: War went badly for the Americans. Effect: Franklin went to France and persuaded the king to aid Americans.

Alexander Hamilton Government Leader

by Susan Bachner

Building Our Country

Chapter: A New Nation

Lexile Measure: 710

Summary

Alexander Hamilton (1757–1804) was born on the Caribbean Island of St. Nevis. His parents were not married and his father left the family when Hamilton was ten. His mother died a few years later, leaving Hamilton and his brother on their own. He emigrated to the Thirteen Colonies where he attended King's College (now Columbia University). He fought in the Revolutionary War and became an advisor to George Washington. Later, his ideas on federalism helped shape the new government under the Constitution. As first Secretary of the Treasury he helped put the country on a firm financial footing. He died at age 47 in a duel with Aaron Burr.

Before Reading

Building Background

Briefly recall with students what they know of the Revolutionary War and the early days of our country. Have them name some of the founders. Display a ten-dollar bill, which has Hamilton's portrait on it. Tell students they will learn why it is appropriate that Hamilton is on a U.S. bill.

Vocabulary

Loyalist, Patriot, constitution, convention, federalism, import, tariff, finances

English Language Learners

Write *federal* on the board and have students pronounce it. Explain that when we talk about the federal government, we mean the government of the United States. (Spanish-speaking ELLs may be familiar with the cognate *federales*.) Write *federalism* and have students pronounce it. Point out that the *–ism* ending is a clue that the word has to do with an idea.

Target Reading Skill: Summarize

Explain that when we summarize, we tell only the most important points or ideas about something. We tell the main points, not every little detail. After students have read the book, allow time for them to work in pairs to complete the Target Reading Skill. Monitor their understanding and provide assistance as needed.

During Reading

Think Critically

1. What impressed Nicolas Cruger about Hamilton? (Sample answer: Hamilton worked hard at his job and wrote reports to Cruger about ways he could save money in his business.)

2. Why did Hamilton write the Federalist Papers? (Sample answer: He wanted to explain the Constitution to New Yorkers so that they would agree to this new form of government; he wanted to promote federalism, an idea that he had long supported.)

3. In what way was Hamilton a good choice for Secretary of the Treasury? (Sample answer: He looked for ways to improve things. He knew how to solve problems. He was smart.)

4. Why did Hamilton want to put a tariff on imported goods (Sample answer: Tariffs make imports more expensive, so Americans would buy goods made here. This would keep American businesses strong and help them grow.)

After Reading

Writing

Have students work in small groups to create a skit showing scenes of important events in the life of Alexander Hamilton. Invite them to perform their skits for the class.

Answers to Target Reading Skill

Students' summaries should cover the key points and accomplishments in Hamilton's life, such as his childhood, education, role in the Revolutionary War, role in forming the government under the Constitution, and contributions as Secretary of the Treasury.

Alexander Hamilton, Soldier and Statesman

by Susan Bachner

Building Our Country

Chapter: A New Nation

Lexile Measure: 800

Summary

Alexander Hamilton (1757–1804) was born on the Caribbean Island of St. Nevis His parents were not married and his father left the family when Hamilton was ten. His mother died a few years later, leaving Hamilton and his brother on their own. He emigrated to the Thirteen Colonies where he attended King's College (now Columbia University). He fought in the Revolutionary War and became an advisor to George Washington. Later, his ideas on federalism helped shape the new government under the Constitution. He was the first Secretary of the Treasury and helped put the country on a firm financial footing. He died at age 47 in a duel with Aaron Burr.

Before Reading

Building Background

Briefly recall with students what they know of the Revolutionary War and the early days of our country. Have them name some of the founders. Display a ten-dollar bill, which has Hamilton's portrait on it. Tell students they will learn why it is appropriate that Hamilton is on a U.S. bill.

Vocabulary

Loyalists, Patriots, military, constitution, convention, federalism, finances, tariff

English Language Learners

Write *federal* on the board and have students pronounce it. Explain that when we talk about the federal government, we mean the government of the United States. (Spanish-speaking ELLs may be familiar with the cognate *federales*.) Write *federalism* and have students pronounce it. Point out that the *–ism* ending is a clue the word has to do with an idea.

Target Reading Skill: Summarize

Explain that when we summarize, we tell only the most important points or ideas about something. We tell the main points, not every little detail. After students have read the book, allow time for them to complete the Target Reading Skill activity.

During Reading

Think Critically

1. How did Hamilton show that he was ambitious and hard-working? (Sample answer: He worked hard for Cruger and looked for ways to improve Cruger's business. When he went to school in the colonies, he studied hard to catch up.)

2. What was wrong with the Articles of Confederation, the first form of government the young United States tried? (They were weak. The federal government didn't have enough power.)

3. Why did Hamilton write the Federalist Papers? (He wanted to explain the Constitution so that people would support it.)

4. What do you think was Hamilton's greatest contribution to the country? Why? (Answers will vary, but students should be able to defend their choice.)

After Reading

Writing

Ask students to imagine they are Alexander Hamilton after the Constitutional Convention. Have them write a short letter to Hamilton's former employer, Nicolas Cruger, explaining why federalism is the system he favors.

Answers to Target Reading Skill

Students' summaries should cover the key points and accomplishments in Hamilton's life, such as his childhood, education, role in the Revolutionary War, role in forming the government under the Constitution, and contributions as Secretary of the Treasury. See the Summary above for a sample.

Alexander Hamilton and the Founding of the Federal Government

by Susan Bachner

Summary

Alexander Hamilton (1757–1804) was born on the Caribbean Island of St. Nevis His parents were not married and his father left the family when Hamilton was ten. His mother died a few years later, leaving Hamilton and his brother on their own. He emigrated to the Thirteen Colonies where he attended King's College (now Columbia University). He fought in the Revolutionary War and became an advisor to George Washington. Later, his ideas on federalism helped shape the new government under the Constitution. He was the first Secretary of the Treasury and helped put the country on a firm financial footing. He died at age 47 in a duel with Aaron Burr.

Before Reading

Building Background

Have students recall what they know of the Revolutionary War and the early days of our country. Have them name some of the founders. Display a ten-dollar bill. Tell students they will learn why it is appropriate that Hamilton is on a U.S. bill.

Vocabulary

Loyalist, Patriot, military, constitution, federalism, ratify, tariff

English Language Learners

Write *federal* on the board and have students pronounce it. Explain that the federal government means the government of the United States. (Spanish-speaking ELLs may be familiar with the cognate *federales*.) Write *federalism* and have students pronounce it. Point out that the *–ism* ending is a clue that the word has to do with an idea.

Target Reading Skill: Summarize

Explain that when we summarize, we tell only the most important points or ideas about something. Ask volunteers to summarize a TV show or movie they have seen recently. Allow students time to complete the Target Reading Skill activity on the inside front and back cover of their Readers.

During Reading

Think Critically

1. How do you think Hamilton's childhood affected his thoughts about money and how to use it? (He knew the value of work and money because from a young age, he had to work to support himself.)

2. Why were the Federalist Papers important? (The Federalist Papers explained the Constitution to the people of New York and helped convince them to ratify it.)

3. Why was the job of first Secretary of the Treasury so important? (The first Secretary of the Treasury had to solve several problems to help the country grow financially.)

4. What do you think was Hamilton's most important accomplishment? Explain your answer. (Students' answers will vary, but accept all answers that can be supported.)

After Reading

Speaking

Divide students into two groups and assign one group to be Loyalists and the other to be Patriots. Have them prepare arguments to use in a debate. They should debate the question, should the Thirteen Colonies seek independence, even at the cost of war?

Answers to Target Reading Skill

Students' summaries should cover the key points and accomplishments in Hamilton's life, such as his childhood, education, role in the Revolutionary War, role in forming the government under the Constitution, and contributions as Secretary of the Treasury. See the Summary above for a sample.

Elizabeth Cady Stanton and the Fight for Women's Rights

by Jeri Cipriano

Building Our Country

Chapter: The Young Nation Grows

Lexile Measure: 750

Summary

Elizabeth Cady Stanton (1815–1902) was the daughter of a successful lawyer and judge. After the death of her older brother, she became aware of the low value as well as the restrictions placed on women by society. She spent time in her father's legal office and learned how few rights the law accorded women. She married an abolitionist, Henry Stanton, and was mentored in the suffrage movement by Lucretia Mott. Working with Mott and others, she established the first women's rights convention in Seneca Falls, New York, in 1848. She worked with Susan B. Anthony for decades on behalf of women. Stanton never lived to see American women get the right to vote in national elections, but her work for the women's rights movement helped make that right a reality.

Before Reading

Building Background

Explain to students that women in this country were not allowed to vote in national elections until 1920. In the early to mid-1800s, when Elizabeth Cady Stanton was growing up, women had few rights. Poor women often worked out of necessity, as laundresses, cooks, or servants, but wealthy women were expected not to work or have careers.

Vocabulary

abolitionist, suffrage, petition, movement, legislature, amendment

English Language Learners

Write the words *abolish, abolition,* and *abolitionist.* Explain that *abolish* means "to put an end to" something. The word *abolition* usually means the end of slavery. Abolitionists were people who worked to end slavery. Give close sentence frames and have students practice using the words.

Target Reading Skill: Generalize

Explain that to make a generalization means to look at several facts about a topic and to make a statement about what these facts have in common. Generalizations often include signal words such as the words *usually, often,* or *generally.* (The previous sentence is a generalization.) After students read the book, work with them to complete the Target Reading Skill activity.

During Reading

Think Critically

1. What effect did the death of Stanton's brother have on her? (Her brother's death showed her that boys were often more valued than girls.)
2. Why did Stanton attend a women's college? (The college she wanted to go to only accepted men.)
3. What was unusual about Stanton's marriage? (Stanton did not promise to obey her husband; she added her married name to the end of her given name; she called her husband "Henry" in public.)
4. Why did Stanton and Anthony make a good team? (Stanton was a good writer, and Anthony had the time to travel and make speeches.)

After Reading

Writing

Have students pretend they are Stanton. Have them write a letter to a granddaughter, telling her why women need the same rights as men.

Answer to Target Reading Skill

Possible generalizations: Women had few rights in the mid-1800s; Stanton was intelligent and determined to affect change; women who worked for women's rights were strong and independent; Stanton helped make many gains for women's rights. Accept any that can be substantiated by the text.

Elizabeth Cady Stanton Founder of the Women's Rights Movement

by Jeri Cipriano

Summary

Elizabeth Cady Stanton (1815–1902) was the daughter of a successful lawyer and judge. After the death of her older brother, she became aware of the low value as well as the restrictions placed on women by society. She spent time in her father's legal office and learned how few rights the law accorded women. She married an abolitionist, Henry Stanton, and was mentored in the suffrage movement by Lucretia Mott. Working with Mott and others, she established the first women's rights convention in Seneca Falls, New York, in 1848. Stanton never lived to see women in the United States get the right to vote in national elections, but her work was the beginning of the fight for women's rights.

Before Reading

Building Background

Explain to students that women in this country were not allowed to vote in national elections until 1920. In the early to mid-1800s, when Elizabeth Cady Stanton was growing up, women had few rights.

Vocabulary

abolitionist, emancipation, movement, suffrage, petition, legislature, amendment

English Language Learners

Write the words *abolish, abolition,* and *abolitionist.* Explain that *abolish* means "to put an end to" something. The word *abolition* usually means the end of slavery. Abolitionists were people who worked to end slavery. Follow the same procedure with *emancipate* and *emancipation.*

Target Reading Skill: Generalize

Explain that to make a generalization means to look at several facts about a topic and to make a statement about what these facts have in common. Generalizations often include signal words such as the words *usually, often,* or *generally.* After students read the book, work with them to complete the Target Reading Skill activity.

During Reading

Think Critically

1. What things in Stanton's childhood made her want to work for women's rights? (Her brother's death was a reminder that girls were less valued than boys; she could not go to the college of her choice; she learned that women had few rights under the law.)

2. What was unusual about Stanton's marriage? (She did not promise to obey her husband; she added her married name to the end of her given name; she called her husband "Henry" in public.)

3. Why did Stanton and Susan B. Anthony make a good team? (Stanton was a good writer, and Anthony had the time to deliver the speeches and speak in front of lawmakers.)

4. Was Stanton successful? (She achieved some success in getting some New York state laws changed. She did not live to see women's suffrage in the United States, but the movement she started did win the vote eventually.)

After Reading

Writing

Have students pretend they are Stanton. Have them write several paragraphs explaining why she did the work she did.

Answer to Target Reading Skill

Accept any generalization that can be substantiated by the text.

Possible generalizations: Women had few rights in the mid-1800s; Stanton was intelligent and determined to affect change; women who worked for women's rights were strong and independent; Stanton helped make gains for women's rights.

More than the Right to Vote: The Story of Elizabeth Cady Stanton

by Jeri Cipriano

Building Our Country

Chapter: The Young Nation Grows

Lexile Measure: 900

Elizabeth Cady Stanton (1815–1902) was the daughter of a successful lawyer and judge. As a young woman she became aware of the restrictions placed on women by society. She learned how few rights the law accorded women. She married an abolitionist, Henry Stanton, and was mentored in the suffrage movement by Lucretia Mott. Working with Mott and others, she established the first women's rights convention in Seneca Falls, New York, in 1848. Stanton never lived to see women get the right to vote in national elections, but her work was the beginning of the fight for women's rights.

Before Reading

Building Background

Explain to students that in the early to mid-1800s, women had few rights. They could not vote or own property. Women and children were considered the property of their husbands. Wealthy women were not expected to work or have careers.

Vocabulary

abolitionist, emancipation, movement, suffrage, petition, legislature, amendment

English Language Learners

Write the words *abolish, abolition,* and *abolitionist.* Explain that *abolish* means "to put an end to" something. The word *abolition* usually means the end of slavery. Abolitionists were people who worked to end slavery. Follow the same procedure with *emancipate* and *emancipation.*

Target Reading Skill: Generalize

Explain that to make a generalization means to look at several facts about a topic and to make a statement about what these facts have in common. Generalizations often include signal words such as the words *usually, often,* or *generally.*

During Reading

Think Critically

1. What experiences did Stanton have as a girl and a young woman that helped shape her life's work? (She wasn't valued as much as her brother; she couldn't go to the college of her choice; she saw how laws treated women unequally compared to men.)

2. What did the abolitionists and the people who worked for women's rights have in common? (Both groups wanted to help people who had few rights and no voice in the government.)

3. One generalization that can be made about Stanton is that "She lived her life according to her beliefs." What facts support this? (She would not promise to obey her husband since she felt they were equal; she worked to change laws she felt were unjust.)

4. Was Stanton successful? (She achieved some success in getting some state laws changed. She did not live to see women's suffrage, but the movement she started did win the vote eventually.)

After Reading

Writing

You read that Stanton wrote a letter to President Theodore Roosevelt, which was never mailed. Write what you think Stanton might have written in that letter.

Answer to Target Reading Skill

Accept any generalization that can be substantiated by the text.

Possible generalizations: Women had few rights in the mid-1800s; Stanton was intelligent and determined to affect change; women who worked for women's rights were determined; Stanton helped make gains for women's rights.

James Polk
American President

by Steven Jay Griffel

Building Our Country

Chapter: Moving West

Lexile Measure: 730

Summary

James Polk was born in North Carolina in 1795. Though he had lifelong health problems, he never let them stop his ambitions. After many years of Tennessee politics, including being governor, he was a surprise nomination as presidential candidate of the Democratic Party. Polk was not expected to win, but he did. As president, he had very specific goals he wanted to accomplish. The most significant goals had to do with national expansion. By acquiring the northwest territory from the British and vast southwest territories from Mexico, Polk was able to expand the United States to the Pacific Coast.

Before Reading

Building Background

Tell students that the United States was once a much smaller country than it is today. Use a United States map to reinforce students' understanding of the country's boundaries before Polk's presidency.

Vocabulary

candidate, legislature, slogan, expand, destined, territory, annex, occupy

English Language Learners

Read aloud and summarize the first two pages of the book. Then have students pair up and summarize another page. Help each pair summarize their page by pointing out the main ideas on the page.

Target Reading Skill: Fact and Opinion

Draw a T-chart on the board or provide copies to the students. Model for students how to complete the chart and use it to separate fact from opinion. For example, a statement in the left column might be: *President Polk helped expand the boundaries of the United States.* A statement in the right column might be: *President Polk was one of the hardest-working presidents the country has ever had.* Discuss why the first statement is a fact and the second statement is an opinion. Allow small groups of students time to complete the Target Reading Skill activity on the inside cover of their Readers. Provide assistance as needed and monitor their understanding of the skill and activity.

During Reading

Comprehension and Critical Thinking

1. Why did so many Americans head west during the mid-1800s? (Travelers to the west were looking for land to settle and to farm.)

2. What dispute did Polk have with Great Britain? (The United States and Britain shared a claim to the Oregon Territory and Polk wanted Britain to give up its claim.)

3. Why did the United States and Mexico go to war? (Troops clashed in disputed lands near the border of Texas and Mexico.)

4. What was Polk's major achievement? (He greatly increased the size of the United States by adding the Oregon Territory and lands purchased from Mexico, including California, after the Mexican War.)

After Reading

Writing

"Who is James K. Polk?" Have students work in pairs to write other slogans for either Polk's or Henry Clay's election campaign in 1844. Invite students to share their slogans with the class.

Answers to Target Reading Skill

Sample facts: James Polk was born in North Carolina; James Polk had health problems; James Polk was elected president in 1844.

Sample opinions: James Polk was a talented speaker; James Polk was a powerful leader.

President James Polk and the Expansion of the United States

by Steven Jay Griffel

Summary

James Polk was born in North Carolina in 1795. Though he had lifelong health problems, he never let them stop his ambitions. He became a lawyer and was very good at public speaking, which lead him into politics. After many years of Tennessee politics, he was a surprise presidential candidate of the Democratic Party. He was not expected to win, but he did. As president, he had very specific goals he wanted to accomplish. The most significant goals had to do with national expansion. By acquiring vast territories from Britain and Mexico, Polk was able to expand the United States to the Pacific Coast.

Before Reading

Building Background

Tell students that the United States was once a much smaller country than it is today. Use a United States map to reinforce students' understanding of the country's boundaries before Polk's presidency. Encourage students to share what they know about early settlers in the west.

Vocabulary

candidate, legislature, slogan, expansion, territory, destined, annex, occupy

English Language Learners

In order to communicate content, paraphrase questions or key ideas and vocabulary. Students should understand that the United States expanded over many years from its original thirteen states to the fifty we have today.

Target Reading Skill: Fact and Opinion

Draw a T-chart on the board or provide copies to students. Model how to complete the chart and separate fact from opinion. For example, a statement in the left column might be: *President Polk helped expand the boundaries of the United States.* A statement in the right column might be: *President Polk was one of the hardest-working presidents the country has ever had.* Discuss why the first statement is a fact and the second statement is an opinion. Allow students time to complete the Target Reading Skill activity on the inside cover of their Readers individually or with a partner.

During Reading

Comprehension and Critical Thinking

1. Why did so many Americans head west during the mid-1800s? (They were in search of land.)

2. What is the meaning of "Manifest Destiny"? ("Manifest Destiny" was the belief in the right of Americans to occupy and acquire western lands, all the way to the Pacific Coast.)

3. What were Polk's biggest achievements? (the acquisition of part of the Oregon Country; the successful outcome of the war with Mexico, and the acquisition of lands from Mexico including California)

After Reading

Writing

Have students write an newspaper or online editorial about President James Polk. What were his accomplishments? Was he a good leader or a poor one? Tell them to include both facts and opinions in their writing.

Answers to Target Reading Skill

Sample facts: James Polk was born in North Carolina; James Polk had health problems; James Polk was elected president in 1844.

Sample opinions: James Polk was a talented speaker; James Polk knew how to win elections; James Polk was a powerful leader.

President James Polk and America's "Manifest Destiny"

by Steven Jay Griffel

Summary

James Polk was born in North Carolina and became a serious and successful student. Though he had lifelong health problems, he never let them stop his ambitions. He became a lawyer and was very good at public speaking, which led him into politics. After many years of Tennessee politics, he was a surprise presidential nomination by the Democratic Party. He was not expected to win, but he did. As president, he had a very specific agenda having to do with national expansion. By acquiring the vast northwest territory from the British and vast southwest territories from Mexico, Polk was able to expand the United States to the Pacific Coast.

Before Reading

Building Background

Tell students that the United States was once a much smaller country than it is today. Use a United States map to reinforce students' understanding of the boundaries of the United States before Polk's presidency.

Vocabulary

candidate, devout, legislature, expansion, annexation, administrator, budget, destined, territory, occupy

English Language Learners

In order to enhance understanding, paraphrase questions or key ideas and vocabulary definitions.

Target Reading Skill: Fact and Opinion

Draw a T-chart on the board or provide copies to the students. Model for students how to complete the chart and use it to separate fact from opinion. For example, a statement in the left column might be: *President Polk helped expand the boundaries of the United States.* A statement in the right column might be: *President Polk was one of the hardest-working presidents the country has ever had.* Discuss why the first statement is a fact and the second statement is an opinion. Allow students time to complete the Reading Skill activity on the inside cover of their Readers individually or with a partner.

During Reading

Comprehension and Critical Thinking

1. Why was Polk called a dark-horse candidate? (He was called a "dark horse" because he was relatively unknown and a surprise winner.)

2. What were Polk's major goals as president? (expansion of the country)

3. What position did President Polk take when negotiating with the British? (The United States would not allow any European nation to stop American expansion.)

4. What is the meaning of "Manifest Destiny"? ("Manifest Destiny" was the belief in the right of Americans to occupy and acquire the westward lands, all the way to the Pacific coast.)

After Reading

Writing

President Polk was known as a good speaker. Have students write and give a brief speech Polk might have given after the Treaty of Guadalupe Hidalgo, expressing his view of the events leading to American expansion.

Answers to Target Reading Skill

Sample facts: James Polk was born in North Carolina; James Polk had health problems; James Polk was elected president in 1844.

Sample opinions: James Polk was a talented speaker; James Polk was a man of fierce determination; James Polk was a powerful leader.

President Ulysses S. Grant

by Susan Bachner

The Growth of Our Country

Chapter: Civil War and Reconstruction

Lexile Measure: 720

Summary

This biography of Ulysses S. Grant (1822–1885) describes his unlikely rise from average student and disinterested West Point cadet to Civil War hero and president of the United States. By the age of 40, he had achieved no material success, but his entry into the Civil War saw him quickly promoted through the ranks of the military. President Lincoln had faith in Grant, regardless of Northern outrage over Grant's loss of many Union troops at the Battle of Shiloh. This faith was rewarded when Grant's leadership as commander of all Union forces helped the Union win the war. As president of the United States, Grant was a proponent of civil rights for those newly freed from slavery. Despite the fact that his second term of office was marked by scandals, he is remembered as a popular president.

Before Reading

Building Background

Build background by explaining to students that Ulysses Grant was a general who helped the North win the Civil War and a president who led the country after the war. Ask volunteers to think about what challenges Grant might have faced, as general and president.

Vocabulary

civil rights, segregation, economy, recession, veto, scandal, memoirs

English Language Learners

Have students take turns reading aloud sections of the reader, and have partners paraphrase what they heard. Explain idioms such as "a crushing blow" (page 7).

Target Reading Skill: Sequence

Explain to students that sequence tells the order in which events happened. Sequence can be signalled by words such as *first*, *next*, and *last* or, as in this case, by dates. Reproduce the graphic organizer on the board. Explain that a timeline is a good way to identify the sequence of events in someone's life. As an example, begin by filling in *Grant's birth* next to the year *1822*. Have students reproduce the timeline graphic organizer on a separate sheet of paper. Tell them that as they read they will write down dates and events in the life of Ulysses S. Grant. Allow students time to complete the Target Reading Skill activity on the inside front and back cover of their Readers. Remind them to refer to their Readers as needed.

During Reading

Think Critically

1. Why did Grant resign from the army in 1854? (He did not like being away from his wife for long periods of time.)

2. Why were there so many scandals during Grant's presidency? (Grant did not have a lot of experience in government. He trusted people he should not have and hired dishonest people.)

3. What ideas did Grant have that made him a good president for the period after the Civil War? (He wanted civil rights for people freed from slavery. Healing the country was important to him.)

After Reading

Writing

Have students imagine they are Grant. Ask them to write a letter to a friend explaining why they rejoined the Army when the Civil War began.

Answers to Target Reading Skill

1822 Grant is born; 1843 graduates from West Point; 1848 marries Julia Dent; 1854 resigns from army; 1861 Civil War begins; 1865 Civil War ends; 1868 is elected president; 1870 Fifteenth Amendment is passed; 1872 is reelected; 1873 Panic of 1873; 1877 leaves office; 1885 dies.

Ulysses S. Grant
General and President

by Susan Bachner

The Growth of Our Country

Chapter: Civil War and Reconstruction

Lexile Measure: 820

Summary

This biography of Ulysses S. Grant (1822–1885) describes his unlikely rise from average student and uninterested West Point cadet to Civil War hero and president of the United States. By the age of 40, he had achieved no material success, but his entry into the Civil War saw him quickly promoted through the ranks of the military. President Lincoln had faith in Grant, regardless of Northern outrage over Grant's loss of many Union troops at the Battle of Shiloh. This faith was rewarded when Grant's leadership as commander of all Union forces helped the Union win the war. As president of the United States, Grant was a proponent of civil rights for those newly freed from slavery. His second term of office was marked by scandals, but he was remembered as a popular president.

Before Reading

Building Background

Build background by explaining to students that Ulysses Grant was a general who helped the North win the Civil War and a president who led the country after the war. Ask volunteers to think about what challenges Grant might have faced as general and president.

Vocabulary

promote, Reconstruction, inaugurate, civil rights, segregation, economy, recession, veto, scandal, bribe, memoirs

English Language Learners

Have students take turns reading aloud sections of the reader, and have a partner paraphrase what they heard. Explain idioms such as "Grant was ahead of his time" (page 15), and paraphrase the meaning of some of the longer quotes in the book.

Target Reading Skill: Sequence

Reproduce the graphic organizer on the board. Ask students to make their own copy on a sheet of paper. Tell them that sequence is the order in which events occur. Tell them that they will use the timeline to note major events in the life of Grant as they read. For an example, begin by writing *Grant's birth* next to the year *1822*. As they read they will note additional key events in Grant's life. Allow students time to complete the Target Reading Skill activity on the inside front and back cover of their Readers.

During Reading

Think Critically

1. What in Grant's childhood may have helped him become a great general and president? (He read a lot; he learned army ways at the military academy.)

2. Why do you think Grant rejoined the army when the Civil War began? (He thought he could help his country.)

3. What ideas did Grant have that may have helped the nation recover? (He believed that both sides should forgive each other.)

4. Do you think Grant was a good president? (Yes; he pushed for the first civil rights laws for African American people. No; his inexperience led to scandals.)

After Reading

Writing

Have students imagine they are Grant and write a section of his memoir about one part of his life.

Answers to Target Reading Skill

Possible events: 1822 Grant is born; 1843 graduates from West Point; 1846 Mexican War begins; 1848 marries Julia Dent; 1854 resigns from army; 1861 Civil War begins; 1862 Battle of Shiloh; 1863 Battle of Vicksburg; 1865 Civil War ends; 1868 is elected president; 1870 Fifteenth Amendment is passed; 1872 is reelected; 1873 Panic of 1873; 1877 leaves office; 1881 moves to New York; 1885 dies; 1897 Grant's Tomb is dedicated.

Ulysses S. Grant
Defender of the Union

by Susan Bachner

The Growth of Our Country

Chapter: Civil War and Reconstruction

Lexile Measure: 880

Summary

This biography of Ulysses S. Grant (1822–1885) describes his unlikely rise from average student and uninterested West Point cadet to Civil War hero and president of the United States. By the age of 40, Grant had not achieved material success, but his entry into the Civil War saw him quickly promoted through the ranks of the military. President Lincoln had faith in Grant, regardless of Northern outrage over the loss of many Union troops at the Battle of Shiloh. This faith was rewarded when Grant, as commander of all Union forces, helped the Union win the war. As president, Grant was a proponent of civil rights for those newly freed from slavery. While his second term was marked by scandals, he was a popular president.

Before Reading

Building Background

Build background by explaining to students that Ulysses Grant was both a general who helped the North win the Civil War and a president who led the country after the war.

Vocabulary

promote, assassin, Reconstruction, inaugurate, civil rights, segregation, economy, recession, veto, scandal, bribe, invest, memoirs, prosperity

English Language Learners

Have more fluent readers paraphrase sections of the book. Have volunteers explain idioms, such as "Grant was ahead of his time" (p. 15).

Target Reading Skill: Sequence

Discuss the idea that sequence conveys the order in which events occurred in someone's life. Sequence can be signaled by words such as *first*, *next*, and *last* or, in this case, by dates.

Ask students to reproduce the graphic organizer on the board. Tell students that as they read they will fill in events in Grant's life next to the year in which they occurred. To provide an example, begin by filling in *Grant's birth* next to the year *1822*. Allow students time to complete the Target Reading Skill activity on the inside front and back cover of their Readers.

During Reading

Think Critically

1. What activities in Grant's childhood may have helped him as an adult? (He read a lot; he worked hard at math.)

2. How do we know that Grant believed in justice and fairness for all people? (He treated the defeated Confederate soldiers with mercy. He wanted to help African American and Native American people.)

3. Do you think Grant could have avoided some of the scandals in his presidency? (No; he had nothing to do with the scandals. Yes; he gave jobs to friends rather than to people who deserved the jobs.)

After Reading

Writing

Have students imagine that they are Grant. Ask them to write a letter describing in one or more paragraphs the achievements of which he is most proud.

Answers to Target Reading Skill

Possible events: 1822 Grant is born; 1843 graduates from West Point; 1846 Mexican War begins; 1848 marries Julia Dent; 1854 resigns from army; 1861 Civil War begins; 1862 Battle of Shiloh; 1863 Battle of Vicksburg; 1865 Civil War ends; 1869 is inaugurated president; 1870 Fifteenth Amendment is passed; 1872 is reelected; 1873 Panic of 1873; 1877 leaves office; 1881 moves to New York; 1885 dies; 1897 Grant's Tomb is dedicated.

Calamity Jane
Star of the Old West

by Bruce T. Paddock

The Growth of Our Country

Chapter: Expanding West and Overseas

Lexile Measure: 750

Summary

As a teenager, Martha Cannary (c. 1852–1903) migrated west to Montana with her family. Within two years, she was an orphan. She spent most of the rest of her life traveling throughout the West, moving from one place to another. She sometimes worked driving teams of oxen, and possibly as a mail rider—jobs that few other women held. She called herself Calamity Jane, although we don't know exactly how she acquired the nickname. She told a story about how she got it, but like most of the stories she told about her life it wasn't true. What is true is that Calamity ignored the restrictions society placed on women at the time and lived her life, a life of adventure.

Before Reading

Building Background

Use a map of the United States to point out lands west of the Mississippi River. Tell students that this region was settled from the end of the Civil War through the 1880s. Later, people looked back on that period of settlement as one of adventure. The Old West or the "Wild West" became the subject of books, movies, and TV shows. Many people who lived then became "larger than life" heroes.

Vocabulary

reinvent, society, gold rush, heroine, legend

English Language Learners

Write the word reinvent and discuss the meaning of the prefix re-. Discuss the meaning of the term calamity and why someone might give themselves such a nickname. Go over the pronunciation and meanings of other vocabulary words.

Target Reading Skill: Compare and Contrast

Remind students that to compare is to find similarities between two or more things. To contrast is to find differences between two or more things. Allow students time to complete the Target Reading Skill activity on the inside cover of their Readers individually or with a partner.

During Reading

Comprehension and Critical Thinking

1. When did the Cannary family move west? (1865)

2. Give an example of things Calamity Jane was skilled at doing. (riding a horse, shooting, caring for people who were sick, telling stories about herself)

3. What is a bullwhacker? Why do you think Calamity Jane took this job? (It was a person who drove a freight wagon pulled by oxen. Calamity may have taken the job because she liked to travel.)

4. Do you think Calamity Jane was like most people who lived in the West in late 1800s? Support your answer with details from the book. (Sample answers: No—It seems unlikely that most Westerners traveled as much or were as well known as Calamity Jane. Yes—Like other Westerners, she reinvented herself and led a life of adventure.)

After Reading

Activity

Ask students to write a paragraph explaining why they think Calamity Jane lived the kind of life she did.

Answers to Target Reading Skill

Possible answers:

Similar: Other women, like Calamity, lived in the West, in small towns, married, and had children.

Different: Women were expected to obey their husbands, but Calamity Jane made her own decisions. Most women used their real names, or the names of their husbands, but Calamity Jane went by her nickname. She also took jobs that women did not normally have.

Calamity Jane
Life of Adventure

by Bruce T. Paddock

The Growth of Our Country

Chapter: Expanding West and Overseas

Lexile Measure: 820

Summary

As a teenager, Martha Cannary (c. 1852–1903) migrated west to Montana with her family. Within two years, she was an orphan. She spent most of the rest of her life traveling throughout the West, moving from one place to another. She sometimes worked driving teams of oxen or bulls, and possibly as a mail rider—jobs that few other women held. She also called herself Calamity Jane, although we don't know exactly how she acquired the nickname. She told a story about how she got it, but like most of the stories she told about her life, it wasn't true. What is true is that Calamity ignored the restrictions society placed on women at the time and lived her life, a life of adventure.

Before Reading

Building Background

Use a map of the United States to point out the land west of the Mississippi. Explain that the West was settled during the years after the Civil War through the 1880s. Later, people looked back on that time of settlement as one of adventure. The Old West or the "Wild West" became the subject of books, and later of movies and TV shows. Many of the people who lived then became "larger than life" heroes.

Vocabulary

reinvent, society, gold rush, nostalgic, heroine, legend

English Language Learners

Write the word *reinvent* and discuss the meaning of the prefix *re-*. Discuss the meaning of the term *calamity* and why someone might give themselves such a nickname. Go over pronunciation and meanings of other vocabulary words.

Target Reading Skill: Compare and Contrast

Review the meaning of *compare* and *contrast*. To compare is to find similarities between two or more things. To contrast is to find differences. Allow students time to complete the Target Reading Skill activity individually or with a partner.

During Reading

Comprehension and Critical Thinking

1. In 1865, how did Calamity Jane spend most of her time on the trip west with her family? (She spent most of the time riding and hunting with the men, rather than spend time sitting in the wagon with the other children.)

2. Do you think Calamity Jane was a typical woman for her times? (No. Most women then got married and did what society expected. Calamity did what she wanted to do.)

3. Give an example of Calamity's kindness. (She took care of friends and neighbors who were ill from smallpox.)

4. Why do you think Wild West shows became popular? (Sample answer: The West was settled, and people looked back on the earlier days with nostalgia. They may have wanted to relive these days by watching the shows.)

After Reading

Activity

Have students work in pairs to prepare a brief, illustrated talk on Calamity Jane. They can find illustrations on the Internet.

Answers to Target Reading Skill

Possible answers:

Similar: Other women, like Calamity, lived in the West, in small towns, married, and had children.

Different: Women were expected to obey their husbands, but Calamity Jane made her own decisions. Most women used their real names, or the names of their husbands, but Calamity Jane went by her nickname.

The Story of Calamity Jane

by Bruce T. Paddock

Summary

As a teenager, Martha Cannary (c. 1852–1903) migrated west to Montana with her family. Within two years, she was an orphan. She spent most of the rest of her life traveling throughout the West, moving from one place to another. She sometimes worked driving teams of oxen and possibly as a mail rider—jobs that few other women held. She also called herself Calamity Jane. She told a story about how she got her nickname, but like most of the stories she told about her life, it wasn't true. What is true is that Calamity ignored the restrictions society placed on women at the time and lived a life of adventure.

Before Reading

Building Background

Explain that the West was settled in the decades after the Civil War. Later, people looked back on that time of settlement as one of adventure. The Old West or the "Wild West" became the subject of books, and later of movies and TV shows. Many of the people who lived then became "larger than life" heroes.

Vocabulary

solitude, reinvent, society, reputation, gold rush, nostalgic, dispatch, heroine, legend

English Language Learners

Write the word *reinvent* and discuss the meaning of the prefix re-. Discuss the meaning of the term *calamity* and why someone might give themselves such a nickname. Go over pronunciation and meanings of other vocabulary words.

Target Reading Skill: Compare and Contrast

Review the terms *compare* and *contrast*. (To compare is to find similarities between two or more things. To contrast is to find differences between two or more things.) Allow students time to complete the Target Reading Skill activity on the inside cover of their Readers.

During Reading

Comprehension and Critical Thinking

1. Why do you think Calamity fit in so well in Deadwood in the late 1870s? (Calamity Jane didn't like living her life by other people's rules. Deadwood had few rules.)

2. Give one example of Calamity's kindness and generosity. (She took care of friends and neighbors who were suffering from smallpox.)

3. Why do you think Wild West shows and novels about the Old West were popular? (People wanted to experience the adventure of living in those times.)

4. Do you think Calamity Jane was a typical Westerner of the late 1800s? Support your answer with details from the book. (No—It seems unlikely that most Westerners traveled as much or were as well-known as Calamity Jane. Yes—Like some other Westerners, she reinvented herself and led a life of adventure.)

After Reading

Activity

Have students imagine that Calamity Jane is appearing on a TV talk show. With a partner have them prepare and act out an interview between Calamity Jane and the show's host.

Answers to Target Reading Skill

Possible answers:

Similar: Other women, like Calamity, lived in the West, in small towns, married, and had children.

Different: Women were expected to live by society's rules, but Calamity Jane made her own decisions. Most women used their real names, or the names of their husbands, but Calamity Jane went by her nickname.

Thomas Edison, American Inventor

by Steven Jay Griffel

Summary

This biography of Thomas Edison (1847–1931) recounts his remarkable life as an American inventor and businessman. As a young boy, Edison showed an early curiosity for how things worked. He read a lot and even set up a laboratory in his basement. Edison, who went on to receive patents for 1,093 inventions, was a model of persistence and hard work. He invented things he believed people would find useful and would be willing to buy. Among his most famous achievements are the phonograph, the movie camera and projector, and the light bulb and electrical system. His laboratories and factories turned his inventions into hugely successful businesses.

Before Reading

Building Background

Build background for the book by asking students to share what they know about Edison and the invention of the light bulb. Ask students to turn to page 7 of the book and read some of Edison's famous sayings. Discuss the meaning of the sayings.

Vocabulary

laboratory, profit, telegraphy, transmitter, generator, manufacture

English Language Learners

Have students page through the book to look at photographs and identify each of the inventions. Say aloud words such as *phonograph*, *kinetograph* (kih NEH toh graf), and *kinetoscope* (ki NEH toh skope) to help students with pronunciation.

Target Reading Skill: Draw Conclusions

Reproduce the graphic organizer on the board. Ask volunteers to fill in facts and details in the first column and information they already know in the second column to form their conclusions. One conclusion might be that Edison succeeded because he worked very hard and tried things over and over again. Allow students time to complete the Reading Skill activity on the inside front and back cover of their Readers.

During Reading

Think Critically

1. What did Edison do as a young boy that may have helped him become a great inventor? (He asked a lot of questions and read a lot. He also set up a laboratory and did experiments.)

2. Why did Edison focus on practical inventions? (He wanted to invent things that people wanted and would be willing to buy.)

3. How was Edison able to invent so many different things? (His laboratories employed many scientists who worked on several different inventions at a time.)

4. Why do you think some people call Edison the greatest inventor ever? (He invented more than a thousand inventions. Many, such as the light bulb, changed people's lives.)

After Reading

Writing

Have students write a short paragraph explaining which Edison invention they think was the most important and why.

Answers to Target Reading Skill

Students' details should support their conclusions.

Sample facts and details: Even as a boy, Edison found ways to make money; Edison built useful things people wanted to buy.

Sample Conclusion: Edison was a businessman as well as an inventor who invented things that would earn money.

The Wizard of Menlo Park
Thomas Edison's Story

by Steven Jay Griffel

The Growth of Our Country

Chapter: Industry and Immigration

Lexile Measure: 870

Summary

This biography of Thomas Edison (1847–1931) recounts his remarkable life as an American inventor and businessman. As a boy, Edison showed an early curiosity for how things worked. He read a lot and even set up a laboratory in his basement. Edison, who went on to receive patents for 1,093 inventions, was a model of persistence and hard work. He invented things he believed people would find useful and would be willing to buy. Among his most famous achievements are the phonograph, the movie camera and projector, and the light bulb and electrical system. His laboratories and factories turned his inventions into hugely successful businesses.

Before Reading

Building Background

Build background for the book by asking students to share what they know about Edison and the invention of the light bulb. Ask students to turn to page 7 of the book and read some of Edison's famous sayings. Discuss their meanings.

Vocabulary

laboratory, profit, telegraphy, patent, transmitter, filament, manufacture, persistence

English Language Learners

Have students page through the book to look at photographs and identify each of the inventions. Give help with the pronunciation for words such as *phonograph, kinetograph* (kih NEH toh graf), and *kinetoscope* (ki NEH toh skohp).

Target Reading Skill: Draw Conclusions

Reproduce the graphic organizer. Use the example provided to students in the Target Skill to guide students in using details to draw a conclusion. An example of a conclusion might be that Edison succeeded because he worked hard and tried things over and over again. Allow students time to complete the Reading Skill activity.

During Reading

Think Critically

1. How did Edison's childhood prepare him to be a great inventor? (He was curious and asked a lot of questions; he read a lot and did experiments; he thought of ways to make money.)

2. Why were so many of Edison's inventions moneymakers? (He invented things that he knew people wanted and would pay for.)

3. What was special about Edison's laboratories at Menlo Park and West Orange? (The laboratories were invention factories. Edison employed many people to work on dozens of inventions at a time, allowing them to produce hundreds of new products he thought people would buy.)

4. Which of Edison's inventions do you think changed people's lives the most? Why? (Answers should serve to spark discussion of Edison's major achievements.)

After Reading

Writing

Have students write a letter as Edison to his children that tells them what they have to do to be a successful inventor.

Answers to Target Reading Skill

Students' details should support their conclusions. Sample facts and details: Even as a boy, Edison found ways to make money; Edison built useful things people wanted to buy; Edison set up his invention factory so that he could work on many inventions at a time.

Sample conclusion: Edison was a businessman who looked for ways to make money.

Thomas Edison
Practical Genius

by Steven Jay Griffel

Summary

This biography of Thomas Edison (1847–1931) recounts his remarkable life as an American inventor and businessman. As a boy, Edison showed an early curiosity for how things worked. He read a lot and even set up a laboratory in his basement. Edison, who went on to receive patents for 1,093 inventions, was a model of persistence and hard work. He invented things he believed people would find useful and would be willing to buy. Among his most famous achievements are the phonograph, the movie camera and projector, and the light bulb and electrical system. His laboratories and factories turned his inventions into hugely successful businesses.

Before Reading

Building Background

Build background for the book by asking students to share what they know about Edison and the invention of the light bulb. Ask students to turn to page 7 of the book and read some of Edison's famous sayings. Discuss what they mean.

Vocabulary

profit, telegraphy, patent, transmitter, filament, socket, manufacture, persistence

English Language Learners

Have students page through the book to look at photographs and identify each of the inventions. Give help with pronunciation of *phonograph*, *kinetograph* (kih NEH toh graf), and *kinetoscope* (ki NEH toh skope).

Target Reading Skill: Draw Conclusions

Reproduce the graphic organizer on the board. Discuss the example provided to students in the Target Reading Skill. A sample conclusion could be that Edison's inventions made people's lives easier and more entertaining. Allow students time to complete the Reading Skill activity.

During Reading

Think Critically

1. How did Edison's curiosity help him become successful? (Edison asked questions because he wanted to understand how things worked. Knowing how things worked helped make him a great inventor.)

2. What lesson did Edison learn when Congress did not want his vote recorder? (He learned to invent things that people want or need.)

3. What was special about Edison's laboratories at Menlo Park and West Orange? (The laboratories employed many people to work on dozens of inventions at a time, allowing them to produce hundreds of new products.)

4. Edison claimed that the key to his success was hard work. What else do you think made him successful? (He was persistent, curious, creative, and intelligent.)

After Reading

Writing

Have students write a speech that Edison might have given on the day that he first lit up part of New York City. Ask students to explain why Edison worked so hard to achieve what he did.

Answers to Target Reading Skill

Students' details should support their conclusions. Sample facts and details: Even as a boy, Edison found ways to make money; Edison built useful things people wanted to buy; Edison set up his invention factory so he could work on many inventions at a time.
Sample conclusion: Edison worked hard to make his invention factory successful.

Ida Wells-Barnett Civil Rights Leader

by Susan Bachner

Summary

Ida B. Wells (1862–1931) was born into slavery in Mississippi during the Civil War. After Wells lost her parents in a yellow fever epidemic, she dropped out of school to teach and to support her younger siblings. An incident while riding the railroad started her on a career as a civil rights journalist and speaker. After a good friend was lynched, Wells turned her energy to a campaign against lynching. Wells married Chicago lawyer and publisher Ferdinand Barnett and was active in the early civil rights movement as well as the campaign for women's suffrage. Her uncompromising views made her a controversial figure and brought Wells-Barnett into conflict with other activists, notably Booker T. Washington and Susan B. Anthony. Her work inspired later generations of civil rights activists.

Before Reading

Building Background

Review with students conditions in the South after the Civil War. Explain that although African Americans were now citizens and males received the vote, the Southern states enacted laws that kept African Americans segregated. In addition there was much violence against African Americans who dared stand up for their rights.

Vocabulary

civil rights, epidemic, suffrage

English Language Learners

Have students preview the vocabulary words in the glossary. Ask them to read the definition of each term. Then, as they read the Reader, students should note the page where the word occurs and study the context to reinforce the meaning of the term. Afterwards, have them use the words in oral sentences.

Target Reading Skill: Summarize

Explain that to summarize means to tell the most important ideas of a story or article. After students have read the book, work with them to complete the Target Reading Skill activity on the inside cover of their Readers. You may also want to go on to have students summarize the later part of Wells-Barnett's life.

During Reading

Think Critically

1. Why was the time after the Civil War a time of hope for African Americans? (After the Civil War, slavery was ended and African Americans gained new rights.)

2. What incident moved Ida Wells toward a career in writing? (When she was physically forced out of the first-class railroad car, she was so angry she wrote an article about it.)

3. Why did Ida Wells leave Memphis? (A mob destroyed her newspaper's office and threats were made against her life.)

4. What caused the conflict between Wells-Barnett and Booker T. Washington? (He thought she was too extreme in her views. She thought he should use his position to speak out about lynching.)

After Reading

Writing

Have students work in pairs or small groups to write questions they would ask Ida Wells-Barnett if they were interviewing her.

Answers to Target Reading Skill

Summaries could include the following:

Ida B. Wells-Barnett was born into slavery during the Civil War. After her parents died, Wells dropped out of school and got a teaching job to support her younger brothers and sisters.

Ida Wells-Barnett Writing for Civil Rights

by Susan Bachner

Summary

Ida B. Wells (1862–1931) was born into slavery in Mississippi during the Civil War. After Wells lost her parents in a yellow fever epidemic, she dropped out of school to teach and to support her younger siblings. An incident while riding the railroad started her on a career as a civil rights journalist and speaker. After a good friend was lynched, Wells turned her energy to a campaign against lynching. Wells married Chicago lawyer and publisher Ferdinand Barnett and was active in the early civil rights movement as well as the campaign for women's suffrage. Her uncompromising views made Wells-Barnett a controversial figure and brought her into conflict with other activists, notably Booker T. Washington and Susan B. Anthony. Her work inspired later generations of civil rights activists.

Before Reading

Building Background

Review with students what they already know about conditions in the South after the Civil War. Explain that although African Americans were made citizens and males received the vote, the Southern states soon enacted laws that kept African Americans segregated. In addition there was much violence against African Americans who dared stand up for their rights.

Vocabulary

civil rights, epidemic, segregated, journalist, discrimination, suffrage, activist

English Language Learners

Write the word *active* on the board and then change it to *activist*. Call attention to the suffix *-ist* and explain that the suffix means "one who is active in something." Explain that an activist is someone who actively works for change. Do the same thing with *journal* and *journalist*.

Target Reading Skill: Summarize

Explain that to summarize means to tell the most important ideas of a story or article. Point out that in informational text such as this biography, the headings can provide a clue to the most important idea of a section. Allow students time to complete the Target Reading Skill activity on the inside cover of their Readers.

During Reading

Think Critically

1. What incident moved Wells-Barnett toward a career as a journalist? (When she was forced out of the first-class railroad car, she was so angry she wrote an article about it.)

2. What were some reasons that some white Americans sometimes committed acts of violence against African Americans? (Racial hatred was one cause, but many wanted to keep African Americans from competing with businesses owned by whites.)

3. What caused the conflict between Wells-Barnett and Booker T. Washington? (He thought that she was too extreme in her views. She thought that he should use his position to speak out against lynching.)

After Reading

Writing

Ask students to write a letter that Ida Wells-Barnett might have written to her father in the last years of her life, telling him what she did with her life.

Answers to Target Reading Skill

Summaries could include:

Ida Wells was born into slavery. When she was sixteen, her parents died. She cared for her younger siblings. She became a teacher and later a journalist and civil rights activist.

Ida Wells-Barnett Civil Rights Journalist

by Susan Bachner

Summary

Ida B. Wells (1862–1931) was born into slavery in Mississippi during the Civil War. After Wells lost her parents in a yellow fever epidemic, she dropped out of school to teach and to support her younger siblings. An incident while riding the railroad started her on a career as a civil rights journalist and speaker. After a good friend was lynched, Wells turned her energy to a campaign against lynching. Wells married Chicago lawyer and publisher Ferdinand Barnett and was active in the early civil rights movement as well as the campaign for women's suffrage. Her uncompromising views made her a controversial figure and brought Wells-Barnett into conflict with other activists. Her work inspired later generations of civil rights activists.

Before Reading

Building Background

Review with students what they already know about conditions in the South for African Americans after the Civil War and during the early 1900s. Explain that the Southern states enacted laws that kept African Americans segregated. In addition there was often violence against African Americans who dared stand up for their rights.

Vocabulary

Reconstruction, civil rights, epidemic, activist, journalism, segregated, discrimination, boycott

English Language Learners

Write the word *active* on the board, and then change it to *activist*. Call attention to the suffix *-ist* and explain that the suffix means "one who is active in something." Use *journalist* as a further example, and compare *journalist* to *journal* and *journalism*.

Target Reading Skill: Summarize

Explain that to summarize means to tell the most important ideas of a story or article. Point out that in informational text, the headings can provide a clue to the most important idea of a section and can help a reader summarize. Allow students time to complete the Target Reading Skill activity.

During Reading

Think Critically

1. How do you think Wells-Barnett's father might have been an important influence in her life? (She saw him stand up for his rights. He taught her to value a good education.)

2. What were some reasons that some white Americans sometimes committed acts of violence against African Americans? (Racial hatred was one cause, but many wanted to keep African Americans from competing with businesses owned by whites.)

3. Why did Wells-Barnett have a conflict with Booker T. Washington? (Washington thought she was too extreme in her views. She thought he should use his influence to speak out more for African American rights.)

After Reading

Writing

Have students write a poem or a short skit that makes a statement about Ida Wells-Barnett's life or expresses the kind of person she was.

Answers to Target Reading Skill

Summaries should include information about the major events and activities of Wells-Barnett's life, including her youth, her journalism career, and her later causes and activities.

Louis Armstrong: A Life in Music

by Bruce T. Paddock

Summary

Louis Armstrong was born in a poor neighborhood in New Orleans, Louisiana, in 1901. He worked hard to help support his mother and sister. He also began teaching himself to play the cornet. At the age of 11, he spent 18 months at a reformatory, where he received his first formal music education. After his release, he began to play in jazz bands. As an adult, he quickly established himself as one of the premier jazz trumpeters and vocalists. He toured constantly, made records, and appeared in films. He usually focused on his music, but he also spoke out against segregation in schools.

Before Reading

Building Background

Tell students that Louis Armstrong was one of the most popular musicians of his day. Use the Internet or a CD to play one of Armstrong's songs, such as "What a Wonderful World" or "Hello, Dolly!" or a song with scat singing, such as "Heebie Jeebies."

Vocabulary

segregation, cornet, reformatory, solo

English Language Learners

Read page 3 of the book to the class. Explain that a nickname is an informal name sometimes given to a person.

Target Reading Skill: Cause and Effect

Write the following sentence on the board: *Because John left the gate open, the dog escaped.* Draw two large boxes on the board, one labeled *Cause*, the other labeled *Effect*. Complete the chart by asking volunteers to tell which part of the sentence shows the cause and which shows the effect. Discuss why the first part is the cause and the second part is the effect. Allow students time to complete the Target Reading Skill activity on the inside cover of their readers individually or with a partner.

During Reading

Think Critically

1. Where did Louis Armstrong get his first music lessons? (at a reformatory)

2. How did Armstrong's coal delivery job lead him to play the cornet as a boy? (Each day he passed a store with a cornet in the window. His boss bought it for him.)

3. Why was Armstrong sometimes unable to find a place to stay when he did shows in the South? (White hotels didn't allow blacks. There weren't many black-run hotels.)

4. What did Armstrong think about segregation in schools? (He believed it was the right of African Americans to go to the same schools as whites.)

After Reading

Writing

Have students choose one cause-and-effect relationship and write why they think that event was important in Armstrong's life.

Answers to the Target Reading Skill

Possible answers:

Cause: Louis Armstrong fired a gun into the air.

Effect: He was sent to a reformatory.

Cause: Armstrong spoke out about segregation in schools.

Effect: Some newspaper writers called Armstrong a troublemaker.

Louis Armstrong, Jazz Man

by Bruce T. Paddock

The Growth of Our Country

Chapter: Good Times and Hardships

Lexile Measure: 770

Summary

Louis Armstrong was born in a poor neighborhood in New Orleans, Louisiana, in 1901. He performed many odd jobs to help support his mother and sister. He also began teaching himself to play the cornet. At the age of 11, he spent 18 months at a reformatory, where he received his first formal music education. After his release, he began to play in jazz bands. As an adult, he quickly established himself as one of the premier jazz trumpeters and vocalists. He toured constantly, made records, and appeared in films. While he usually focused on his music, Armstrong also spoke out against segregation in schools.

Before Reading

Building Background

Tell students that Louis Armstrong was one of the most popular musicians of his day. Use the Internet or a CD to play one of Armstrong's songs, such as "What a Wonderful World" or "Hello, Dolly!" or a song with scat singing, such as "Heebie Jeebies."

Vocabulary

segregation, slang, cornet, reformatory, solo, controversy, innovator

English Language Learners

Review the vocabulary terms and definitions with students. Have student pairs write sentences using a vocabulary word. Ask volunteers to share them.

Target Reading Skill: Cause and Effect

Write the following sentence on the board: *Because John left the gate open, the dog was able to escape from the yard.* Ask volunteers to tell which part of the sentence shows the cause and which shows the effect. Discuss why the first part is the cause and the second part is the effect. Allow students time to complete the Target Reading Skill activity on the inside cover.

During Reading

Think Critically

1. Why did Armstrong call people "Pops"? (He liked to talk in slang.)
2. Why did Armstrong move to Chicago in 1922? (Joe Oliver invited Armstrong to join his band.)
3. What event caused Armstrong to speak out against segregation? (Black students were not allowed to attend an all-white high school.)
4. What changes were happening in music later in Armstrong's career? (Other forms of jazz as well as rock and roll were becoming popular.)

After Reading

Writing

Have students write a letter to a friend describing Louis Armstrong's style of performance. Students should then exchange letters with a partner and discuss their similarities and differences.

Answers to the Target Reading Skill

Possible answers:

Cause: Louis traveled the town delivering coal.

Effect: He heard many different forms of music.

Cause: Louis Armstrong fired a gun into the air to celebrate New Year's Eve.

Effect: He was sent to a reformatory.

Cause: Armstrong helped create a new type of singing called scat, and it became popular.

Effect: Other jazz musicians started scat singing.

Students should share their charts with a partner.

How Louis Armstrong Brought Jazz to the World

by Bruce T. Paddock

Summary

Louis Armstrong was born in a poor neighborhood in New Orleans, Louisiana, in 1901. He performed odd jobs to help support his mother and sister. He also began teaching himself to play the cornet. At the age of 11, he got into trouble and spent 18 months at a reformatory, where he received his first formal music education. After his release, he began to play in jazz bands. As an adult, he quickly established himself as one of the premier jazz trumpeters and vocalists. He toured constantly, made records, and appeared in films. While he primarily focused on his music, he also spoke out against segregation in schools. Armstrong remains a beloved musician.

Before Reading

Building Background

Tell students that Louis Armstrong was one of the most popular musicians of his day. If possible, use the Internet or a CD to play "What a Wonderful World" or "Hello, Dolly!" or a song with scat singing, such as "Heebie Jeebies."

Vocabulary

standard, segregation, producer, slang, cornet, reformatory, solo, improvise, controversy, innovator, promote

English Language Learners

Explain to students that some words signal a cause-and-effect relationship. Have pairs skim the book and look for uses of the word *because*. Ask them to write down a sentence that uses the word. Have them circle the cause and underline the effect.

Target Reading Skill: Cause and Effect

Write on the board: *Because John left the gate open, the dog was able to escape.* Draw two large boxes, one labeled *Cause* the other labeled *Effect*. Complete the organizer by asking volunteers to tell which part of the sentence shows the cause, and which shows the effect. Discuss why the first part of the sentence is the cause and the second part is the effect. Have students complete the Target Reading Skill activity on the inside cover of their readers.

During Reading

Think Critically

1. Why did Armstrong have nicknames like "Gatemouth" and "Satchelmouth"? (because of his huge smile)

2. What is one way that Armstrong influenced other musicians? (He helped create scat singing, and soon after other jazz singers tried it too.)

3. What was the result of Armstrong speaking out against segregation in Arkansas schools? (Newspapers attacked him and an advertiser tried to get him fired from a television show, but his fans stood by him.)

4. Why was Armstrong no longer an innovator by the 1960s? (New styles of music, such as rock and roll, were becoming more popular.)

After Reading

Writing

Have students write a short essay describing ways that Louis Armstrong influenced music.

Answers to the Target Reading Skill

Possible answers:

Cause: Louis Armstrong fired a gun into the air.

Effect: He was sent to a reformatory.

Cause: In the South, white hotels did not allow blacks.

Effect: Sometimes Armstrong couldn't find a place to sleep when he played shows in the South.

Cause: Armstrong spoke out about school segregation.

Effect: Newspapers attacked Armstrong.

Harry S. Truman
American President

by Steven Jay Griffel

Summary

Harry Truman was born in Missouri in 1884. As a boy, Truman was an avid reader, especially of history. After high school, he worked on his father's farm. He distinguished himself as a captain fighting in France during World War I. Afterward, he was elected twice as a United States senator. In 1944, he was elected vice president, and he became president after Franklin Roosevelt's death in 1945. Truman was initially unprepared for the job, but he was smart and unafraid to make tough decisions. The Truman Doctrine and Marshall Plan were major parts of his foreign policy, meant to deal with the rising threat of communism. Some of his policies were unpopular, but he continued to fight for them. Truman returned to Missouri after his presidency in 1953. He died in 1972.

Before Reading

Building Background

Build background by telling students that Harry Truman was president of the United States during the mid-1900s. Explain that at that time, after the end of World War II, Russia and many of its neighbors were part of the large communist nation called the Soviet Union. Point to Russia and other former Soviet republics on a map.

English Language Learners

Reinforce the idea that certain words can tell readers in what order events took place. Read the first four pages of the book to the class. Pause when you reach the sequence clue words *after*, *then*, and *later*. Each time you pause, explain which event came first and which came second.

Vocabulary

politician, artillery, campaign, minimum wage, communist, economy, assassinate

Target Reading Skill: Sequence

Write the following on the board: "Marta works in Washington. Before she started working, she graduated from high school in Illinois and then went to college in New York." Ask volunteers to underline the sequence clue words (*before*, *then*) and place the events of Marta's life in sequence (high school, college, work). Allow students time to complete the Target Reading Skill activity on the inside cover of their readers individually or with a partner.

During Reading

Think Critically

1. What boyhood dream did Truman fulfill? (He became a great soldier when he went to fight in France during World War I.)

2. How did Truman become president? (He was vice president when President Franklin Roosevelt died.)

3. What was the Fair Deal? (Truman's ideas to help Americans in need)

4. Why was Truman's decision to use the atomic bomb during World War II a tough one? (If he didn't use it, many American soldiers might be killed. Using it would, and did, result in the deaths of many Japanese people.)

After Reading

Activity

Have students write down several events from a typical day on sheet of paper. The events should be written out of order. Students should then exchange papers and place their partner's events in the correct order.

Answers to Target Reading Skill

Students' organizers should include at least four events from Truman's life placed in correct sequence, with dates included if possible, such as born in Missouri, 1884; was elected as a senator for the first time, 1934; became president after Franklin Roosevelt's death, 1945; moved back to Missouri, 1953.

131

Harry S. Truman Plain-Speaking President

by Steven Jay Griffel

The Growth of Our Country

Chapter: World War II

Lexile Measure: 770

Summary

Harry Truman was born in Missouri in 1884. As a boy, Truman was an avid reader, especially of history. After high school, he worked on his father's farm. He distinguished himself as a captain fighting in France during World War I. Afterward, he was elected twice as a United States senator. In 1944, he was elected vice president, and he became president after Franklin Roosevelt's death in 1945. Truman was initially unprepared for the job, but he was smart and unafraid to make tough decisions. The Truman Doctrine and Marshall Plan were major parts of his foreign policy, meant to deal with the rising threat of communism. Some of Truman's policies were unpopular, but he continued to fight for them. Truman returned to Missouri after his presidency in 1953. He died in 1972.

Before Reading

Building Background

Build background by telling students that Harry Truman was president of the United States from 1945–1953. Explain that at that time, after the end of World War II, Russia and many of its neighbors were part of the large communist nation called the Soviet Union. Point to Russia and other former Soviet republics on a map.

Vocabulary

politician, artillery, economy, efficiency, financial, campaign, minimum wage, unemployment, communist, assassination

English Language Learners

Write each vocabulary word on the board. Pronounce each word and say their definitions. When pronouncing the word *campaign*, point out to students that the *g* is silent.

Target Reading Skill: Sequence

Write these sentences on the board: "Marta works in Washington. Before she started working, she graduated from high school in Illinois and then went to college in New York." Ask volunteers to underline the sequence clue words (*before*, *then*) and place the events of Marta's life in sequence (high school, college, work). Allow students time to complete the Target Reading Skill activity on the inside cover of their readers individually or with a partner.

During Reading

Think Critically

1. How did Truman first become president? (In 1944, Franklin Roosevelt was president, and Truman was vice president. When Roosevelt died suddenly in 1945, Truman became president.)

2. What lesson did Truman learn from reading about history? (He learned that a good leader is someone who can get other people to do what they don't want to do and to like it.)

3. How did Truman respond to his assassination attempt? (He responded calmly, and in his plain, direct way said that presidents should expect such things.)

After Reading

Writing

Have each student write down two events they think were important in Truman's life. Ask students to write two paragraphs explaining why they think these events were important to Truman.

Answers to Target Reading Skill

Students' organizers should include at least five events from Truman's life placed in correct sequence, with dates included if possible, such as born in Missouri, 1884; was elected senator for the first time, 1934; became president after Franklin Roosevelt's death, 1945; issued the Truman Doctrine, 1947; moved back to Missouri, 1953.

President Harry S. Truman
"The Buck Stops Here"

by Steven Jay Griffel

Summary

Harry Truman was born in Missouri in 1884. As a boy, Truman was an avid reader, especially of history. After high school, he worked on his father's farm. He distinguished himself as a captain fighting in France during World War I. Afterward, he was elected twice as a United States senator. In 1944, he was elected vice president, and he became president after Franklin Roosevelt's death in 1945. Truman was initially unprepared for the job, but he was smart and unafraid to make tough decisions. The Truman Doctrine and Marshall Plan, major parts of his foreign policy, were meant to deal with the rising threat of communism. Some of his policies were unpopular, but he continued to fight for them. Truman returned to Missouri after his presidency in 1953. He died in 1972.

Before Reading

Building Background

Build background by telling students that Harry Truman was president of the United States from 1945–1953. Explain that at that time, after the end of World War II, Russia and many of its neighbors were part of a large communist nation called the Soviet Union. Point to Russia and other former Soviet republics on a map.

Vocabulary

politician, invest, artillery, economy, finances, efficiency, unemployment, minimum wage, communist, poll, assassination

English Language Learners

Have students pair up with other readers to create flash cards with vocabulary words on one side and definitions on the other. Students should quiz each other until they know the words and their meanings.

Target Reading Skill: Sequence

Write these sentences on the board: "Marta works in Washington. Before she started working, she graduated from high school in Illinois and then went to college in New York." Ask volunteers to underline the sequence clue words (*before*, *then*) and place the events of Marta's life in order (high school, college, work). Allow students time to complete the Target Reading Skill activity on the inside cover of their readers individually or with a partner.

During Reading

Think Critically

1. Why was the Truman Committee important? (Truman gained respect for his cost-cutting measures, and because of this, President Roosevelt asked him to run as his vice president.)

2. Why did Truman decide to use the atomic bomb? (He wanted to end World War II and prevent the deaths of Americans.)

3. What did Truman hope to accomplish with the Truman Doctrine and the Marshall Plan? (He hoped that by improving the economies of many countries in Europe, the U.S. would gain trading partners and the nations could better resist communist takeovers.)

After Reading

Writing

Have students reread pages 2 and 7 of the reader. Then ask them to write a letter to a friend from the point of view of Harry Truman, explaining how he felt after becoming president.

Answers to Target Reading Skill

Students' organizers should include at least six events from Truman's life placed in correct sequence, such as born in Missouri, 1884; returned home to work on family farm, 1906; was elected as a senator, 1934; became president after Franklin Roosevelt's death, 1945; issued the Truman Doctrine, 1947; moved back to Missouri, 1953; died, 1972.

President John F. Kennedy

by Vanessa Walker

Summary

John Fitzgerald Kennedy was born on May 29, 1917, into a wealthy Irish Catholic family that valued success and competition. Kennedy attended Harvard, where he was an average student, and joined the navy in 1941. As commander of a PT boat, he led his shipwrecked crew to safety. In 1946, he ran for Congress and in 1952, the Senate. A year later, he married Jacqueline Bouvier. In 1960, he was elected president, the first Catholic to be elected. His presidency, which took place during the height of the Cold War, was marked by several international crises, most notably the Bay of Pigs fiasco, the Cuban Missile Crisis, and the Berlin Crisis. Achievements included a civil rights bill passed in 1964, the Peace Corps, and the space program. Kennedy was assassinated by Lee Harvey Oswald in Dallas on November 22, 1963.

Before Reading

Building Background

Build background by introducing or reviewing the term *Cold War* and explaining that Kennedy was president during this time. Ask students to suggest what challenges Kennedy might have faced during his presidency, and to tell what they might know about him.

Vocabulary

discrimination, ambassador, campaign, Cold War, inauguration, communist, missile, blockade, civil rights

English Language Learners

Have students skim for key terms and other important words in the text. Use visuals to communicate the meaning of some terms, such as *blockade* and *missiles*. Give help with pronunciation of vocabulary, especially multisyllabic words.

Target Reading Skill: Fact and Opinion

Reproduce the graphic organizer. Ask volunteers to fill in examples of facts and opinions from the book. For instance, under Facts, students might record that Kennedy was born May 29, 1917. Allow students time to complete the Target Reading Skill activity on the inside front and back cover of their Readers.

During Reading

Think Critically

1. How was John Kennedy different from his older brother Joe? (He was not a good student, he was weaker and not such a good athlete.)

2. How did his visit to Europe just before World War II influence Kennedy? (He became interested in what was happening and followed events closely. Then he wrote a paper about England's role that was later published as a book.)

3. What traits did Kennedy have that may have helped him succeed? (He was funny and smart and people liked him.)

4. What do you think Kennedy should be most remembered for? Explain. (Students may suggest he should be remembered for standing up to the Soviets and avoiding nuclear war, for the civil rights bill, and for starting the Peace Corps.)

After Reading

Writing

Write a paragraph that tells your opinion of Kennedy's presidency. Was he a good president? Support your opinion with facts from the book.

Answers to Target Reading Skill

Sample facts: Kennedy was born to an Irish American family in Brookline, Massachusetts; attended Harvard University; was elected president in 1960.

Sample opinions: Kennedy was funny and fun; Jacqueline Bouvier was beautiful; one of Kennedy's most important accomplishments was the civil rights bill; Kennedy bravely faced a powerful enemy overseas.

John F. Kennedy American President

Vanessa Walker

Summary

John Fitzgerald Kennedy was born on May 29, 1917, into a wealthy Irish Catholic family that valued success and competition. Kennedy attended Harvard, where he was an average student, and joined the navy in 1941. As commander of a PT boat, he led his shipwrecked crew to safety. In 1946, he ran for Congress and in 1952, the Senate. In 1960, he was elected president, the first Catholic to serve in that office. His presidency was marked by several international crises, most notably the Bay of Pigs fiasco, the Cuban Missile Crisis, and the Berlin Crisis. Achievements included a civil rights bill passed in 1964, the Peace Corps, and the space program. Kennedy was assassinated by Lee Harvey Oswald in Dallas on November 22, 1963.

Before Reading

Building Background

Review the term *Cold War* with students. Explain that Kennedy was president during this time. Discuss with students what they know about President John F. Kennedy. Ask students to predict what challenges he might have faced during his presidency.

Vocabulary

discrimination, ambassador, campaign, frontier, Cold War, inauguration, communist, missile, blockade, civil rights, assassination

English Language Learners

Have students skim for key terms and other important words in the text. Use visuals to communicate the meaning of some terms, such as *blockade* and *missiles*. Give assistance with pronunciation of multisyllabic words.

Target Reading Skill: Fact and Opinion

Reproduce the graphic organizer on the board. Review that a fact can be proved, and an opinion is what someone thinks or feels about something. Have students skim to find examples of each. Allow students time to complete the Target Reading Skill activity on the inside covers of their Readers.

During Reading

Think Critically

1. How did Kennedy's family help him succeed? (His parents pushed their children to compete and to win. His family worked for his campaigns, helping to get him elected.)

2. How did the death of his brother change Kennedy's life? (The family thought his brother Joe would run for office, but after Joe's death, Kennedy decided to run for office.)

3. What traits did Kennedy have that may have helped him succeed? (He was funny and intelligent, and people liked him.)

4. Do you think Kennedy acted wisely during the Cuban Missile Crisis? Explain. (Students may think that Kennedy acted wisely to take a stand against the Soviets, but he was also wise to compromise and avoid war.)

After Reading

Writing

Have students write a letter that Kennedy might have written to young people thinking of entering the Peace Corps.

Answers to Target Reading Skill

Sample facts: Kennedy was born in Brookline, Massachusetts; attended Harvard University; and was elected president in 1960.

Sample opinions: Kennedy acted bravely; was funny; had a charming personality; was handsome; most important accomplishments.

John F. Kennedy and the New Frontier

by Vanessa Walker

Summary

John Fitzgerald Kennedy was born on May 29, 1917, into a wealthy Irish Catholic family that valued success and competition. Kennedy attended Harvard and then joined the navy in 1941. As commander of a PT boat, he led his shipwrecked crew to safety. In 1946, he ran for Congress and in 1952, the Senate. A year later, he married Jacqueline Bouvier. In 1960, he was elected president, the first Catholic to serve in that office. His presidency was marked by several international crises, most notably the Bay of Pigs and the Cuban Missile Crisis. Achievements included a civil rights bill passed in 1964, the Peace Corps, and the space program. Kennedy was assassinated on November 22, 1963.

Before Reading

Building Background

Review the term *Cold War* with students. Explain that Kennedy was president during this time. Ask students to predict what challenges Kennedy might have faced during this time.

Vocabulary

ambassador, campaign, nomination, Cold War, inauguration, communist, exile, blockade, Allies, assassination

English Language Learners

Read each section aloud to students and call on volunteers to summarize. Give help with pronunciation of vocabulary, especially with multisyllabic words.

Target Reading Skill: Fact and Opinion

Reproduce the graphic organizer on the board. Review the difference between fact and opinion.

Allow students time to complete the Target Reading Skill activity on the inside front and back cover of their Readers.

During Reading

Think Critically

1. How did Kennedy's family help him succeed later in life? (His parents pushed their children to compete and to win. His family worked for his campaigns, helping to get him elected.)

2. How did his brother's death change the course of Kennedy's life? (His brother Joe had been expected to run for office. After Joe's death, Kennedy decided to run for office.)

3. How did television possibly help Kennedy become president? (During the television debate, he looked tanned and relaxed.)

4. Do you agree with the author's opinion that the Bay of Pigs was one of the biggest mistakes of Kennedy's presidency? Explain. (Answers will vary. Students may suggest that the incident made the United States look weak.)

After Reading

Writing

Write a letter that Kennedy might have written to students, about what it means to "do for your country."

Answers to Target Reading Skill

Sample facts: Kennedy was born in Brookline, Massachusetts; attended Harvard University; was elected president in 1960.

Sample opinions: Kennedy stood up bravely to the Soviet threat; was funny; had a charming personality; was handsome; inaugural speech was inspiring; president's home was beautiful; without Kennedy, landing on moon might not have been possible; one of most important accomplishments.

Bob Dylan
Singer for His Times

by Bruce T. Paddock

Summary

Bob Dylan was born Robert Zimmerman on May 24, 1941, and was raised in a small Minnesota town. He became interested in music as a child and changed his name to Bob Dylan when he began performing as a young man. He first became famous as a leader of the folk music scene, but over the decades he has recorded albums with a mix of sounds that include rock, blues, rhythm and blues, and country. His innovative, personal style of songwriting continues to influence musicians today.

Before Reading

Building Background

Build background by asking students to name some famous musicians today. Discuss which of these artists write most or all of their own material. Explain that Bob Dylan writes his own songs, sings, and plays several instruments. If possible, find a video on the Internet that shows Dylan performing one of his songs and display it for the class.

Vocabulary

critic, press, civil rights, cover, acoustic, introspective, genre

English Language Learners

Take a "picture walk" through the biography and explain to students what each picture shows. For some pictures, point to the instruments and say them by name, such as *harmonica*, *acoustic guitar*, and *electric guitar*.

Target Reading Skill: Main Idea and Details

A main idea is the most important idea of a topic. Details help support the main idea. Write the following sentences on the board: *Bob Dylan grew up in Minnesota. Bob Dylan plays the guitar and the harmonica. Bob Dylan has written many songs. Bob Dylan was in a motorcycle accident.* Ask students which of these details support the main idea "Bob Dylan is a musician" (second and third sentences). Allow students time to complete the Target Reading Skill activity on the inside cover of their Readers individually or with a partner.

During Reading

Think Critically

1. What musicians did Dylan like when he was younger? (Little Richard, Woody Guthrie.)

2. Why did a record company get in touch with Dylan? (There was a story praising Dylan in *The New York Times*.)

3. What was happening in the country at the time "Blowin' in the Wind" became a big hit? (Protests against the Vietnam War, and the civil rights movement)

4. What was special about the song "Like a Rolling Stone"? (It's one of Dylan's best-known songs, and at six minutes long, it broke the three-minute-long tradition for most songs of the time.)

After Reading

Writing

Have students write a paragraph that describes the different kinds of music that influenced Bob Dylan, and explains why Dylan's own music kept changing.

Answers to Target Reading Skill

Possible main idea: Dylan played many different types of music.

Possible details: He played folk music. He played rock and roll music. He played country music.

The Singing Life of Bob Dylan

by Bruce T. Paddock

Summary

Bob Dylan was born Robert Zimmerman on May 24, 1941, and was raised in a small Minnesota town. He became interested in music as a child and changed his name to Bob Dylan when he began performing as a young man. He first became famous as a leader of the folk music scene, but, over the decades, has recorded albums with a mix of sounds that include rock, blues, rhythm and blues, and country. His innovative, personal style of songwriting continues to influence musicians today.

Before Reading

Building Background

Build background by asking students to name some famous musicians today. Discuss which of these artists write most or all of their own material. Explain that Bob Dylan writes his own songs, sings, and plays several instruments. If possible, find a video on the Internet that shows Dylan performing one of his songs and play it for the class.

Vocabulary

genre, critic, publicize, press, cover, civil rights, acoustic, introspective, memorial, soundtrack

English Language Learners

List the vocabulary words on the board. Pronounce then one at a time and have students repeat them after you. Then have students locate each word in the Reader. Have students read the sentence containing each vocabulary word.

Target Reading Skill: Main Idea and Details

A main idea is the most important idea of a topic. Details help support the main idea. Write the following sentences on the board: *Bob Dylan grew up in Minnesota. Bob Dylan plays the guitar and the harmonica. Bob Dylan has written many songs. Bob Dylan was in a motorcycle accident.* Ask students which of these details support the main idea "Bob Dylan is a musician" (second and third sentences). Allow students time to complete the Target Reading Skill activity on the inside cover of their Readers individually or with a partner.

During Reading

Think Critically

1. Why did Dylan move to New York? (He became restless in Minnesota. New York had an exciting folk scene. He wanted to meet Woody Guthrie.)

2. How did Dylan and Joan Baez help each other in their music careers? (He wrote some of her biggest hits, and she introduced him to more fans when he played at her concerts.)

3. Why did people in the audience boo Dylan when he performed at a Rhode Island folk music festival? (Dylan played an electric guitar instead of the expected acoustic guitar.)

4. In what ways did Dylan influence other musicians? (Many musicians covered Dylan's songs. He wrote some of Joan Baez's biggest hit songs. The Beatles were inspired by Dylan to write more personal songs in the late 1960s.)

After Reading

Writing

Have students find the lyrics to a Dylan song such as "Blowin' in the Wind" or "The Times They Are a-Changin'" Have them read and discuss the words with a partner. Have them write a paragraph about what the song is about.

Answers to Target Reading Skill

Possible main idea: Dylan's musical style changed over the years.

Possible details: He first gained fame as a folk singer. He released a rhythm and blues album in 1964. His next album had heavy rock influences. In 1967, he released an album with a country sound.

Blowin' in the Wind
The Bob Dylan Story

by Bruce T. Paddock

Summary

Bob Dylan was born Robert Zimmerman on May 24, 1941, and was raised in a small Minnesota town. He became interested in music as a child and changed his name to Bob Dylan when he began performing as a young man. He first became famous as a leader of the folk music scene, but, over the decades, has recorded albums with a mix of sounds that include rock, blues, rhythm and blues, and country. His innovative, personal style of songwriting continues to influence musicians today.

Before Reading

Building Background

Build background by asking students to name some famous musicians today. Discuss which of these artists write most or all of their own material. Explain that Bob Dylan writes his own songs, sings, and plays several instruments. If possible, find a video on the Internet that shows Dylan performing one of his songs and play it for the class.

Vocabulary

genre, critic, publicity, press, cover, civil rights, acoustic, innovative, introspective, memorial, soundtrack, induct

English Language Learners

Explain to students that some words have multiple meanings, and some can be used as a verb, a noun, and an adjective. Discuss various meanings of the word *cover*. Then be sure students understand the meaning of the word as used by the music industry.

Target Reading Skill: Main Idea and Details

A main idea is the most important idea of a piece of writing. Details help support the main idea. Write the following sentences on the board: *Bob Dylan grew up in Minnesota. Bob Dylan plays the guitar and the harmonica. Bob Dylan has written many songs. Bob Dylan was in a motorcycle accident.* Ask students which of these details support the main idea "Bob Dylan is a musician" (second and third sentences). Allow students time to complete the Target Reading Skill activity on the inside cover of their Readers.

During Reading

Think Critically

1. In what ways was Dylan influenced by other musicians when he was young? (Dylan imitated Little Richard when he performed at high school dances, and Jesse Fuller inspired Dylan to use a harmonica rack.)

2. Why did Columbia Records seek out Dylan? (There was a story praising Dylan in *The New York Times*.)

3. In what ways did Dylan influence other musicians? (Many musicians recorded his songs. He wrote some of Joan Baez's biggest hit songs. The Beatles were inspired by Dylan to write more personal songs in the late 1960s.)

4. Dylan kept changing styles. What does this tell you about him? (He was always learning and growing. He wanted to stay creative.)

After Reading

Writing

Have students find and read the lyrics to several of Dylan's songs. Then ask them to try their hand at writing their own song lyrics.

Answers to Target Reading Skill

Possible main idea: Dylan's musical style changed over the years.

Possible details: He first gained fame as a folk singer. He released a rhythm and blues album in 1964. His next had heavy rock influences. In 1967, he released an album with a mellow country sound. In 1979, he recorded religious music.

Condoleezza Rice
United States Diplomat

by Steven Jay Griffel

Summary

Condoleezza Rice was born in segregated Birmingham, Alabama, in 1954, at the start of the civil rights movement. She excelled in school, finished high school early, and entered college at age 15. She focused her studies on international politics. After receiving a doctorate, she became a professor at Stanford University and worked with the U.S. military during the Reagan administration. From 1989 to 1991, she advised President George H. W. Bush about Soviet affairs. In 2001, she became George W. Bush's national security advisor, and later became his secretary of state. Rice worked on issues of national security in the post-9/11 era. After Bush's second term, Rice returned to Stanford, where she teaches and writes.

Before Reading

Building Background

Build background by asking students to share what they know about the events of September 11, 2001. Tell students that since the terrorist attacks on that day, the government has taken steps to further protect Americans. For example, the country has been fighting wars in Afghanistan and Iraq, created the Department of Homeland Security, and increased security measures in airports.

Vocabulary

segregation, racism, terrorism, communist, diplomat, foreign, policy, foreign policy, campaign, security

English Language Learners

Take a picture walk through the book with students. On each page, tell the class what is being shown in the photograph, illustration, or map. Explain that most of the pictures generally show scenes from Rice's life—her childhood, education, and career—in chronological order.

Target Reading Skill: Generalize

Tell students that the skill of generalizing helps them determine how different facts are linked. For example, if students read a book about the Civil War, they might generalize that *the Civil War was a difficult time in American history* based on facts they'd read. Caution students to avoid false generalizations, unsupported by facts. Allow students time to complete the Target Reading Skill activity on the inside cover of their Readers individually or with a partner.

During Reading

Think Critically

1. What did Rice learn from her parents? (She learned to value education and to succeed.)

2. What was Rice an expert in by the time she finished her studies? (international politics)

3. How did Rice help President George H. W. Bush? (She helped him prepare for meetings with leaders of the Soviet Union.)

4. What was Rice's job as national security advisor? (She told the President George W. Bush about issues that could threaten the nation's security.)

After Reading

Writing

Have partners work together to create a three-column chart about Rice's career. The columns should be labeled: Reagan administration, George H. W. Bush administration, and George W. Bush administration. Have partners write at least one fact about Rice's job during each administration. Have them generalize based on those facts.

Answers to Target Reading Skill

Possible Facts: Rice advised the military on how to use weapons to protect the country from attacks; she helped prepare President George H. W. Bush for meetings with Soviet leaders; she gathered information about the attacks after September 11.

Possible generalization: Rice has done many things to protect Americans from outside threats.

Madame Secretary, Condoleezza Rice

by Steven Jay Griffel

Summary

Condoleezza Rice was born in segregated Birmingham, Alabama, in 1954, at the start of the civil rights movement. She excelled in school, finished high school early, and entered college at age 15. She focused her studies on international politics. After school, she became a professor at Stanford University and worked with the U.S. military during the Reagan administration. From 1989 to 1991, she advised President George H. W. Bush about Soviet affairs. In 2001, she became George W. Bush's national security advisor, and later became his secretary of state. Rice worked on issues of national security in the post-9/11 era. After Bush's second term, Rice returned to Stanford, where she teaches and writes.

Before Reading

Building Background

Build background by asking students to share what they know about September 11, 2001. Tell students that since the terrorist attacks, the government has taken steps to further protect Americans. For example, the country has been fighting wars in Afghanistan and Iraq, created the Department of Homeland Security, and increased security measures in airports.

Vocabulary

segregation, foreign, policy, foreign policy, racism, terrorism, communist, administration, nuclear, campaign, security, cabinet, occupation

English Language Learners

Go through each page of the biography with the class. Summarize the main ideas of each page. Explain that most of the pictures generally show scenes from Rice's life—her childhood, education, and career—in chronological order.

Target Reading Skill: Generalize

Tell students that the skill of generalizing helps them determine how different facts are linked. For example, if students read a book about the Civil War, they could generalize that *the Civil War was a difficult time in American history, as many soldiers died in battle.* Caution students to avoid false generalizations, unsupported by facts. Allow students time to complete the Target Reading Skill activity on the inside cover of their Readers individually or with a partner.

During Reading

Think Critically

1. What obstacles did Rice face as a child? (She dealt with racism, segregation, and the threat of violence.)

2. Why do you think Rice was a popular teacher at Stanford? (Students may have liked that she explained war strategies in terms of football and also that she gave students advice.)

3. What was Rice's main goal after September 11, 2001? (To protect the United States against more terrorist attacks.)

4. What was Rice's job as secretary of state? (She was head of U.S. foreign affairs. She worked with the leaders of many countries, trying to promote peace.)

After Reading

Writing

Have students pair up and write five interview questions that they would ask Rice about her life and career.

Answers to Target Reading Skill

Possible facts: Rice advised the military on how to use nuclear weapons to protect the country from attacks; she helped prepare President George H. W. Bush for meetings with Soviet leaders that focused on peace; she gathered information about the September 11 attacks.

Possible generalization: Rice has done many things to protect Americans from outside threats.

Condoleezza Rice
Foreign Policy Expert

by Steven Jay Griffel

Summary

Condoleezza Rice was born in segregated Birmingham, Alabama, in 1954, at the start of the civil rights movement. Young Rice excelled in school, finished high school early, and entered college at age 15. She focused her studies on international politics. After school, she became a professor at Stanford University and worked with the U.S. military during the Reagan administration. From 1989 to 1991, she advised President George H. W. Bush about Soviet affairs. In 2001, she became George W. Bush's national security advisor, and later became his secretary of state. Rice worked on issues of national security in the post-9/11 era. After Bush's second term, Rice returned to Stanford, where she teaches and writes.

Before Reading

Building Background

Build background by asking students to share what they know about September 11, 2001. Tell students that since the terrorist attacks, the government has taken steps to further protect Americans. For example, the country has been fighting wars in Afghanistan and Iraq, has created the Department of Homeland Security, and has increased security measures in airports.

Vocabulary

segregation, foreign, policy, foreign policy, politics, racism, terrorism, integrated, communist, administration, nuclear, provost, campaign, security, superpower, cabinet, occupation

English Language Learners

Go through the biography with the class. Choose difficult sentences from each page and rewrite them simply on the board.

Target Reading Skill: Generalize

Tell students that the skill of generalizing helps them determine how different facts are linked. Caution students to avoid false generalizations, unsupported by facts. Allow students time to complete the Reading Skill activity individually or with a partner.

During Reading

Think Critically

1. How did Rice's parents prepare her for success? (They discussed politics, encouraged her to focus on education, and provided her with lessons in many things.)

2. Why did Rice give up her dream of being a piano player? (She felt she didn't have what it takes to succeed at a high level of competition.)

3. What was Rice's main goal after September 11th? (to protect the United States against terrorist attacks)

4. What were some of Rice's successes during her service as secretary of state? (She helped improve communications among government groups that gather information about terror threats.)

After Reading

Writing

Have partners do research in the library or on the Internet to find an interview that Rice gave during the George W. Bush administration. Students may find an article, transcript, or video of a television interview. They should then write up a short news article that summarizes the interview.

Answers to Target Reading Skill

Possible facts: Rice helped prepare President George H. W. Bush for meetings with Soviet leaders that focused on peace; she gathered information about the September 11 attacks; she improved communications among groups that gathering information; she worked with many leaders to help promote peace.

Possible generalization: Rice has done many things to protect Americans from outside threats.

K-W-L Chart

What We **K**now	What We **W**ant to Know	What We **L**earned

Web

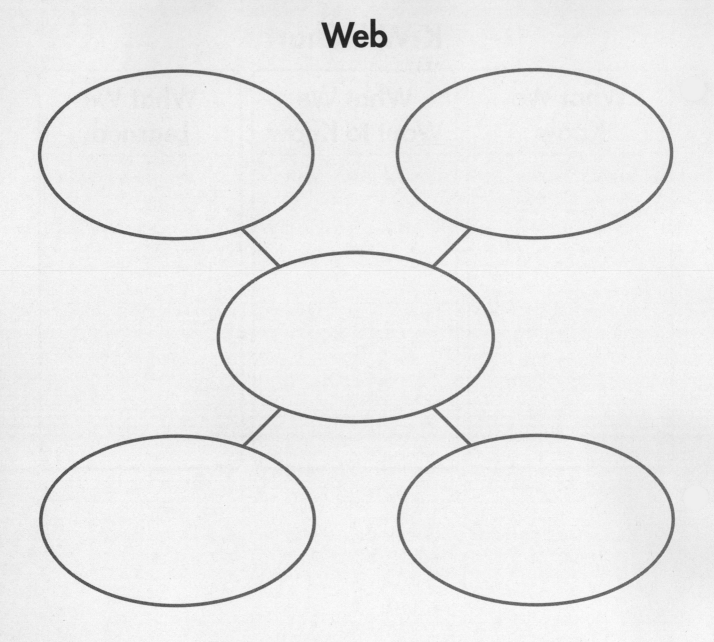

Main Idea and Details

Main Idea

Supporting Detail

Supporting Detail

Supporting Detail

Venn Diagram

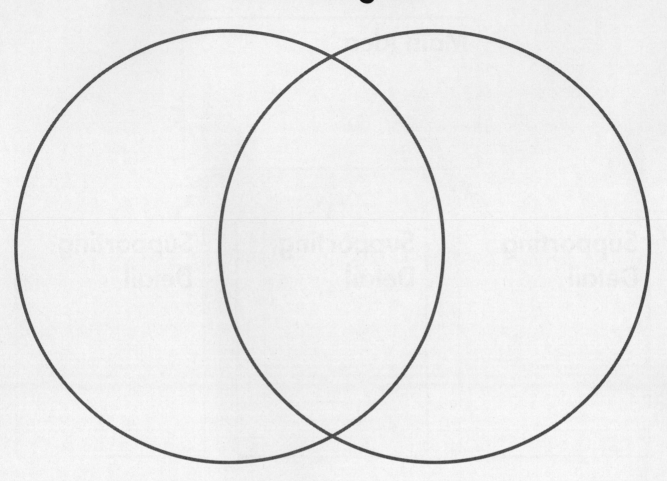

Compare and Contrast

Topics

Alike

Different

Cause and Effect

Causes	**Effects**
Why did it happen?	What happened?
Why did it happen?	What happened?
Why did it happen?	What happened?

T-Chart

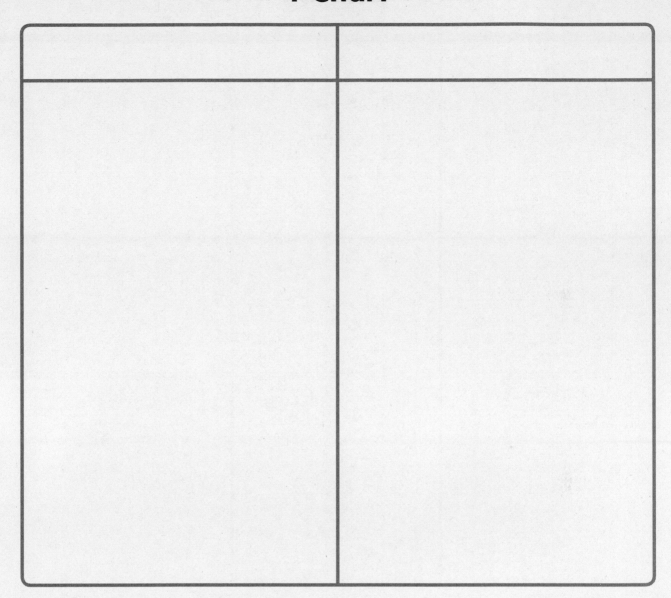

Three-Column Chart

K-W-L Chart

What We <u>K</u>now	What We <u>W</u>ant to Know	What We <u>L</u>earned

Web

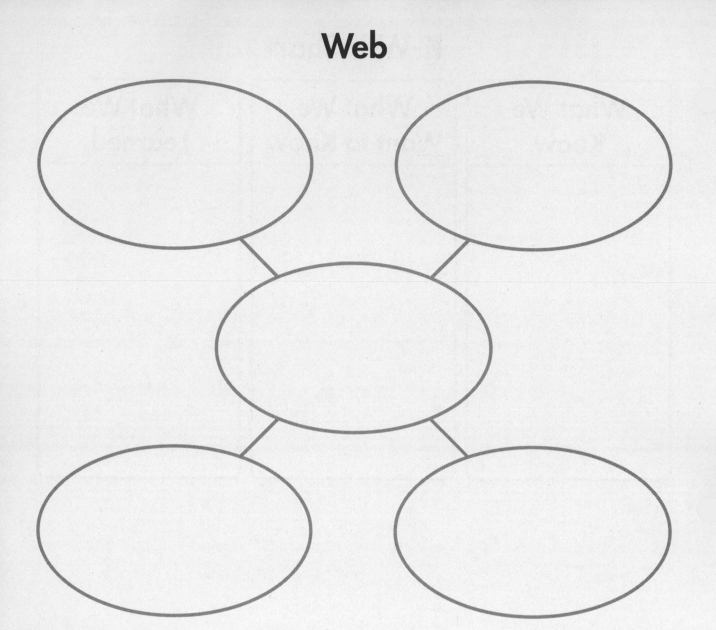

Main Idea and Details

Main Idea

Supporting Detail

Supporting Detail

Supporting Detail

Venn Diagrams

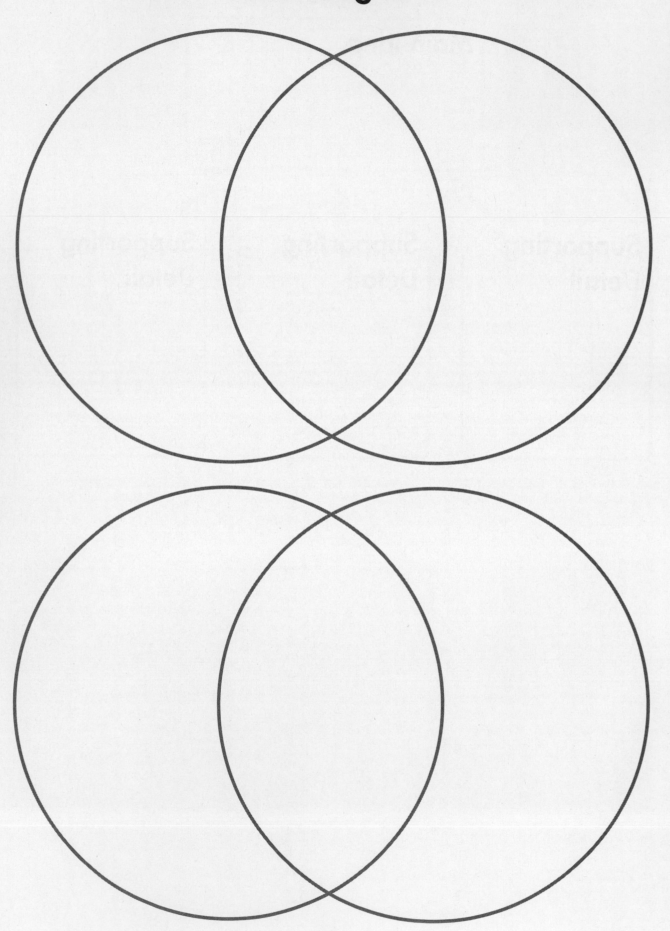

Compare and Contrast

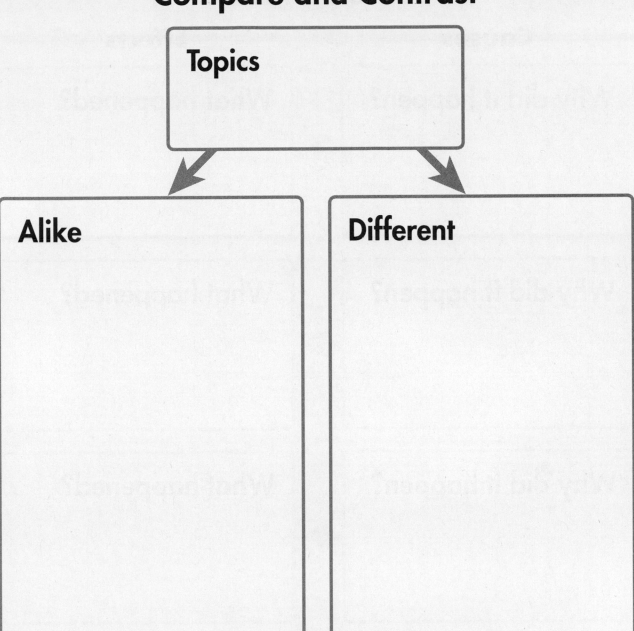

Topics

Alike

Different

Cause and Effect

Causes   **Effects**

| Why did it happen? | → | What happened? |

| Why did it happen? | → | What happened? |

| Why did it happen? | → | What happened? |

T-Chart

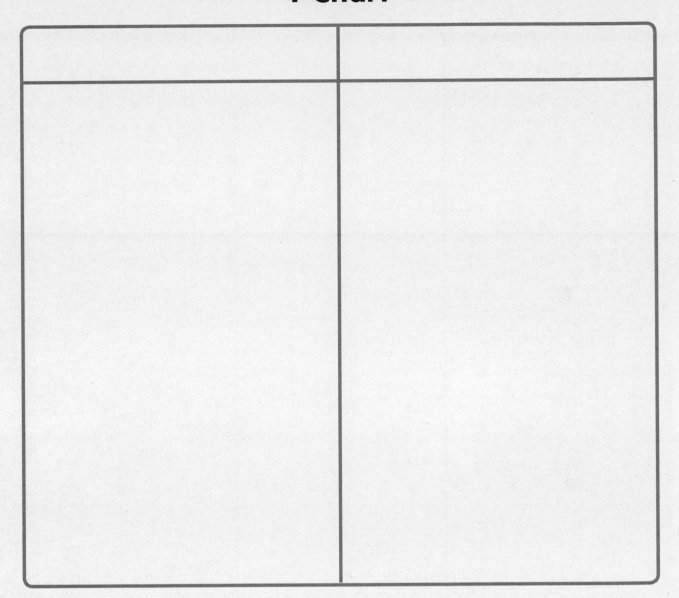

Three-Column Chart

K-W-L Chart

What We **K**now	What We **W**ant to Know	What We **L**earned

Web

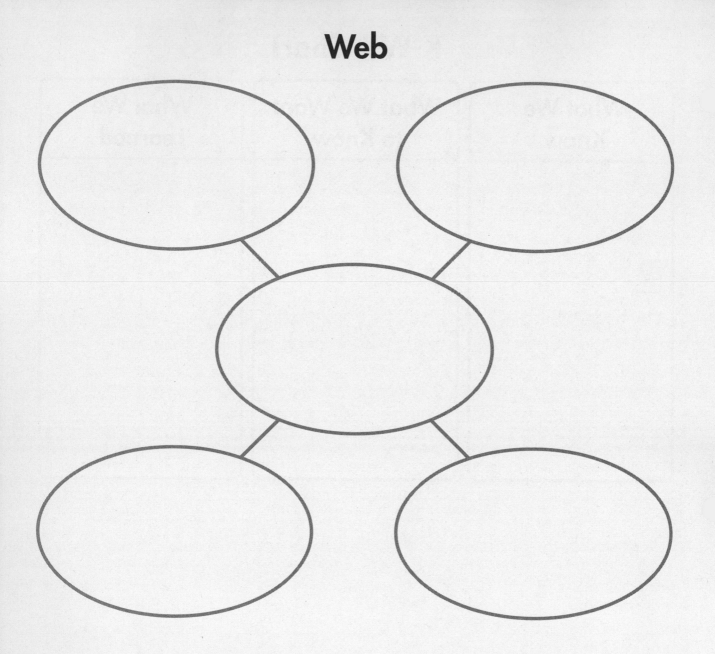

Main Idea and Details

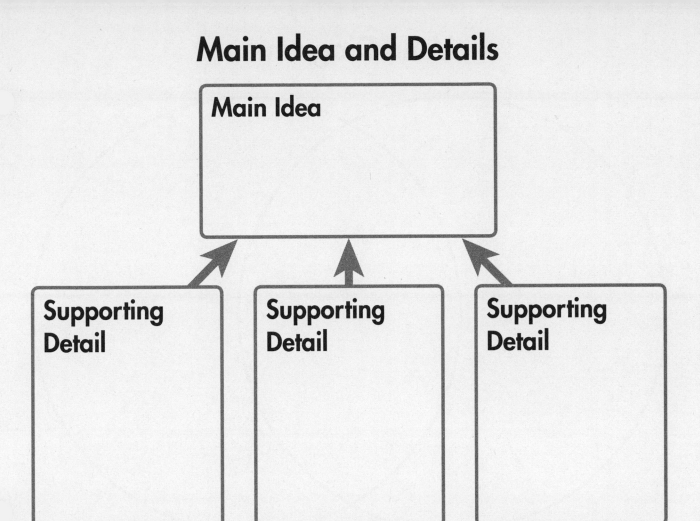

Main Idea

Supporting Detail

Supporting Detail

Supporting Detail

Venn Diagrams

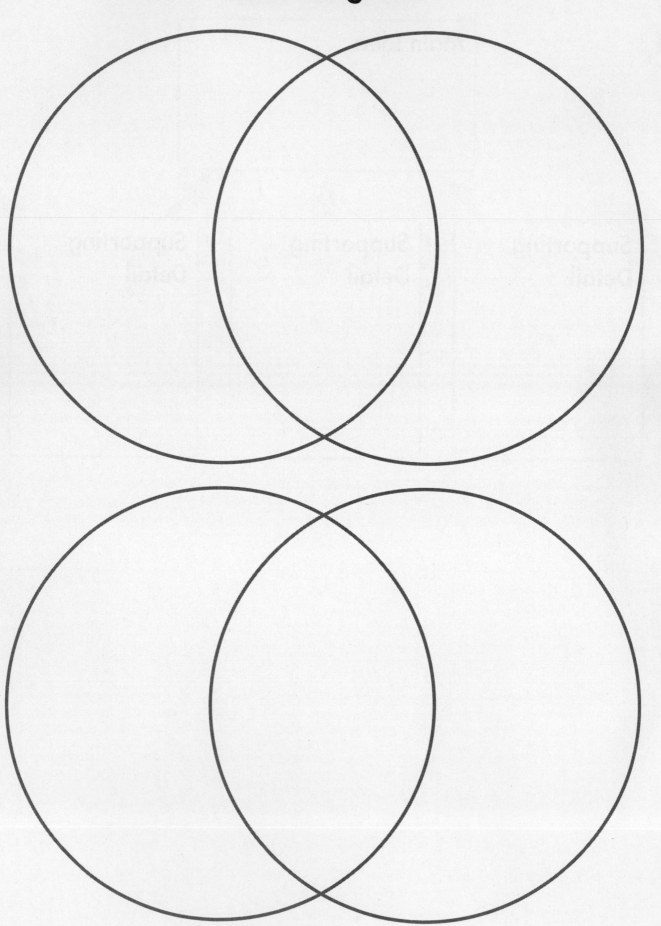

Compare and Contrast

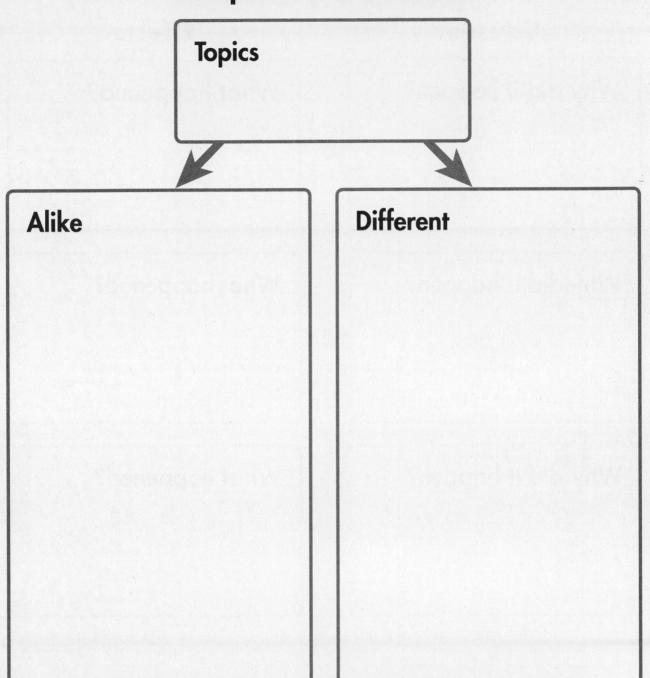

Topics

Alike

Different

Cause and Effect

Causes

Effects

| Why did it happen? | What happened? |

| Why did it happen? | What happened? |

| Why did it happen? | What happened? |

Problem and Solution A

Problem

Solution

Problem and Solution B

Problem

How I tried to solve the problem

Solution

Steps in a Process A

Process

....

....

Step 1

Step 2

Step 3

Steps in a Process B

Process

....

....

Step 1

Step 2

Step 3

Step 4

T-Chart

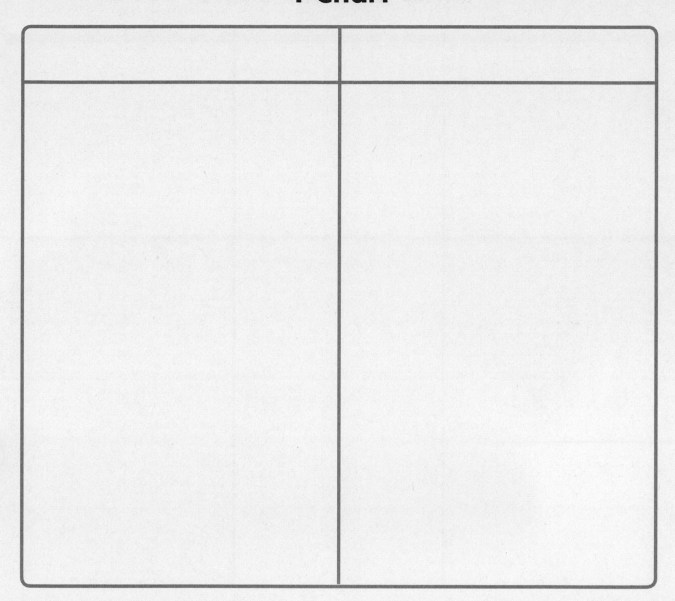

Three-Column Chart

Four-Column Chart

Outline Form

Title

....

....

A. ....

    1. ....

    2. ....

    3. ....

B. ....

    1. ....

    2. ....

    3. ....

C. ....

    1. ....

    2. ....

    3. ....